PIPELINES: FLOWING OIL AND CRUDE POLITICS

RAFAEL KANDIYOTI

I.B. TAURIS

LONDON · NEW YORK

I.B. Tauris & Co Ltd has no responsibility for the persistence or accuracy of the URLs for websites referred to in this publication, and does not guarantee that any content on such websites is, or will remain, accurate or appropriate.

Published in 2008 by I.B. Tauris & Co Ltd
6 Salem Road, London W2 4BU
175 Fifth Avenue, New York NY 10010
www.ibtauris.com

In the United States of America and Canada distributed by
Palgrave Macmillan a division of St. Martin's Press, 175 Fifth Avenue,
New York NY 10010

ISBN: 978 1 84511 390 2

A full CIP record for this book is available from the British Library
A full CIP record is available from the Library of Congress

Designed and Typeset by 4word Ltd, Bristol, UK
Printed and bound in India by Thomson Press India Limited

Contents

List of Maps

(See maps for original sources; all maps redrawn by Spatial Technologies)

Preface

This book is the product of my professional interest in energy production and my long-standing fascination with geopolitical contests. The two strands come together naturally in the study of
transnational oil and gas pipelines. The subject connects with the
stuff of politics at dizzying heights, whether Russia, China and
India can draw together, to provide diplomatic ballast against the
superpower in aggressive mood. At the other extreme, we can
watch agents rushing around Damascus carrying suitcases full of
money, plotting to bring down a government preparing to charge
high transit fees for the trans-Arabian oil pipeline. The lovely
Amur snow leopard enters the life of pipelines, as indeed does the
inebriated hunter who took a few pot-shots at the giant trans-
Alaskan oil pipeline; his last high velocity round did not miss.
There is much to tell!

In handling complex problems, the approaches we select are
inevitably tinged by our formative experiences. The reader of
'Pipelines' will no doubt be aware of an engineer hovering in the
background. In small doses, that can be useful. Certainly, it helped
me compare the magnitudes of things, but it is not just a matter of
numeracy. I was captivated to watch political horse-trading among
powerful international actors, whilst keeping tabs on the constraints that technical requirements and limitations place on their

policy options. The approach has helped me to shed light on a few dark corners that others might have passed over. In this sense, 'Pipelines' may be considered a little different from works that consider the geopolitics of oil and gas transmission in isolation.

I would like to thank Fred Halliday, whose friendship and support helped me to see this project through. I would also like to express my appreciation to Iradj Bagherzade, my publisher, who has been generous with guidance and encouragement. My wife Deniz Kandiyoti helped me to formulate the tetrarchy of factors that dominates the life of pipelines. She has also put up with me for the greater part of a lifetime. Anne Burley, Velisa Vesovic and Deniz Kandiyoti have all braved early drafts and tried hard to keep me on the straight and narrow. Abigail Fielding-Smith of I.B.Tauris and my students Cedric Charpenteu and Revata Seneviratne have done their best to support me in my work. My thanks also go to the Department of Chemical Engineering at Imperial College London, for allowing me time to finish what I had started.

R. Kandiyoti
London

Introduction

By now, most of us are keenly aware of the vital importance of *energy supplies* for the daily running of modern societies. Events of the past few years have also demonstrated the crucial impact of *energy transmission* on our daily lives. Vast amounts of fuels are conveyed every day, over long distances, often across entire continents. Despite worries about environmental pollution and global warming, most nations are looking to consume increasing amounts of fossil fuels, in order that their economies can function and grow. Among these fuels, coal is more uniformly distributed across the continents, but the geographic distribution of oil and gas is uneven. With rapidly expanding trade, the long-haul transportation of these fuels has ballooned into a major industry in its own right.

Most oil and gas is transported in tankers or through pipelines. By and large, tankers run through open seas. Many pipelines, on the other hand, need to cross territories belonging to 'other' states, sometimes a succession of 'other' states. That is where problems often begin. The vital nature of fuel transmission ranks among key geopolitical elements that now regulate relations between states. In this book, I have attempted to outline the many ways in which the stories and histories of oil and gas pipelines intertwine with the way that interstate relations function and, at times, cause blockages and fail.

1 Pipeline Problems and Problem Pipelines. What is in this Book?

Keeping an eye on issues relating to energy and fuel transmission can at times be deceptive. On the ground, new facts may be created every day, but the effect that these transformations have on the geopolitical realities around us is relatively slow, almost imperceptible. These changes nonetheless steadily shape and reshape power relations between states. That is why most books on pipelines quickly become out of date. In attempting to lend the present account a level of continuity with the relentlessly changing landscape it attempts to describe, I have tried to combine several otherwise disparate elements.

The first of these is an attempt to provide the historical backdrop and the geopolitical context of major problem pipelines and of contentious projects under discussion. I have also presented some of the physical and geographic background needed for talking about pipelines in their geopolitical contexts (Chapter I: 'The Ground Rules'). It is important to keep track of four key factors that determine the evolution of pipeline projects. These are the 'physics of fuel transmission', 'fuel demand', 'geopolitical blockages' and the ramifications of the major 'epochal change' of our time, the dismemberment of the Soviet Union. In the next section, I will attempt to describe the place that these four elements occupy in my account of pipeline geopolitics. Chapter II ('Pipelines and Their Problems') outlines some major physical concerns regarding energy production and transmission. At another level, hydrocarbon extraction and conveyance often causes pollution; there are health hazards and risks of fires and explosions. We will need to examine the impact of environmental concerns on the politics and the geopolitics of pipelines.

Limitations of space do not allow the vital 'resource curse' question to be discussed in sufficient detail. Very briefly, this refers to the social, economic and political distortions caused by the process of exploitation in resource-rich countries. Similarly, it was only possible to outline elements of the 'militarization debate', the invariably destructive effect on local communities of the defence of pipelines and other energy-related installations, against military interference or insurgency.

It is hoped, nevertheless, that the background provided will lend stability to the narrative and give the reader an understanding of the undercurrents, as well as the overt mechanisms of future developments. Clearly, the longer-term relevance of the analysis presented in these chapters will depend on whether it has been correctly aligned with the vital axes of geopolitical competition in our era.

2 Pipelines as a Focus in Struggles for Power, Influence and Economic Advantage

Four key factors repeatedly come up in discussions about transnational pipelines.[1] Their interplay profoundly affects the planning, construction, operation and eventual demise of oil and gas transmission projects.

(i) The physics of fuel transport

The first of these factors arises from constraints imposed by the physics of fuel transport, i.e. by 'the exigencies of matter'. One interesting set of problems relates to synchronizing volumes of production at the well-head, available transmission capacity and the eventual level of consumer demand. In this respect, the rest of us owe rather more than most people realize to engineers who try to match the disparate elements of this supply chain. It also makes sense to be aware of the trade-offs involved in transporting fuels in tanker ships versus conveyance by pipelines. For shorter distances, gas usually seems cheaper to transmit by high-pressure pipelines, compared to transport as a liquid in refrigerated tanker ships. By contrast, crude oil is usually cheaper to transport by tanker than by pipeline. Approximately 60 per cent of all crude oil is transported by tanker ships.

In trying to distinguish between the transport of natural gas and crude oil, we must also remember that natural gas, even when compressed, carries less energy per unit of volume, compared to liquid phase hydrocarbons (e.g. crude oil). This makes oil pipelines more lucrative to operate. It is also important to realize the relevance of pumping stations, and that pumping pressure affects the throughput of pipelines.

Finally, we need to be conscious that some pipelines are constructed to higher safety standards than others and are therefore more expensive to build. Natural gas is a more dangerous fuel to transport (Chapter II). Gas pipelines are therefore constructed to more stringent safety standards, which incidentally usually become stricter as pipelines approach human habitation.

In short, the physics of fuel transport defines the constraints over what we can or cannot do and how we should or should not build our conveyance systems. The physics of fuel transport also helps to define the factors that allow us to compare the efficiencies and costs of competing transmission systems.

(ii) Fuel demand

Another key factor affecting pipeline projects is fuel *demand*, the key driver of the whole transmission chain. During the past few decades, global demand for crude oil has risen slowly but steadily. Meanwhile, production naturally depletes oilfields, and transmission of crude oil from newly developed fields requires new pipelines. Similarly, demand may shift from one region to another. The Soviet pipeline system (Chapter V) shows how an extensive pipeline network has the ability to match supply to geographically shifting demand.

It is the new hunger for natural gas, however, that has been driving much of the recent pipeline construction activity. The high costs of transporting liquefied natural gas (LNG) by refrigerated tanker ships tends to shift attention to gas pipelines. For example, India has been importing oil by tanker as a matter of course. Meanwhile, state-owned energy companies as well as the multinationals have hesitated when faced with the high costs of importing gas by tanker in the form of LNG. We will see in Chapter IV that the large *demand* for gas in India is not matched by sufficient purchasing power on the part of the customer base. Several of the multinationals that were drawn to the Indian LNG market are now beginning to sell and are pulling out. Talks about several cross-border gas pipeline projects are also moving slowly, due to hard bargaining about the price of gas.

Elsewhere, an explosion in the volume of gas production and transmission bears testimony to the overall profitability of these operations. Among the great new lines under consideration at present, we can count the trans-Alaska *gas* pipeline, the 'Nord Stream' gas line from Russia to Germany running under the Baltic Sea, the Iran–Pakistan–India gas pipeline and the schemes expected to carry gas and oil from Russia and Central Asia to China. A trans-Saharan line is also being talked about, for pumping Nigerian gas to Europe. In the Caucasus, the Baku–Tblisi–Erzurum gas pipeline running partway alongside the new Baku–Tblisi–Ceyhan oil pipeline is already operational. Despite Russian resistance, the latter is likely to be the first of several pipelines constructed with western finance, to convey Caucasian and trans-Caspian oil and gas exports.

(iii) Geopolitical bottlenecks

Much of this book will be taken up with the evaluation of geopolitical issues raised by the present or potential trajectories of oil and gas pipelines. Energy transmission projects may be driven by demand and guided by physics but, ultimately, they are determined by the geopolitical context. We will review and attempt to analyse – however partially – the instances of energy transmission that have become the subjects of geopolitical competition for power, influence and, eventually, for economic advantage.

Nowhere is this more clearly discernible than in the sequence of pipelines constructed in the last century to convey Iraqi oil to world markets. The earliest pipelines ending at Haifa were lost to the Arab–Israeli conflict. The functioning of the northern pipelines from Iraq across Syrian territory to the Mediterranean coast (Chapter III) has been plagued by feuds between these two countries. After the 2003 invasion of Iraq, it was this line that US forces denied blowing up a segment of, even though they controlled the pumping station upstream of the breach. A third Iraqi pipeline crossing the Arabian Peninsula to reach the Red Sea has been 'confiscated' by the Saudis following Saddam's invasion of Kuwait. The only other line out of Iraq crosses into Turkey and carries oil to the Mediterranean port of Ceyhan. That line was reduced in capacity by US bombing during the invasion in 2003. Remaining capacity now operates sporadically, during intervals between hasty repairs and insurgent attacks.

(iv) The epochal change

No epochal change since the Second World War has transformed the geopolitical landscape of Europe and Asia more radically than the dissolution of the Warsaw Pact and of the Soviet Union. There followed a comprehensive partitioning of Soviet-era oil and gas pipeline networks, with each new post-Soviet republic claiming ownership over installations on its own territory. We will discuss the myriad of new relationships that have emerged and try to analyse the tensions that have developed around the use of this now fragmented network.

After 1990, Russian influence in Eastern Europe receded quite dramatically. In two successive waves of accession, NATO has absorbed *all* the Warsaw Pact countries and three former *Soviet* republics: Estonia, Latvia and Lithuania. Meanwhile, Belarus has adhered to her close, if problematic, links with Moscow, whilst Ukraine is being powerfully pulled by both East and West. In the Caucasus and the Caspian basin, strategic penetration by the western powers has manifested itself, among others, in the form of new pipelines for transporting Caspian oil and gas to the open seas. Present US policy aims to 'wean' these countries from control by the former imperial power. These moves are being met with strong resistance by Moscow. In this region, great power competition centred on energy transmission is barely disguised.

Since 1992, Russian policy has tended towards attempting to recapture her ascendancy over former Soviet territories. Russia's so-called *'near abroad'* broadly corresponds to the lands bequeathed to the Soviets by the Romanov Empire. In several of the former Soviet republics, notably Moldova, Georgia and Azerbaijan, Russia has encouraged separatist movements, initiated military confrontations and assumed the mantle of arbiter. This has served Moscow as a re-entry vehicle into these contested regions, where the archipelago of Soviet-era military bases now occupied by the *Russian* Army have served as instruments for exerting pressure on independent-minded local governments. In many former Soviet republics, Russia is also using her oil and gas sales – combined with the inability of most of the new republics to pay – as a policy tool to enhance her strategic and economic posture.

In the post-Soviet space, struggles between Moscow-centric forces and those attempting to break away are thus in great part being played out along oil and gas transmission axes. We will study them with care.

3 The Selection of Regions

A word of explanation may be useful regarding the regional scope of this book. The selection has been guided by our focus on controversies over pipelines in Eastern Europe and the Eurasian basin, and on pipelines being actively considered for South Asia and East Asia. The regional accounts begin with the Middle East (Chapter III), home to some of the oldest, largest (for their time) and most stricken cross-border pipelines in the world. The account almost naturally leads to South Asia, where possibilities of importing gas from Iran are slowly, very tentatively bringing together India and Pakistan. Meanwhile, India's efforts to import gas from Myanmar through Bangladesh await difficult political decisions in Dhaka. Chapter V describes the Russian nexus and the fuel transmission difficulties that are rooted in the dissolution of the Soviet Union. Russia's hydrocarbon exports towards the West will be reviewed within the framework of contests for influence in Eastern and Central Europe and above all in Ukraine, home to pipelines carrying some 80 per cent of Russian gas exports to the West. Chapter VI reviews Caspian and Central Asian oil and gas transmission problems, in the context of Russia's ambition to take a share of the region's riches and a background of great power rivalry. Our grand tour of Asia will finally take us to the Eastern rim of the continent, where competition for Russian fuel resources is being played out by way of tense and intricate manoeuvring between China, Japan and the two Koreas (Chapter VII). The last chapter aims to provide a short overview.

Chapter I

Oil and gas pipelines: The ground rules

Despite several major discontinuities, global demand for oil and gas has increased more or less steadily since the end of the Second World War. During the past two decades, however, neither extraction and transmission infrastructure nor refinery capacity have been expanded at the same pace. We will see below that this has happened for some very sound economic reasons. The gradual decline in spare capacity and lag in infrastructure construction had hitherto gone largely unnoticed. However, these elements combined in 2004 and 2005, with massive havoc created by several hugely damaging storms over the oil- and gas-rich Caribbean. It was all brought home in the form of a step increase in oil and gas prices.

Intrinsically, rising fuel prices have a relatively minor effect on the cost of fuel transportation. Meanwhile, the increased value of the cargo makes haulage over longer distances more affordable. Within the context of expanding demand, oil and gas transmission thus plays a critical role for the functioning and development of hydrocarbon importing economies. Much effort is devoted to keeping an eye on 'choke-points' of busy tanker lanes:[1] Hormuz, the Turkish straits, the Suez and Panama Canals and the Straits of Malacca. In times of crisis or war, these waterways might be easily blocked by a determined protagonist. It is also important to keep

1

an eye on hydrocarbon transmission through transnational (and occasionally 'national') pipelines that may be prevented from functioning in case of conflict or disagreement.

The sheer volume of media reporting on fuel transmission bears testimony to the near universal concern and attention it has recently commanded. Let us take a quick look at pipeline stories during the course of just one month: the admittedly eventful month of January 2006.

Throughout 2005, Gazprom had insisted on a higher price for gas to be sold to Ukraine during 2006. The Ukrainians had stalled. The government in Kiev had also been drawing away from its strategic alliance with Russia that, as we shall see, the Russians consider crucial to their own security. With Ukraine courting NATO membership, Gazprom was not willing to sell them gas at subsidized prices and Ukraine was unwilling to pay the high price demanded. On 1 January 2006, the Russians reduced the volume of gas pumped into the pipelines that serve Ukraine and parts of Eastern and Central Europe, by just the amount that Ukraine would have drawn from the system.

The turn-down occurred during one of the coldest winters of the past 30 years and was intended to punish Ukraine. In the event, deliveries to Slovakia and the Czech Republic were reduced. Germany and France protested because their supplies were curtailed. There were shortfalls in Italy, and large, potential future buyers in Britain looked on with dismay. Meanwhile, Gazprom claimed that Ukraine had 'stolen' the missing gas and Ukrainian ministers shrugged and blamed the giant Gazprom. Within four days, the Russians were forced to settle on a smaller increase of the gas price for Ukraine and observers in the West came to question Russia's reputation as a reliable supplier. Would they use gas transmission as a political weapon, the Europeans asked themselves? Would they?

Barely three weeks later, two gas pipelines and an electricity transmission line successively feeding Georgia and Armenia were blown up. Georgia is another post-Soviet republic drifting from the Russian political orbit. Only the day before, the Russian Information Agency Novosti had quoted Georgian President Saakashvili as saying '... Georgia should become independent of Russia in terms of energy ...'.[2] Clearly, someone had duly obliged.

The apparently well-coordinated attacks took place in a zone of North Ossetia controlled by the usually dependable Russian border guards. It seemed almost as if the leaders were taunting each other – and it was still the same coldest January for quite some time. The Georgian president personally blamed Russian intelligence for the incident and the Russians blamed Chechen guerrillas. The United States (USA) expressed concern, while Iran offered to make up for some of the missing gas by means of a disused pipeline running from Iran into Azerbaijan. The offer was gratefully accepted. To dampen down the ensuing furore, Russia also provided extra supplies through Azerbaijan, and the US State Department expressed satisfaction that a semblance of normality had returned.

Before the end of the same turbulent month of January 2006, Mani Shankar Aiyar, India's Minister of Petroleum and Natural Gas, was discreetly asked to take charge of 'rural bodies and sports'. *Express India* reported this news under the headline 'Iran gas pipeline is now dead'.[3] For some years, Aiyar had effectively campaigned for a gas pipeline carrying Iranian gas through Pakistan to India. Both countries need more gas and, through this opening, they were beginning to talk to each other very sensibly. Russia's Gazprom had shown interest in providing engineering support for the venture. It was known that the USA opposed the project – with the aim of isolating Iran. However, up until his demotion, Aiyar seemed to be proceeding with the approval of his Prime Minister. The minister who replaced him, Murli Deora, ' … currently co-chairs an India-US parliamentarian forum … is known to have "deep contacts" in the US Senate and business circles'.[4] There is now a promise of US technological assistance for India's nuclear energy sector, proposed in lieu of Iranian natural gas. In fairness, Deora cannot be said to have acted in ways detrimental to the already problematic Iran–Pakistan–India pipeline since assuming office. Nevertheless, the shift worried observers in Russia and China, keen to enlist Indian diplomatic support as a counterweight to the USA. It was feared these were signs of India's shifting position in world affairs.

And all the Indians did was to move their Minister of Petroleum sideways!

1 From Firewood to Gasoline: A Very Short History of Fuels

Human beings have needed fuels ever since they discovered fire. Our caveman ancestors must have been incessantly searching for firewood. By the time charcoal was invented, agrarian communities were largely in the ascendancy. Although a relentless agent of deforestation, charcoal-making is still practised in parts of Africa and Asia, and charcoal is still prized as a domestic fuel. In classical times, vegetable oils and animal fats served as luxury fuels for the lamps of the profligate rich. Fire itself was precious! Temples were erected around the sites of natural tar seepages from the ground, to worship the 'eternal' flame.

During the early modern era, much European steel was made by firing charcoal with iron ore. However, coal could be mined in far greater quantities. It is also denser and cheaper to transport. Coincidentally, the evolution of technology in the late eighteenth century had produced some surprisingly sophisticated machinery. The latter only needed a concentrated source of energy to make a far greater impact. The age of coal and steam led to a revolution in manufacturing.

Coal and steam also led to a revolution in transportation and warfare. It has often been said that Napoleon's armies could move no faster than Caesar's legions. Railways and steamships dramatically cut transit times. Warship designs were revolutionized whilst on land, men and munitions could be moved by rail at speeds inconceivable for the commanders of Austerlitz and Borodino. Applications of steam – and the new wonder, electricity – quickly multiplied. Progressively greater amounts of energy were required to satisfy new, 'modern' needs. Eventually, energy utilization became a yardstick of economic advancement and a means of comparing living standards.

The advent of petroleum

When Edwin Drake sank his first successful oil well near Titusville in Pennsylvania (1859), he probably had no idea of what was to become of his discovery. Petroleum turned out to be a vastly more convenient source of energy than coal. It could be refined to give 'illumination' oil and heating oil, and other fuels that could be pumped rather than shovelled. In the latter part of the nineteenth century, prospectors returned to look for natural tar seepages as indications of petroleum deposits in the bowels of the earth. Such seepages had previously been considered as nuisances, polluting sources of fresh water. Drake became ill and died a poor man. He probably never imagined that his humble derrick was the first to produce the dark, greasy fluid that would alter the course of history in the twentieth century and probably well beyond.

Not long afterwards, Robert Nobel made his first oil investments in Baku in present-day Azerbaijan – then a distant province of the Russian Empire. By 1879, there were nine oil wells in the town. Development accelerated once the railway from Baku to Batumi on the Black Sea coast was completed (1883). Financed by the 'English' Rothschilds, the railway provided a commercially viable export route. For its time, it answered a vital question still relevant in our day: how to get Caspian oil to world markets? By 1900, there were 1,710 wells. Baku and Grozny produced over half the world's oil. The heart of the industry was Chiornyi Gorod, the sooty 'Black Town' on the outskirts of Baku.

What do you do with 'this stuff'?

The first product distilled from petroleum was kerosene, for lighting and heating. At first, oil did not impinge greatly on technologies geared to the use of coal. In part, the use of petroleum was restricted by the geography of its supply. After the USA, production started in a big way first in Mexico, and then in Venezuela. In the 1880s, Shell struck oil in Sumatra, whilst Baku and hapless Grozny were the early oil centres of the Russian Empire. By 1914, production levels in Burma, Iran and India had not yet caught up with the volumes of oil coming from the Americas. Only Russia claimed a comparable share of world production.[5] Coal, on the other hand, could be mined on all continents and, at the time, in much greater quantities than oil could be extracted from the ground.

However, oil was a more practical fuel. It could be pumped and there were other advantages. Oil-fired furnaces were smaller than those built for coal *and* coal-fired furnaces could be easily adapted to burn oil. Then, towards the end of the nineteenth century, a development took place that changed everything. The new internal combustion engine was smaller and lighter. It could be used in mobile vehicles that could travel on roads rather than rails. In fact, it could go anywhere!

The dilemmas provoked by the transition to oil are described in Churchill's war memoirs.[6] In 1912, the Royal Navy wanted bigger 15-in guns on faster ships. Churchill wrote of the advantages: '... conferred by liquid fuel ... speed to be attained with far greater rapidity ... 40 per cent greater radius of action for the same weight of coal ...'; and for the crews: '... The ordeal of coaling exhausted the whole ship's company ... robbed them of their brief period of rest ... .' But the transition was not going to be an easy one, as '... oil was not found in appreciable quantities in our islands ... we must carry it by sea in peace or war from distant countries. We had on the other hand the finest supply of the best steam coal in the world safe in our mines under our own hand.'

He was also worried because '... The oil supplies of the world were in the hands of vast oil trusts under foreign control ... '. He neither trusted American companies nor the Anglo-Dutch company Shell, with its East End London and foreign (Dutch) connections. However, oil would allow him to build better warships: ' ... it was decided to create the fast division ... based irrevocably on oil ... '.

The experiences of the First World War transformed the entire machinery of war. By 1918, the tank had become as vital to land armies as the field gun, whilst the Royal Air Force was operating some 5,000 warplanes; but the conquests of petroleum did not stop on the battlefields. Less than ten years after the end of the Great War, the UK alone boasted nearly 1 million civilian-owned motor vehicles on the roads.

2 The Hydrocarbon Game: Transportation is King

Crude oil is not worth much at the well-head. It needs to be moved, refined and delivered to the point of distribution. In the early days, even moving the crude from well-heads to a railhead was an adventure. Pees[7] describes how, during the Pennsylvania oil boom, oil was stored and moved in wooden barrels. Roads were primitive, often made impassable by mud and the sheer number of wagons on the road. When a road could no longer be used, a new one would be opened through nearby fields and, sometimes, through *ploughed* fields. The teamsters appear to have had the edge of violence over local farmers: 'Indispensable to the business, they [the teamsters] became the tyrants of the region – working and brawling as suited them …'; and sometimes they would charge three or four dollars a barrel for a five- or ten-mile haul.

From the beginning, piping the oil appeared to be a desirable option, but the first few pipelines were failures. They spluttered and leaked at the joints. Real trouble began, however, '… when in late 1865 Henry Harley, a commission dealer, commenced to lay two 2-inch lines from Benninghoff City to his tanks at the Shaffer railroad yard, a distance of two miles … The teamsters were aghast when they learned that *one* 2-inch pipe could deliver up to 2000 barrels per day to the storage tanks … '. They attacked the pipeline; they pulled the joints apart with '… their teams and heavy chains …'. Harley persevered. When a second line was laid, the teamsters torched his installations. Everybody was armed. Men were hurt and lives were lost. Eventually, Harley called in detectives from New York. Some 20 of the arsonists were sent to prison; others became fugitives from justice. The pipeline won. Defeated, thousands of teamsters drifted away. The first gathering lines began to be laid for conveying oil to storage areas and then to railheads.

Initially, railroads served as the main arteries for transporting crude oil over long distances. J. D. Rockefeller and his ubiquitous Standard Oil Company owed much of their spectacular commercial success to the attention they paid to the transportation of oil, first by rail and then by pipelines. Gradually, advantages conferred by longer pipelines were appreciated. By 1914, the USA was far ahead of the rest of the world in pipeline construction, with 7,000 km of trunk lines in operation.

In the 1870s, most of Russia's pipeline construction was undertaken to convey crude oil from well-heads to refineries, usually relatively short distances away. The oil bonanza in Baku and Grozny quickly led to a proliferation of privately-owned gathering lines,[8] led by the Nobel Brothers (enterprising sons of the inventor of dynamite), who imported their 3-in pipes from the USA.

Overland transport of refined kerosene to the port of Batumi on the Black Sea coast was done by railway until the first decade of the twentieth century, when a small consortium built the first 8-in line.

In the Middle East, the first commercial oil was found in south-western Iran (1908). A 130-mile pipeline was constructed from Masjid-i-Sulaiman to Abadan Island, on the Shatt-el-Arab waterway, where the newly formed Anglo-Persian Oil Company hastily set up a refinery. In these early stages, the industry found it easier to build its refineries closer to centres of oil extraction. As the oil-refining process itself was improved and the variety of products prepared from crude oil multiplied, it became more economical to transport the crude oil to refineries built closer to industrial and population centres, where the product mix could be tailored to the needs of the local customer base. By the 1920s, tanker ships were shifting massive quantities of crude oil from production areas to far-away refineries.

When overland oil transport is needed, rail or roads can be put to use. However, pipeline transport usually costs less. 'Gathering lines' are short; they connect production fields to collection areas or nearby shipping facilities. In the Gulf,[9] distances between oil wells and tanker terminals are rarely longer than several hundred miles. By contrast, oil pumped to tankers at Novorossiysk on the Black Sea coast is carried by trunk pipelines from as far away as the Caspian, the Urals or Western Siberia. In the territories of the former Soviet Union, the average distance for oil transmission was over 1,500 km.[10]

As a rule of thumb, tankers, compared to pipelines, usually provide a somewhat cheaper service for moving large tonnages of crude oil. Clearly, tanker rates can fluctuate, depending on the availability of ships and the volume of business. On the other hand, pipeline transit fees can also change erratically, particularly when they cross into a third country. In this respect, the tribulations of the cross-border pipelines of the Middle East tell a story all their own. Similarly, many pipelines cross from Russia into former Soviet republics, giving rise to sharp conflicts of interest. Before we tackle these difficulties, however, it would be useful to take a quick look at pipeline ownership patterns in different parts of the world.

Who owns the pipelines?

In the inter-war years, Europe emerged rapidly as a large market for oil producers in the Middle East. Pumping the oil to the Mediterranean could help save part of the cost of transport by tanker around the Arabian Peninsula, the Red Sea and the Suez Canal crossing. Oil companies operating in the region were already vertically integrated to handle production and transmission, refining and retail. Almost inevitably, they took on the construction, ownership and operation of new pipelines. Following the nationalizations of the 1970s, pipeline ownership in the Middle East passed into the hands of the oil-producing states and the governments of the transit countries. We will see in Chapter III that, on the whole, the new owners did not make the best use of their new transmission networks.

In the Soviet Union, it was the State that took charge of the rapidly expanding pipeline business. After 1945, a massive pipeline system was constructed to carry the vast output of the new oil and gas fields. The Soviets constructed the single largest interconnected network in the world. A state monopoly over crude oil and natural gas transmission has been maintained in the *Russian* Federation. The state-owned gas production and transmission giant Gazprom has continued its existence, while 'Transneft' took over from the state-owned giant pipeline monopoly 'Glavtransneft' of Soviet times as the oil pipeline monopoly of the Federation.

By contrast, a multipartner ownership configuration has evolved for conveying *Kazakh* oil across Russian territory. The 28 million-ton Caspian Pipeline Consortium (CPC) pipeline links the Tengiz fields in Western Kazakhstan with Novorossiysk, the Russian tanker terminal on the Black Sea. The Consortium includes Transneft (Russia), alongside Kazakhstan, Oman and a rainbow of participating companies. True to form, Transneft has retained the role of operating company and maintains overall control on behalf of the consortium. We will see later that the post-2004, cash-rich Russia has come to view such collaborations with rather less favour than previously, requiring modifications to previous agreements and often pushing to take greater control of these operations.

Meanwhile, in America, the ownership of oil transmission has had a long and distinctively colourful history. By 1872, oil was big business, with crude oil and its products ranked as the fourth largest US export item. At the time, J. D. Rockefeller was a prosperous oil refiner in Cleveland, Ohio, whose control over the industry was expanding rapidly. In a book entitled *The History of the Standard Oil Company*[11] (1904), Ida Tarbell, a well-known journalist of her day, has outlined the nature of this expansion. Parts of the story still make interesting reading.

In 1871–2, Rockefeller joined forces with several other refiners and formed the 'Southern Improvement Company'. As Tarbell explains, this company made a series of agreements with regional railroad companies for rebates in transporting *their* crude oil and refined products. The agreement stipulated *increased* freight charges for refiners who were not members of the Southern Improvement Company. Unusually, the extra income was to be passed back to the Southern Improvement Company.

Ida Tarbell was dubbed 'Miss Tarbarrel' by Rockefeller's friends in the press. Undaunted, she produced the names of railroad company officers and stockholders who were given shares in the Standard Oil Company at about the time when these preferential tariff changes came into effect. Within a short time, the 25 or so competing crude oil refineries in the area faced higher freight charges, on the one hand, and seemingly attractive offers for the sale of their refineries, on the other. Payment took the form of cash or Standard Oil Company stock. They were advised to take the stock ' ... for your good!' According to Tarbell, ' ... almost the entire independent oil interest of Cleveland collapsed in three months'. Of the 26 refineries, 21 sold out. At the time, this represented about a fifth of the refining capacity in the USA. Rockefeller is then said to have turned his penetrating gaze towards the refiners of the so-called Oil Regions, Titusville and Oil City, closer to the production areas. Mounting public anxiety about the methods of the Standard Oil Company eventually led to its break-up in 1911.

Whatever they tell us about business practices in the USA in the nineteenth century and beyond, these stories point to one basic fact about the oil business: oil is nearly worthless at the well-head. It must be moved and moved again after refining and in those days, the most effective mode of transport in mid-western America was by railway. All Rockefeller had done was to corner the railroad transit trade. Later, he would do the same in California.

The problems of conveying oil from well-heads to collection points, to refineries and to market are still with us today. With vastly improved tanker and pipeline infrastructure, the distances that can now be covered are enormous. The vital role of the energy transport industry, and the conflicting technical, commercial and geopolitical pressures upon it, make it the object of constant public and political attention and (often) of interference.

3 Problems on the Pipelines

Building and operating pipelines is nearly always a profitable business and most of the world's pipelines are only discussed in relation to routine engineering or financial matters. When a pipeline crosses parts of another country's territory, transit fees need to be negotiated. Often, the host country expects to 'lift' some of the transmitted fuel, usually at some preferential rate. In the European Union (EU) and North America, such matters are negotiated as ordinary commercial transactions. Formal agreements are generally respected and, in case of disagreement, some tractable recourse to law or arbitration is always possible. On the other hand, many pipeline systems have the potential to become part of the fabric of regional or international conflict.

In the case of the former Soviet network, international boundaries were placed in the paths of oil and gas pipelines many years *after* the system had been constructed. Soviet engineers had put together a pipeline system of mind-numbing proportions and complexity. They moved enormous, landlocked hydrocarbon wealth closer to industrial and population centres. During long decades, Glavtransneft supplied crude oil to all the Soviet Republics and erstwhile Warsaw Pact allies. It also provided conduits for exports of crude oil further afield.

In building this system, little regard was paid to internal frontiers between Soviet Republics. Indeed, deliberate interdependence was sometimes built into the system. However, after the dissolution of the Soviet Union, each of the new republics laid

11

claim to pipelines on its own territory. There must have been no more painful spectacle for Soviet pipeline engineers than to see their amazing edifice fragmented and disfigured through the erection of frontiers across their lines of flow. The new configuration has given rise to endless squabbles over transit fees, fuel prices and interference in energy transmission, as well as straightforward political blackmail.

For its part, the Middle East has seen some of the worst quarrels over cross-border pipelines. In the 1960s and 1970s, Syrian transit-fee demands made the Trans-Arabian pipeline ('Tapline'), from Saudi Arabia into Jordan, Syria and Lebanon, economically unworkable. Damascus also wreaked havoc with the operation of the Iraq Petroleum Company (IPC) pipelines, which connect the northern Iraqi fields to the Mediterranean. The actions gave the Syrians a rather unique record as a transit state and convinced Iraq to build alternative, albeit longer and more expensive, lines through Turkey and Saudi Arabia.

Whatever the wisdom of these past squabbles, it is difficult to view them as being driven by commercial considerations alone. The operations of the IPC-lines and the Tapline were repeatedly interrupted by the Syrians, who stood to benefit by many hundreds of millions of dollars through combined packages of 'off take' rights, preferential tariffs and transit fees. In a similar vein, Russian pressure for dominance over former Soviet republics in Eurasia has been perceived at once as high-handed and erratic. The Caucasian and the trans-Caspian republics have thus rediscovered the cardinal rule of energy transmission, valid for producers and consumers alike: the necessity to maintain alternative transmission routes.[12]

What do we make of all this? Like most industrial investments, much of the money for the construction of a pipeline is spent upfront. Operating costs are comparatively small, involving routine maintenance and some energy for pumping. An operator who also owns the line is, thus, vulnerable to pressure by transit countries.[13] On the other hand, much depends on the business climate. Owners and operators of European pipeline systems would expect contracts and common legal frameworks to govern what in effect are large but routine business transactions.[14] However, when political passions are inflamed, as has so often happened in the Middle

East, or geopolitical calculations take precedence, as between Russia and former Soviet republics or former Warsaw Pact countries, prior agreements tend to become only one component of a constantly shifting reality.

Pipelines may also face problems from indigenous elements. In India's north-eastern state of Assam, separatist forces miss no opportunity to blow up regional oil pipelines. Similarly, in Pakistan, the tribesmen of Baluchistan show their displeasure at central government policies with worrying regularity by blowing up gas pipelines. Constructing the economically attractive Iran–Pakistan–India gas pipeline does not, therefore, merely involve solving problems *between* the three regional powers and dealing with diplomatic opposition from the USA. In the South Asian subcontinent, there are immense internal political tensions as well.

Further west, in war-torn Iraq, attacks on oil and gas transmission lines have become part of a struggle likely to determine the country's post-occupation settlement and, indeed, the eventual control of Iraq's vast untapped oil resources. By disrupting pipeline operations, the insurgents have been trying to deprive successive post-Saddam administrations of large amounts of income that could have been used to stabilize the government's hold on power. Instead, several years after the invasion, the situation on the ground would appear to be nothing short of the first ever full-scale pipeline war – in tandem with an accelerating, largely sectarian civil war.

The new wave of construction

Despite these difficulties, much new oil and gas transmission equipment is currently under construction or at advanced stages of planning. Planned expenditure on pipelines in the USA scheduled to begin construction in 2007 was estimated at a little over $11 billion, spread across 93 projects with an average value of $120 million.[15] Elsewhere, the burst of activity is due partly to an emerging customer base for natural gas in expanding economies such as Turkey, India and China, where cleaning up urban air-pollution has become a priority.

The construction of gas-fired electricity generating plants has been another major driver. Since the 1990s, gas-fired power station

construction costs have fallen to about half that of a modern pul-
verized *coal*-fired power plant of comparable output.[16] Gas-fired
combined cycle plants are technically more efficient,[17] can be built
in half the time and payback times – depending on the price of gas
– could be as short as three years: 'This is all the more relevant
when considering the high cost of capital [i.e. high interest rates]
in developing countries.'[18] In addition to producing electricity, the
expanded use of natural gas also provides attractive process routes
for fertilizers and other bulk chemicals such as methanol.

To supply the sharply rising need for gas and the more slowly
but steadily increasing demand for oil, remote new production
areas are being brought on stream. New gas from the Yamalo-
Nenetskiy region of Western Siberia and new production in the
Caspian basin are notable examples. There are, furthermore, vast
untapped gas reserves in Southern Iran, oil *and* gas in Eastern and
North-eastern Siberia and parts of Africa and Latin America, that
are being considered for development. Much new transmission
infrastructure will be needed. The new pipeline trajectories will
invariably reveal much about current thinking around regional
geopolitics and its potential lines of evolution.

Comparing crude oil and natural gas transmission

In general, the engineering of natural gas production and transmission is more complex and expensive than infrastructure for
conveying crude oil. Natural gas field development requires longer
lead-times than corresponding crude oil projects. Greater and
longer-term financial commitments are required, because of the
high gas pressures used and the more stringent safety standards
required. Moreover, gas must be brought to the customer's 'gate',
which commits the owner-operator of the pipeline to the particular customer. On the other hand, securing investment capital for
gas pipelines requires firm, middle- to long-term contracts, often
upwards of ten years. Municipalities, power plant operators and
fertilizer manufacturers are typically customers who are able to
offer such long-term purchasing agreements. The consumers, in
turn, require long-term supply guarantees.

Natural gas transmission differs from the transportation of
crude oil and oil products in several significant respects. First, rail-

cars and trucks are not practical for large-scale operations and are rarely used. Over large distances, natural gas can be piped or conveyed by large cryogenic (refrigerated) tanker ships. For the latter, the gas is pressurized and cooled to very low temperatures; it liquefies and occupies less volume. At the end of the tanker's journey, the LNG is landed, re-gasified and piped to consumers. Usually, about 20 per cent of the fuel is used to liquefy, transport and re-gasify the cargo. Longer distances in LNG tankers lead to further expense and consumption of the cargo for its own refrigeration. All this requires very large capital outlays:

> For a 6 million tons/year ... (about 8.4 billion cubic meter/year) liquefaction plant, LNG tankers, receiving and storage terminals, and regasification facilities can typically cost over four billion dollars. Because of this, for relatively short distances – under about 2,000 miles – pipelines are less expensive than LNG.[19]

Alternatively, natural gas can be compressed, depending on the line, to between 70 and 150 bar,[20] and piped, uninterrupted, from producer to consumer. The need for continuity makes gas transmission more difficult and exacting than crude oil conveyance. Furthermore, in case of rupture, natural gas does not *just* spill or catch fire as crude oil does. It explodes! Gas lines are, therefore, more expensive to build and safety is always a more critical issue. Casually shuffling through daily dispatches, it is not uncommon to find items such as:

> Six months after Sydney was faced with gas shortages caused by the explosion at the Moomba gas complex, cracks in the main Moomba–Sydney gas pipeline have raised the prospect of supply disruptions during a prolonged cold spell this winter.[21]

Or, better, 'A ... man digging a hole escaped serious injury Tuesday when his backhoe ruptured a natural gas pipeline ... and sent up ten-foot flames ... the six-in gas line was buried three to four feet deep...he didn't know natural gas lines ran through the area ... .'[22] In Chapter II, we will outline some of the dangers associated with pipeline operation, even in the absence of war or insurgency.

4 The Oil Shocks and the Rise of Natural Gas

The changing price of oil

In many ways, gas is a newcomer to the world energy scene. In the early 1970s, demand for crude oil was rising worldwide. At that time, OPEC countries put forward demands for a larger share of revenues and greater control over the wealth from oil extracted on their land. In early 1973, the price of crude oil had already started to drift upwards from about $2.80 to $3 per barrel. In that heady atmosphere, even (then) cautious Iraq mustered the courage to nationalize the IPC.[23]

In the autumn of that year, war returned to the Middle East. The pressures on oil prices combined with Arab horror at Egyptian losses on the battlefield and open US support for Israel. The mixture was explosive. The consequences of the ensuing oil embargo have been studied with much care.[24] Essentially, quite suddenly, oil was in short supply. The price of crude jumped to approximately $14–16 per barrel. One auction was actually said to have fetched $22. Suddenly, oil was no longer quite so cheap!

Up until then, the combination of low extraction costs and low crude prices had kept numerous non-OPEC producers at the margins of the oil business. The step increase in prices allowed potential producers with relatively high extraction costs to enter the market. Notable among these were the North Sea producers. The first oil from the UK sector of the North Sea flowed in 1975.[25] After the second oil shock of 1979–80, such high-cost extractors entered the oil business well and truly.

As became apparent later, higher oil prices also allowed many oil consumers to look for alternative sources of energy. Up until the early 1970s, natural gas had not been considered worth trading over long distances. It has been estimated[26] that using the same 20-in pipe diameter, a fuel oil line could carry four times the energy load of a gas pipeline. The transport cost 'per unit of energy per mile' would be almost four times greater for natural gas. Stauffer[27] estimates what he terms the 'gas disability' at a factor between six and 12. Clearly, in times of cheap oil, gas had to be cheaper still and the larger transport costs per unit of energy made gas transmission over long distances unprofitable. It was simply not worth the investment. It is said that the gas flare at Ras Tanura (in Eastern Arabia), burning off unwanted associated gas,[28] could be seen from space.

The major exception to this indifference to gas was the USA, where gas from oil wells had for decades been piped and used as fuel in power stations. After the Second World War, gas from Texas and Louisiana was cheap and credits for 'natural gasoline', the liquid condensate recovered during the processing of natural gas, kept these operations in profit.[29] However, when, during 1973, the price of oil tripled over a relatively short period, the economics of conveying gas over longer distances was transformed.

There has since been much debate about where profits lie in the extraction, transmission and trading of natural gas,[27] but clearly much depends on its price, which has fluctuated by nearly a factor of two in the last two months of 2005 alone.

In the first decade of the twenty-first century, we have also seen sharp increases in oil prices, and an overall economic slow-down has been predicted further down the line. However, the consequences of this latter-day 'oil shock' for industrial economies is observed to be less cataclysmic than during 1973–4 or 1979–80. This appears to be due to the reduced energy component in the value of manufactured products *and* the reduced *oil* component in the overall energy mix. Not unlike what happened in the 1970s, however, high crude oil prices have also altered the economics of a number of alternative fuel conversion routes. In Canada, liquid fuel production from the Athabasca oil sands had begun before the price hikes of 2004. Interested parties in these ventures now include potential partners from as far afield as China. Liquid fuel manufacture from coal has also gained a new lease of life, with China building three demonstration plants to test alternative technologies at near-production scale. Many biomass options have also been reviewed, although actual amounts of fuel from these

PIPELINES: FLOWING OIL AND CRUDE POLITICS

latter processes are bound to be limited. Notwithstanding, the secondary consequences – and the wisdom – of growing plants for manufacturing massive amounts of fuel are very much open to debate.[30]

New gas for old?

A feeling of deja vu seems inevitable when considering the new rush to gas. In reality, the urban environment has been familiar with the use of fuel gas for domestic illumination, heating and cooking for nearly 200 years. The city of Baltimore, Maryland was the first to install commercial gas lighting for residences, streets and businesses back in 1816.[31] Commercial gas plants were subsequently erected by small groups of local entrepreneurs in increasing numbers of towns and cities across the USA. They used mainly standard gaswork kits built in New York City and shipped west by any means available, from freight wagons and canals to rivers and rail. In the latter half of the nineteenth and early part of the twentieth century, gasworks spread to all self-respecting towns and cities the world over. Hatheway[32] has estimated that in the USA alone, some 52,000 local gasworks were constructed over the period, in most towns with 10,000 or more residents. Usually fuelled with coal, these were heavily polluting installations. Some of the by-products of these processes, such as tars and effluent streams containing aromatic compounds, are today considered highly toxic. When reclaiming the land, these fields are now usually simply concreted over.

The 1864-vintage Istanbul gasworks provides an interesting example. The plant had originally been meant for the illumination of the new Imperial Palace at Dolmabahçe. Once electricity became available for the Palace, the gas was piped to homes instead. The installation remained unchanged throughout the following century, while the city's population grew from nearly 700,000 inhabitants in the late nineteenth century to over 5 million in the early 1980s. By then, Istanbul householders had despaired of the low gas pressure and mostly switched to high-sulphur local lignite for heating and liquefied petroleum gas (LPG)[33] for cooking. A visit to the gasworks in 1977, at its second home in the district of Kağıthane, revealed the evils of nineteenth-century industry there for all to see. Labourers walked over cold ash, manually poking the coke charge out of honeycomb ovens into water channels, breathing the emanating dust and smoke, laden with ash (aluminosilicates) and polynuclear aromatic chemicals. Whatever the temperature outside, the men were scorched by the heat radiating from the furnaces. Alive to their danger, the plant engineers complained of putting on weight and considered themselves as men condemned to premature death by various forms of cancer.[34]

Natural gas in the USA

During the Second World War, the US government had constructed large oil pipelines to link the Texas oilfields with the Eastern Seaboard. At the end of the war, these lines were bought by the natural gas industry and converted for gas-transmission. Natural gas was cheap and convenient. Coupled with the post-war discoveries of large gas fields in Texas and Louisiana, it spelled the end of the market for manufactured 'town-gas' in America. In Western and Northern Europe, a similar changeover took place when North Sea gas became available; the switch was mostly completed by the mid-1970s. To satisfy rising European demand, pipeline systems were built to import gas from Russia and Algeria.

Natural gas is a cleaner fuel. It can be rendered nearly free of sulphur and other pollutants with relative ease. For those who would link climate change to carbon dioxide releases, natural gas also produces less carbon dioxide per unit of energy released. It is not surprising, therefore, that in the first decade of the twenty-first century, many great cities of the world are queuing up to import natural gas. Delhi needs to be rid of burning charcoal and cow dung, Beijing of high-sulphur coal and Istanbul from nasty Thracian lignite.

Does gas replace oil?

Before moving on, it is also worth discussing several related points about the increasingly large volumes of natural gas exports from the Gulf countries, in the form of LNG. It has been suggested that these exports have been detrimental to oil sales by OPEC countries and, more specifically, detrimental to oil sales by the Gulf oil states. It has been argued that '... gas displaces oil ...'.[35] The general picture, however, seems a little more complicated.

In the EU, natural gas was not used for power generation prior to 1992. It was considered a premium fuel, to be conserved for *domestic* use by future generations. In 1992, this ban on the use of natural gas for power generation was lifted. Much new gas-fired plant came on stream. Within a short time, the share of natural gas in UK power production grew from nil to about 40 per cent, of a total electricity production capacity of over 70 GW. The new plants have mostly replaced some of the country's ageing *coal*-fired power stations. Thus, in the UK, the main loser from the expanded use of natural gas has been coal, not oil. This is but one example where gas has displaced fuels other than oil.[36] Incidentally, successive UK governments have famously claimed credit for reductions in carbon dioxide emissions, occasioned by the commercially driven switch to gas-fired electricity production in the country after 1992.

Halfway across the world, in energy hungry China, the rules of the game are entirely different. In relatively developed economies, small increments in energy consumption may suffice to power far larger increases in economic growth. For example, the gross domestic product of the UK has nearly doubled since 1970, whilst energy consumption only rose by about 15 per cent during the same period.[37] This was due, at least in part, to the shift away from heavy industries. However, at earlier stages of development, energy utilization appears to increase more in proportion to economic growth. Chinese power-generating capacity is expected to nearly double from its 2005 base, to 900 GW by 2020.[38] More than 80 per cent of this expansion is expected to come from coal. Meanwhile, China is looking to import all the natural gas it can buy at reasonable cost.

In this particular but important case, gas will neither replace oil, nor coal, but merely contribute as one more component in an energy mix that is expanding in total size. In China, natural gas is already being piped over long distances [e.g. from Xinjiang province and from Northern Shaanxi] and will also be imported as LNG. In all of these cases, it will be expensive. Due to the flexibility of natural gas-fired power stations, Chinese engineers anticipate using gas-fired electricity mainly for 'peak load' power production; that is, during periods of surge in electricity demand. If more gas is discovered or can be imported, it would probably first displace some of the older, less efficient and more polluting coal-fired power stations. Either way, the utilization of gas would not *replace* Chinese oil utilization, still less directly reduce China's oil imports.

5 Pipeline Works: Successful Lines and Near Misses

What makes pipelines interesting in terms of our story are the dysfunctional interfaces, usually along geo-political fault lines. Before entering the world of problem pipelines, however, it is important to recall that most pipelines, including a great many cross-border pipelines, do not ordinarily become the focus of international argument or conflict. Such installations are no different than any other component of industrial infrastructure.

Europe's energy infrastructure in brief

Many of Europe's oil and gas companies are wealthy and stable giants. Among these, we can count ENI (Italy), Transco and BG (UK, gas transmission), as well as several of the elder 'sisters', CFP of France, Shell and BP. The industry receives nearly 90 per cent of its crude oil imports by tanker and shifts it around using a complicated web of transnational pipelines, boasting exemplary efficiency and minimal spillage rates.[39] Furthermore, Europe is at present supplied by some 40 transnational gas transmission lines, including five major lines from Russia and two distinct pipeline systems from Algeria.[40] Ostensibly, it all seems to work rather well. Despite the solidity of its infrastructure and the unprecedented prosperity of its constituent nations, however, the EU occasionally manages to sound worried.

In fact, there has always been an underlying problem in the European energy balance and it is simply stated: from the Treaty of Rome onwards, Europe, in all its incarnations, has always been a net importer of oil and gas and the gap is growing. Arguments in an EU Green Paper (November 2000) were fashioned around several worrying facts concerning the European energy equation.[41] The EU was dependent on imports for about 50 per cent of its energy needs. On present trends, ' ... If no measures are taken...', this will rise to about 70 per cent in the next 20 to 30 years. Furthermore, ' ...in geopolitical terms ...', 45 per cent of oil imports come from the Middle East and 40 per cent of gas imports from Russia. By 2030, the overall share of gas (in total energy used) was expected to rise and, at the time, it was considered that this would mainly be at the expense of nuclear energy. Overall, EU dependency on Russian gas was expected to increase as the various Eastern European 'accession' countries joined the Union.[42] It was deemed worrying that some of the new members were dependent on a 'single gas pipeline that links them to a single supplier country'. The ' ... single supplier country ...' was, of course, Russia.

It was noted, furthermore, that competition between the main gas suppliers, Norway, Algeria and Russia, is reduced by the rigidities inherent in the nature of gas transmission and trading infrastructure. These include long-term take-or-pay agreements, without which gas pipeline construction would have been too risky to undertake. It also includes gas price indexing to the price of oil or a combination of fuels, a common feature of many long-term gas supply contracts. The text obsessively returns to ponder Europe's dependence on Russia, all the while praising the 'exemplary stability' of Russian gas supplies over the past quarter of a century. That was before Russia cut gas supplies to Ukraine and Georgia in early 2006, and interrupted oil supplies to Belarus and through Belarus to Eastern Europe in early 2007 (see Chapters V and VIII).

Europe ' ... should keep a watchful eye on the development of oil and gas resources in the Caspian Sea basin and in particular on the transport routes to open up oil and gas production'. These are intriguing comments for the year 2000, about the *now completed* Baku–Tblisi–Ceyhan (BTC) oil pipeline and the Baku–Tblisi–Erzurum gas pipeline (Chapter VI). The EU report singled out Iran and Qatar as possible alternative sources for natural gas imports. With hindsight, these worries seem reasonable. In the intervening five years, demand for gas has continued to rise and the price paid to Russia has nearly doubled to $255 per 1,000 cubic metres (in late 2006), comparable to the customarily high New York City 'gate' price.

Whatever the perceived new threat from Russia as an unreliable supplier, the short-to-medium term alternatives appear to be restricted to reverting to more nuclear-based power generation, probably combined with increased dependence on Russian gas. Indeed, the new Russian-German 'North European' pipeline has an impressive design capacity of 60 billion cubic metres. The UK, with its ageing coal-fired power stations and dwindling gas supplies from the North Sea, must also be considered as a potential customer for more Russian gas.

We will return to Europe's energy prospects in Chapter V. Let us now take a brief look at other continents.

In Latin America

The city of Punta Arenas, near the southern tip of South America, is a bleak and windy place, 2,200 km south of the Chilean capital, Santiago. It has a chequered history of land clearance, European colonization and the extermination of native Patagons. When the Spanish first arrived in these parts, they saw the large island across the straits (Isla Grande) occasionally discharge huge balls of fire. They named it 'Tierra del Fuego', the Land of Fire. The ancient Gods of the Patagons must surely have been angered by the violence and greed of these pitiless invaders, but of late, divine wrath has been soothed with a thoroughly modern twist.

The natural gas fields near Punta Arenas and on Tierra del Fuego have been developed. Reservoir pressures have dropped and the land no longer bursts into flame. In 1984, the place was teeming with young technicians and engineers, paid too well for their own good. There was much gambling and the rest that is part and parcel of boom towns. There was also something else in this strange outpost. There was a light dusting of nerves. Punta Arenas was just the breadth of the Strait of Magellan away from Argentina,[43] from where a military invasion had been expected for some time.

Many years later, in 1998, I was taken to the coal-fired power plant at Tocopilla, nearly 1,300 km north of the capital Santiago. With its small coal port overlooking the Pacific Ocean, the plant quietly sits on the edge of the Atacama Desert, producing power for the gigantic copper mines further inland. It seemed to me that the future of the plant was assured, but I was told, the coal-fired power plants in the North of Chile would switch to peak load only. In other words, coal-fired electricity would be used only when consumption surged above the base load, which was to be produced more economically from natural gas ... and the gas was coming from over the Andes. 'The Andes?' I asked. My patient host explained that one way of keeping Chileans and Argentineans from squabbling was to give both sides a stake in joint ventures. The pipeline coming across was to be jointly owned.

I was also told that our old friends in Punta Arenas were now importing natural gas via a little pipeline from across the Straits of Magellan. The logic was simple. Down there, the Chileans have natural gas but no one to sell it to. The Argentines have a well-developed inland pipeline system. The Chileans *could* have sold gas to Argentina, but the Argentines had enough gas of their own. On the other hand, making methanol (methyl alcohol) from natural gas is known technology. It is a useful chemical that can be shipped in tankers. A company called Methanex in Punta Arenas now operates one of the largest ('*the* largest', I was assured) methanol plants in the world. One third of the gas used in Chile's 'Zona Austral' is now imported from Argentina. That was not all. In the centre of the country, the city of Concepción and the capital Santiago are now also supplied with gas from across the Andes, using two modestly sized 24-in pipelines. The Gas Andes line comes into Santiago from Mendoza, across the mountains, and the Gas Pacifico line feeds the Concepción area from Neuquen in Argentina.

By the standards of Russian gas exports, the quantities of gas involved in these projects are clearly not enormous.[44] Nevertheless, these lines represent sizeable investments, each costing several hundreds of millions of dollars, enabling a profitable trade, bringing a clean fuel to two formerly very polluted cities and several regional power stations, as well as a methanol synthesis plant. The projects also seem to have promoted closer collaboration between the two countries, whose elites, to an outside observer, look equally intelligent, urbane and refined. Might we draw a provisional conclusion that, in Latin America at least, pipelines could also unite?

Not always! The already completed gas pipeline between Bolivia and Brazil has caused dissention in the Bolivian administration, focused on exactly who would benefit from the export of the gas. It has cost the President his job and appears to have ended in tears just when the new incumbent, Evo Morales, was settling into his new job: the Brazilian federal energy company Petrobras is reported to have cancelled investment plans for the expansion of natural gas and oil production in Bolivia. Instead, a decision has been announced to ' ... speed up studies on importing liquefied natural gas (LNG) to guarantee future supplies for Brazil's fast growing gas market ...'.[45] That particular ploy seems to have worked ... to bring Presidents Lula of Brazil and Morales of Bolivia to agree a gas purchase price. How the brief military occupation of oil and gas production facilities within Bolivia affects the medium-term investment climate among oil companies, however, remains to be seen.

Then again, more recently, the presidents of Venezuela and Colombia have signed an agreement for a 177-km line bringing gas to Venezuela's western Lake Maracaibo district. What is interesting about this line is the future intent to network this segment into a system for joint exports of gas to Central America. Another fascinating aspect of the dialogue between the two countries is the expression of interest to build a crude oil line from Venezuela to Colombia's Pacific coast. This would give Venezuela tanker access to East Asian markets, with no less eager customers than China, Japan and Korea. Of course, much would hinge on the security of the pipeline. Presumably, *it* will not be protected by US Special Forces who train Colombian troops detailed to defend the Chevron-owned oil pipeline running to the Gulf of Mexico. We will return to the Colombian pipelines in Chapter II.

In Southern Africa

The construction of a new gas pipeline at the far end of Africa serves as harbinger for another kind of new peace. For over a generation, the Republic of South Africa (RSA) waged covert war on Angola and Mozambique. Mercenary bands were trained and the RSA army staged incursions in support of their proxies. In the heyday of the Cold War, this aggression was aligned with regional

US policy and dressed up as 'fighting communism'. In Mozambique, the undeclared war destroyed much of the limited infrastructure left behind by the Portuguese. However, in the late 1980s, the massive flight of capital, coupled with the disintegration of the Soviet Union, made the 'apartheid' regime both economically unsustainable and strategically expendable.

Much has changed in Southern Africa since the bad old days. The new South Africa has taken care not to undo what they felt to be of value to the community as a whole. They also embraced IMF and World Bank policies which deepened poverty in the country. SASOL is the company originally founded to make synthetic petroleum products from coal, to mitigate the effects of the UN-sponsored oil embargo. It is one of the largest energy companies in Africa and now part-owns a gas pipeline[46] from Mozambique to SASOL's Secunda centre.

Aspects of this infrastructure project make interesting reading. It is calculated that Mozambique has a hydropower potential of about 14,000 megawatts (MW), of which 2,500 MW have so far been developed.[47] However, *internal* demand for electric power is a meagre 200 MW. Nearly the entire output of the Cabora Bassa dam on the Zambezi river is exported to the RSA and Zimbabwe. In Mozambique, about 6 per cent of households have electricity, while energy needs in the countryside are met with wood, charcoal and animal dung. There is significant deforestation, coupled to harmful indoor pollution due to smoke from badly designed and inefficient hearths. The use of ' ... modern cooking fuels is limited ... by their high cost in relation to incomes ...'. In other words, much of the population is still too poor to buy ordinary kerosene or LPG.

According to the International Bank for Reconstruction and Development (IBRD) report, the proposal was ' ... to initiate the development and export of Mozambique's substantial natural gas resources in an environmentally sustainable manner, thereby contributing towards economic growth and poverty reduction ...'. Agreements have been signed between the Government of Mozambique and SASOL for the development of the Pande and Temane gas fields. The construction of a 26-in diameter, 865-km-long pipeline has been completed. It is owned and operated by ROMPCO, a wholly owned SASOL subsidiary.

How to secure cross-border pipelines – Mozambique to Secunda?[48]

This is the first cross-border infrastructure project of its size undertaken in Southern Africa for quite some time. By all accounts, there is reasonable harmony between the present governments of RSA and Mozambique. Commercial lenders have nevertheless approached the project somewhat gingerly.[49] They have made the commercial debt facility conditional on the availability and scope of political risk cover. It seems interesting briefly to review what legal frameworks can be made available for a modern transnational pipeline, constructed between countries that are not hostile, but whose economies and legal frameworks are not integrated to any great extent.

First, the project was designed to give Mozambique a significant stake. The Mozambican National Oil Company (ENH) has invested in the project through two of its subsidiaries. For its part, SASOL spread the 'political risk' by involving export credit agencies in Australia and South Africa, in addition to the European Investment Bank and the Development Bank of South Africa (DBSA). The

'DBSA is assuming full Mozambican political risk for a bridge facility and for the long-term financing'.

The IBRD has been asked to take on the role of guarantor of last resort. Efforts have also been made to achieve the simplest possible package and reduce the complexity of implementing cover by four different underwriters.

The agreements signed by the parties have also attempted to mitigate some of the more asymmetric aspects of this relationship. Provision was made for Mozambique to take a share of the gas, and of the investment possibilities, when her circumstances improve. The system is designed to allow for five gas take-off points within Mozambique, for eventual possible use of some of the gas within the country. The Mozambican (State) Hydrocarbon Company already has a 30 per cent interest in the gas fields and an option to acquire a 30 per cent interest in the Central Processing Facility (CPF), one of the more capital-intensive component parts of the installation. Much appears to depend on when and how the badly mauled Mozambican economy can become strong enough to take advantage of some of these opportunities. More recently, there have been indications that Mozambique is beginning to activate some of these mechanisms.

In this chapter, we have discussed the many ways in which pipelines are necessary components of global, regional or national infrastructure. But are they always desirable? Do they have their down-sides? In the next chapter, we will visit some communities that would *not* like to have pipelines of *any* description anywhere near where they live – *ever, at any price*!

Chapter II

Pipelines and their problems

1 Not In My Backyard!

On Saturday 31 July 2004, the Associated Press reported a gas explosion in the village of Ghislenghien, about 20 miles south-east of Brussels:[1] 'About a half-hour before the explosion, construction workers alerted fire-fighters that they had damaged the underground gas pipeline ...' There was no time to carry out an evacuation: 'A towering wall of fire roared after the blast sent a series of fireballs boiling high into the sky. Everything within 400 yds of the crater caused by the explosion was melted or incinerated.' Some 15 people were killed and more than a hundred injured.

Industrial accidents happen all the time. For the victims, it matters very little that this particular accident was caused by people who should not have been interfering with the pipeline at all. It turns out, over a third of *all* pipeline accidents are caused by 'third-party action'. In other words, it is not sufficient for the pipeline and its contents to quietly mind their own business. Someone may come along, driving an excavator or wielding a pickaxe or, indeed, an explosive, at times, for the perfectly valid reason of seismic mapping for oil or gas exploration.

Corrosion is another major cause of pipeline accidents. There are technical means for suppressing corrosion, but the key to keeping pipelines in good order is routine maintenance. It is normally reasonably expensive. As BP was painfully reminded in Alaska during the summer of 2006, however, a policy of savings based on reduced maintenance eventually costs far more than the intended savings. Mechanical and material failures can also lead to fractures and leaks. Often, statistics are kept for accidents due to earthquakes and, less frequently, due to storm damage. In 2004 and 2005, several exceptionally violent hurricanes wreaked havoc with oil and gas installations in the Gulf of Mexico, but modern pipelines are increasingly designed to withstand such occurrences – or so we were told before Hurricane Katrina. There are, moreover, legal obligations to minimize the risk of accidents, pollution and loss, but in truth, no installation can be totally free of risk. Therefore, when pipeline operators assure us that *their* pipeline is safe for those living nearby, it is entirely legitimate to ask 'how safe is "*safe*"?'

Crude-oil pipelines are no less prone to accidents than gas lines. One routine news item in the *Guardian* newspaper (London, 2 February 2004) reported that (in Kazakhstan) the

> Novyi Uzen-Atyrau-Samara pipeline burst Sunday because of rust ... [and that] ... it was unclear how much oil had leaked. On Thursday, a rupture of the Kalamkas–Karazhanbas–Aktau pipeline, also in the west, caused a leak of more than 220 tons of oil. The leak was stopped within hours.

The poor state of maintenance of the vast Soviet-era pipeline network is often mentioned in the news. It appears, after nearly 16 years of independence, that neither the new Kazakh owners nor the various multinationals collaborating in new local production had significantly improved matters.

There is, however, an additional dimension to this. Post-Soviet Russian statistics show that the greater part of large-diameter pipelines and much of the more recent pipeline construction took place on territory that now falls within the Russian Federation. Partly, at least, this was due to new discoveries of very large fields in Western Siberia and elsewhere, on what is now Russian territory. This is one of the reasons why far fewer pipeline failures are reported per ton-mile within the Russian Federation, compared to the rest of the post-Soviet space.[2]

Some of the Nigerian pipeline incidents similarly make terrible reading. Many of the lines carrying crude from the oilfields towards the north go through rural hinterland that is populated by some of the earth's poorest fellow creatures. These are people who have seen precious little benefit from the more than 350 billion dollars of oil wealth that has (or *not*, as the case may be) passed through the coffers of the Nigerian state in the past several decades.[3] Instead, some locals vandalize the lines, hoping to retrieve a little of what is owed to them. On 30 July 2004, the crude-oil pipeline

> from Port Harcourt to Enugu [was] vandalized at kilometer 190.5 in Ogbeke Agbani ... by unknown persons Wednesday night who scooped fuel into petroleum tankers through a valve drilled into the pipeline ... after the vandals left the scene, fuel continued to flow from the valve until the entire area was flooded and thereby attracted residents of the town who continued to scoop fuel till the early hours of yesterday. [4]

The report then describes how someone approached the oil spill with a lantern and ignited the fuel flowing into a nearby stream. Seven people were killed and scores more were severely burnt. Sadly, this is but one of many similar reports regularly emanating from the area. It is also possible to come across enticing revelations of how to steal fuel from pipelines.

> First, they drill a hole most of the way through, and then they use a rubber mallet to crack open the pipe without making a spark. They insert a valve into the hole and then attach it to a tanker truck with a hose. The whole procedure takes about 20 minutes. You can also tap into a pipeline to steal natural gas.[5]

More recently, however, events in Nigeria have taken a nastier turn, with guerrilla-style attacks on oil installations, abductions of key personnel, bombings and arson.[6] Careless operation by the oil companies has polluted their land and poisoned their water, and the region's poor are angry!

Elsewhere, pipelines have become direct victims of great power competition. In 1982, there were media reports about an explosion involving a Soviet pipeline in the Tyumen region of Siberia. It created an immense crater, uprooting many thousands of large trees that piled up like so many matchsticks. This was one of a series of major accidents in the early-to-mid 1980s that made the Soviets look rather vulnerable. A recent book by a former US Air Force Secretary in the Reagan administration makes the incident sound even more sinister. According to T. C. Reed, this was one disaster the Russians might have spared themselves. Reed claims that this explosion was caused by defects deliberately introduced into a computer code, which the Russians secretly acquired as part of their effort to pilfer technology from the USA:

> In order to disrupt the Soviet gas supply, its hard currency earnings from the West, and the internal Russian economy, the pipeline software that was to run the pumps, turbines, and valves was programmed to go haywire, after a decent interval, to reset pump speeds and valve settings to produce pressures far beyond those acceptable to pipeline joints and welds...The result was the most monumental non-nuclear explosion and fire ever seen from space.[7]

Reed claimed that the Soviets were panicked by this incident into looking for other 'Trojan horses', within the mass of other technology covertly 'acquired' from the West. Russian intelligence officers then responsible for the area have dismissed the story as routine misinformation. Whether this account is true or a more recently minted piece of skulduggery, it highlights the status of oil and gas pipelines as vital pieces on the global geopolitical chessboard.

Are pipelines safe?

In the final analysis, designers can only attempt to minimize the probability and eventually the actual number and severity of accidents, but no pipeline, indeed no industrial installation, can ever be entirely accident-free. In parts of the developed world where public scrutiny is reasonably effective, reducing the numbers of incidents and accident severity can earn a degree of public acceptance, as well as incur savings on payouts for damages. On the other hand, ensuring pipeline safety *can* be costly. In general, capital outlays rise steeply with increasing margins of safety.

'Ultimate' safety can mean an expensive state of near or total paralysis. Safety procedures also tend to place restrictions on the way operators are allowed to work. On a day-to-day basis, such measures tend to irritate – even if the procedures are designed to protect the operators themselves. For all these reasons, working designs usually represent compromises between desired levels of safety, rising costs and ease of operation. This is not an exact science and, in any given situation, there is rarely a single correct solution to a given problem. Much 'sound judgement' and 'experience' is brought to bear.

For perfectly sound reasons, therefore, the presence of a pipeline nearby rarely makes householders very happy. It might adversely affect property prices. Others might worry that security considerations would lead to increased police or military presence in their living space. The latter may not be a problem for the gas pipeline running under Hampstead Heath, in London, but in rural Colombia, or indeed in occupied Iraq, much military action revolves around pipeline trajectories. For civilian bystanders, furthermore, the rights and wrongs of attacking pipelines matter considerably less than risks to personal safety. They could be excused for thinking of life near pipelines as less than salubrious. Even in the absence of violent conflict, newspaper headlines such as 'No gas pipeline deaths in state 1986–2005' do not really inspire confidence.[8]

Despite these difficulties, oil and gas are still desirable fuels. We live in an age when even Bedouins in Arabia have abandoned their trusty old camels for the noise and pollution of Nissan-Datsun pickups. The transport of oil and gas to points of need has thus become a critical function and pipelines have an essential role to play. What is more, they invariably run through somebody's backyard. At the beginning of the twenty-first century, pipelines have become ubiquitous features of the landscape. We are all learning to live with them.

The watchdogs

Two types of organization are charged with safety matters regarding the operation of pipelines. Industry-led 'voluntary' associations have their counterparts in public regulatory bodies. In Europe, Conservation of Clean Air and Water in Europe (CONCAWE) acts as the major industry-led association monitoring pipeline related incidents. Before the accession of ten new countries in 2004, CONCAWE covered virtually all cross-country oil pipelines in the European Union, with a total length of about 35,000 km.

In its Report No 4/96, the organization admits ten incidents during 1995, with a net spillage of about 654 cubic metres of oil and oil products. The document claims a long-term downward trend in both the number of spillage incidents and in volumes of liquids spilt. Interestingly, the organization notes *no* link between pipeline age and failure rates. They consider, with – apparently justifiable – satisfaction, that this 'can be attributed to continually improving maintenance and inspection techniques'. Effectively, a comparison of five yearly accident statistics suggests a decline of spillages per 1,000 km p.a. by a factor of four between 1971–5 and 1996–2000. In the same period, the share of incidents due to third-party activity had climbed from 38 to nearly 55 per cent, whilst the total *number* of other incidents had diminished.[9] By 2004 (the last available year), the number of spillages had stabilized at five p.a., with only 65 cubic metres of unrecovered spillage.[10] In the USA, the Association of Oil Pipelines (AOPL) boasts 200,000 miles of pipeline to 'supply us with a commodity that is fundamental to the American way of life'. They publish safety records, as well as policies on accident prevention and results of clean-up and response operations. At Federal level, the Office of Pipeline Safety acts as the regulatory body, in conjunction with several lower tiers of regulatory bodies at state and county level.

Pipeline monitoring in the former Soviet Union presents a very different picture. Post-Soviet Russian statistics admit a nearly seven times greater rate of pipeline-related accidents compared to their European counterparts.[11] The breathless Soviet pipeline construction programmes of the 1950s and 1960s have left a legacy of low-grade, low-technology installations. The same source explains that ' ... national standards of design and construction of main oil pipelines are no less stringent than their foreign counterparts, but controls which ensure that they are adhered to are obviously inadequate ... .' It had been insistently reported, furthermore, that maintenance was not given high priority during the latter years of the Soviet Union.

There is an added twist to this picture of messy, rapid expansion of pipeline construction in the Soviet Union. Before 1975, 'a considerable number of pipelines were constructed and commissioned

34

without any remote control of the pipe-line facilities ... the necessary equipment and communication lines did not exist'.[12] Such control instrumentation would have been extremely useful, not to say indispensable, in steering as vast a pipeline network as that of the Soviet Union, intended as it was to work as a single integrated unit. After the mid-1970s, the gap with the West widened even more, as process control industries in the USA and Europe moved rapidly to exploit developments in the use of small, fast microprocessors. I feel we owe respect to our Soviet colleagues in these matters. Western engineers, schooled in a world of relative plenty, would probably have pronounced these tasks as 'impossible', a turn of phrase probably best used with circumspection in the Soviet Union of old.

The truth is that every pipeline has its history of spills, incidents and accidents. Even the spectacularly expensive trans-Alaska oil pipeline (TAPS) is not immune to mishaps. In 2001, a man returning from a hunt went for a few drinks and on the way home took a few shots at an elevated stretch of the pipeline. He seems to have missed with his first four, but scored a direct hit with his last high-velocity bullet. Some 6,800 barrels of crude leaked from the hole (285,600 gallons). It was TAPS's biggest spill ' ... since the 16,000-barrel (672,000-gallon) spill when the line was bombed with plastic explosives at Steel Creek near Fairbanks in February 1978 by parties still unknown. (The *Exxon Valdez* spill was far larger at 260,000 barrels.)'.[13] Not surprisingly, the offender received a prison sentence and an astonishingly large fine, which he will never be able to pay. The line's operator, BP, might well argue that one cannot legislate against such mishaps, but it appears that the problems that overtook them in the spring and summer of 2006 were entirely avoidable.

In March 2006, over 200,000 gallons of crude oil leaked from a pipe on the western side of Prudhoe Bay. Corrosion was blamed. In August of the same year, following another leak and the discovery of further corrosion in the gathering lines, BP shut down much of the production at Prudhoe Bay and the trans-Alaska pipeline.[14] There appeared to have been a whiff of panic. About 8 per cent of US crude oil production was taken off-line for several days, before flows were gradually restored. It made the news! Oil prices, already at record highs in anticipation of new storms in the

Gulf of Mexico, rose by over two dollars on the day's news to almost $77 a barrel![15]

For some years, there had been rumours and reports that BP, part-owner and sole operator of the trans-Alaska pipeline, was cutting corners in maintaining the TAPS and its other installations near the Prudhoe Bay oilfields.[16] There were allegations of intimidation against employees and government inspectors who had pointed out defects in maintenance.[17] A draft report by an engineering firm, written in 2001 warning of corrosion, was said to have been toned down after a request by BP.[18] The emerging picture is one which suggests that the company had instituted a policy (at what level remains unclear) to economize on maintenance.

In the summer of 2006, the matter was finally taken up by the various regulatory bodies which, it appears, should have been asking questions some years earlier.[19] In the event, there were also accusations that the shutdown was timed to maximize profits,[20] although the State of Alaska records indicate a difference from expected production of no more than 9 per cent,[21] since summertime would have been a period of scheduled maintenance. If anything, media interest appeared to have exacerbated apprehensions and boosted the oil price for a short spell. By mid-September 2006, production was restored to nearly full capacity.

2 Standards of Safety and Environmental Care in Rich and Poor Countries

The great accumulation of wealth and increased prosperity of the past 50 years has changed many things in Japan. Safety and environmental standards have improved in ways that reflect the quality of life citizens come to expect in an affluent society. The energy requirements of the country have increased proportionately, to reflect the needs of a wealthier population. Natural gas is the fuel of choice, for domestic use as well as for firing in power stations. Japan imports some 12 per cent of its total energy needs in the form of LNG, using refrigerated tankers. The development of offshore gas fields near Sakhalin Island, in the Russian Federation, provides a convenient new source of supply (see Chapter VII), and in May 2003, the City of Tokyo signed a purchasing agreement for 1.1 million p.a. of LNG from the Sakhalin-II project, about 12 per cent of total project capacity.

Even in Japan, however, environmental consciousness did not always claim such high priority. Only 25 years ago, UK chemical companies considered that investments in new plant generally cost less in Japan ' … because *they* do not have to worry about emissions as much as we do …'. At the time, we were engaged in examining the design of plant components for the manufacture of PTFE (i.e. 'Teflon'). The effluent streams that the Japanese counterparts were not barred (*at that time*) from discharging to air and sea happened to contain some very nasty compounds indeed. In time, the country chose to require higher environmental standards of its industry.

Within this context, whether projects undertaken in newly industrialized countries should be required to conform to higher environmental norms adopted by already industrialized countries poses a complicated dilemma. Standards *presently* in force in Western Europe or North America, or indeed in Japan, are clearly desirable everywhere, yet they are likely to impair the potential attractions (read profitability) of projects under consideration in many Third World countries.

This is an interesting problem. Could levels of pollution by some of the Third World's nascent industries be perceived as less sinister and deadly than they really are? For example, what to think of the large steel mill within the city limits of Taiyuan (capital of Shanxi Province, China) or of the pair of power plants on the rim of Ulaan Bataar City in Mongolia? The former Soviet Union has also had its share of riding roughshod over the health and well-being of its population, at the expense of hasty industrialization, in many instances exacerbated by careless planning. Not all industrializing countries, however, are poor. Paper mills around Recife, in North-east Brazil, discharge directly into small rivers crossing the residential areas of the less well-off.

It is as well to recall that, as late as the mid-twentieth century, coal-fired power plants were operating well inside the grand metropolitan centres of the far wealthier West. The now disused Battersea Power Station, with its *Art Deco* architecture and remarkable quadrille of smokestacks, is a popular Central London landmark. Another disused power station in the heart of London, just across the River Thames from St Paul's Cathedral, now houses the celebrated Tate Modern Museum. New York has its own closed-down power stations along the East river, right inside Manhattan Island. These power plants ceased to operate a good long time after the UK and the USA had reached very high levels of industrialization and prosperity. Present-day China has also commenced her own analyses of environmental pollution problems, with a new readiness to invest in clean technologies and to clean up past pollution. The move appears consistent with improving living standards, increasing wealth and industrial sophistication.

Within this framework, the contrast between modes of operation of the same companies in industrialized and less developed countries is a legitimate object of concern. Many developing countries accept lower safety and environmental standards than inward investors would face in their own countries. BP in Colombia and in Alaska, and Shell in Nigeria and in Indonesia, have faced allegations of human rights violations in addition to environmental irresponsibility, in a way that does not (usually) arise in the European or North American operations of these companies.

However, even under reasonably democratic regimes boasting transparency in governance, it is often difficult for individuals to square up to the legal and political might of oil and gas companies. Experience suggests that it is one thing to be allowed to say 'not in my backyard!' and quite another to make it stick. Opponents of the Corrib gas pipeline in north County Mayo, in the Republic of Ireland, have had a taste of just how worrying life can become when a company the size of Shell brings their overseas habits nearer to home. The company's intransigence and the local anxiety about high-pressure lines very near the village have brought matters to the courts and to ' … demonstration outside the Dáil today to protest at the latest activities of Shell …'.[22] It took *years* to finally persuade Shell to re-route the pipeline, by not very much at all, and that story is still running.

The case of the Baku–Tblisi–Ceyhan pipeline

A booklet published by Amnesty International in May 2003, about the Baku–Tblisi–Ceyhan pipeline (BTC) and its *likely* effects on human rights in Turkey, makes interesting reading.[23] At the time of the report's publication, construction of the (now completed) pipeline had not commenced.

This is the first and, apart from a subsequent report on the Chad–Cameroon oil pipeline,[24] only Amnesty International report focused specifically on a single pipeline project. The organization has given no explanation for this, or any reason why Turkey was signalled out for attention among the several countries on the trajectory of the BTC pipeline. The report, nevertheless, raises some perfectly valid points. The first is an objection to clauses in the contract that fix the environmental obligations of the companies involved to present-day local legislation. In other words, future legal improvements in environmental standards would not be enforceable.

Some of these issues may appear a little arcane to the ordinary reader. They are nonetheless vital. The report explains that Turkey presently adheres to the European Social Charter of 1961, but has entered reservations relating to health and safety in the workplace. In plain language, this means that at present, the health and safety of Turkish workers are not as well protected as their European counterparts. The report goes on to speculate (probably correctly) that ' … looking towards EU accession, Turkey will be forced to drop [these] reservations … '. However, the Host Government Agreement between the BTC Consortium, led by British Petroleum and the Government of Turkey, states '… if the economic equilibrium of the project is negatively affected by any such [legislative] changes, then the Turkish state must compensate the project for the loss … '.

The same report cites several instances in different parts of the country, where Turkish authorities have reacted harshly to press opposition and to public protests by environmental activists against mining and hydroelectric projects. During the past decade, such cases have been taken up by diverse non-governmental organizations (NGOs). The report alleges that, often, protesters are brought to court and charged with unconnected and rather grave offences, apparently designed to deter future protest.

Looking after safety and pollution prevention can cost a great deal of money. In countries where indemnity payments for damage to third parties are not very large, it is tempting for local industries to let matters slide. Apart from its terrible record of pipeline vandalism, Nigeria provides numerous examples of careless operation in oil and gas exploration, production and transmission, of rusty pipelines, and of frequent pipeline spills, fires and explosions. The country also provides an example where close association between an entrenched political elite and the oil companies has allowed maximizing profits to be at the expense of a degrading environment and neglect of public health.

It may be recalled how protests against environmental damage caused by Shell's operations in Ogoniland led to mass *executions* by the Nigerian government. One of the victims, the author Ken Sarawiwa, was a literary figure. Many observers still hold Shell morally responsible for those deaths. The tragedy is intriguing, as the company has an exemplary health and safety record when operating in countries requiring higher standards,[25] particularly in countries where indemnity payments could be high. However slowly, all this seems to be changing. Lawyers have claimed that, in the light of recent rulings, ' ... All British companies have to be clear if they act abroad and do damage they can find a case brought against them in the High Court in London'.[26]

Particular combinations of internal factors thus appear likely to bring about a mix of neglect, endemic poverty and environmental pollution. Public scrutiny may not always be a panacea, but considering the catastrophic failures, say, in Nigeria or in parts of the former Soviet Union (FSU), it seems certain that a measure of local representation and control might help improve matters. News filtering out of Nigeria suggests that local communities no longer expect assistance from the Federal Government. One report from the Niger Delta explains how five towns that make up the Brass Kingdom in Bayelsa State have decided to 'take on the Italian oil giant Agip-Nigeria Limited over the incessant spill of oil in their waters', which poisons the water and kills the fish, threatening their health and their livelihoods.[27] Elsewhere, in Ilaje (Ondo State), the residents were reported to be preparing 'to rise up in self-defence' against oil companies that have failed to address the frequent oil spillages.[28] The elements of local armed resistance that have since taken hold in the Niger Delta were quite long in coming. It seems difficult to see how peace can be re-established before the oil producers clean up their act.

The point at issue is the degree to which the state allows the agents of resource extraction to maximize profits at the expense of environmentally sound and socially equitable exploitation. In this sense, home-grown private and state-owned companies of the FSU or, indeed, of transitional Third World economies such as Turkey and Brazil[29] seem to trespass just as ruthlessly as multinationals operating, say, in Colombia or Nigeria. In the absence of legal mechanisms for effective public scrutiny, failings relating to revenue sharing and poor environmental protection inevitably spill over into problems of governance.

For a decade or more, business leaders and politicians have been telling us that the drive to globalize capital investment and access to markets requires a 'level playing field'. We have yet to hear the voice of the common man, demanding an equally level playing field in matters concerning health and safety standards and some level of social protection, if not necessarily equal pay. Remember, however, that the strengthening of civic power and rising social costs in industrialized economies had contributed to the push for exporting capital to the less-developed world in the first place. This is one of the defining contradictions of present-day globalization.

3 Resource Blessing or Resource Curse: Does Anybody Win?

It is well known that when Major Frank Holmes promised King Abdelaziz al-Saud the heady sum of £2,000 p.a. in return for permission to drill for oil in his parched domains, the nomad King was hoping they might instead find a little water by mistake. Holmes failed to find oil and failed to find water as well. He missed his last two payments. By the time Socal arrived,[30] the stakes had been raised, not least by the efforts of H. St John B. Philby acting as an advisor to the King. The now famous settlement cost Socal an immediate loan of £30,000, plus a first annual rent of £5,000, all in gold. The 35,000 English sovereigns sent to Jeddah on a P&O steamer were counted, one by one, by Abdullah Sulaiman, the King's Finance Minister.

The sale of oil exploration licences in the Kingdom of Arabia plugged a hole in the King's perennially disorganized finances. It is equally well known that once the Americans struck oil, the increased income they provided disappeared from the King's treasury as water droplets on hot sand. His expenses nearly always ran ahead of his income, to maintain in some sort of regal style his constantly growing household, and to pay for presents a great king was expected to bestow upon chiefs of friendly tribes and to bribe those of uncertain loyalty. His Minister of Finance was always asking for more money. The hard-nosed oilmen hummed and hawed, but in the end they invariably provided that little more than they had previously agreed to pay. No one ever questioned, however, that all this was God-given bounty, meant for disposal by the will of the King alone.

At the other end of the spectrum, Norway's democratic, parsimonious and very Protestant institutions invest part of the oil income for the future and distribute public wealth through a meticulously conceived social security apparatus. However, state revenue is only part of the vast sums associated with the oil trade. It would take a brave man to dissect the accounting practices of vertically integrated oil companies. They are known to be adept at moving expenses and profits, gains and losses from one part of the chain to the other, to minimize tax and maximize overall profit.

The resource curse argument

It has often been argued that the discovery of oil and gas in the North Sea has been detrimental to industrial development in the UK. The positive effect of North Sea oil and gas production on the balance of payments, so the argument runs, has helped to maintain the currency at too high a level for British industry to compete with rivals in other industrialized countries. In other words, the 'high pound' made British industrial products more expensive compared to those of their competitors.

It would be naive to explain the great historical decline of British industry in terms of a single factor, which occurred quite late in the life of the industry. Events from recent history suggest, however, that we may safely consider the 'resource curse argument' as at least one of the factors that shaped British industrial trends in the last quarter of the twentieth century. It is difficult to remember the incompetence of Mrs Thatcher's governments with anything but astonishment. In 1980–1, the value of the currency was allowed to drift as high as $2.44, combined with interest rates held at around 15–16 per cent. Vast swathes of British industry were forced to shut their gates and several million workers lost their jobs. Public accounts of these events later given by the then Chancellor and the minister responsible for industry suggest that what little they understood of the consequences of their own actions, they themselves did not approve of. In this unbelievable experiment, the salient factors were the high value of the pound and the high level of interest rates, and it *was* indeed all done on the back of oil and gas production.

It is not possible to do justice to this subject in the space available. Before moving on, however, it is worth pointing out that large incomes from oil have allowed ruling elites in many oil-producing countries to decouple their regimes from the tax-paying multitude. The ruler may recruit an army and structure the state with no need for public consent. The argument applies equally well to any other naturally occurring commodity that provides the central power with a large income. Some of the examples are perverse. Angola's diamonds served to maintain Jonas Savimbi fighting in the field against the government in Luanda long after the CIA had any further need of him. It is widely rumoured that in the end, they had to betray his whereabouts to central government forces and the Angolan military did the inevitable.

An important part of this inevitably simplified argument is that oil and gas discoveries in poor countries rarely benefit the population at large and that the political elites tend to appropriate the surplus income. In the next section, we will examine the proposition that the exploitation of these resources regularly leads to conflicts, often centred on transmission lines.

4 Contentious Pipelines and the Militarization Debate

> … what is particularly obscene is that corporations – knowing the threat of death on their pipelines – go ahead and build them anyway.[31]

A little carelessly, this particular proposition bundles together two distinct problems. The first is the matter of wars over resources, as has been taking place for decades in the Middle East, in Angola and the

Congo, over oil, over copper, over diamonds, over the vast mineral wealth of so many pitifully war-torn African countries. The second argument concerns injury to communities that live near pipelines under attack. It must be admitted that, for the local inhabitants, the difference between war over resources and fighting that spills over from infrastructure projects may appear somewhat subtle. As one approaches crisis situations, the mechanisms underlying events on the ground become increasingly blurred. Nonetheless, these differences are important. Variations on the theme that 'war is caused by pipelines' appear with frequency and it seems useful to address this in a book about problem pipelines. Let us see how the record reads in respect of the ' ... threat of death on their pipelines ... '.

In Colombia

According to a despatch dated 25 August 2003:

> rebels bombed the Caño Limón pipeline Saturday afternoon near the village of Arauquita in Colombia's war-torn Arauca province ... the 23rd time this year that guerrilla fighters have blown up a section of the tube, compared with 42 bombings during 2002 ... jointly owned by state oil firm Empresa de Petroleos de Colombia, or Ecopetrol, and U.S. company Occidental Petroleum Inc. ... Last year, U.S. lawmakers approved $98 million in military aid to pay for U.S. training for Colombian troops guarding the pipeline... The 780-kilometer pipeline transports roughly 110,000 barrels of crude a day from the Caño Limón field in the north-eastern state of Arauca to the Atlantic port of Covenas for export.[32]

Earlier, in 2001, these attacks cost Occidental $75 million in profits, whilst the Colombian government lost $430 million in oil revenue.[33] It is not difficult to imagine the many ways in which local people can be dragged into nearby fighting during a civil war. The despatch of US marines was, no doubt, an additional and politically significant portent of measures being considered in response to these attacks and to Colombia's wider, 40-year-old, drug-infested multiple civil wars.

Whilst, admittedly, the $430 million lost in oil revenue is a respectable sum, the $98 million military aid budget provided by the US government for protecting the pipeline does appear as a rather large proportion of the potential prize. According to the San Francisco Chronicle:

> U.S. officials say training a battalion of 1,000 men to guard a petroleum pipeline is not part of the war on terrorism but rather an effort to preserve Colombia's economy, which derives about one-third of its export earnings from oil. The pipeline is 'important for the future of . . . our (U.S.) petroleum supplies and the confidence of our investors,' said U.S. Ambassador Anne Patterson in a recent interview with the leading Bogota daily *El Tiempo*. Critics, including community leaders in towns alongside the pipeline and the guerrillas, say the shift will intensify the conflict in Colombia's oil-rich northeast.[34]

Let us first dispose of one obvious difficulty in the previous paragraph. It seems easier to believe that the phrases 'our petroleum supplies' and 'our investors' attributed in this article to the US ambassador resulted from mistakes in translation, although one can no longer be certain of such matters. The overall picture suggests that the escalation of fighting along this and possibly other pipelines had resulted directly from an overall intensification of the civil war, rather than the conflagration being stoked-up by the existence of the pipeline itself. On the other hand, for the peasants living in the vicinity, this is clearly a case where they would not have asked for a pipeline in their own backyard, if only somebody would have cared to consult them.

In Iraq and Sudan

Another major fight over pipeline facilities is taking place in Iraq, where well over a hundred major attacks have been recorded every calendar year from 2004. Many of the breaches can be repaired in a matter of days. However, the frequency of attacks has tended to reduce the overall flow of oil and reportedly affected the volume of exports (Chapter III). The Saddam Hussein administration had a policy of paying local tribes to 'protect' the pipelines, which the occupation administration had discontinued, apparently as part of their policy of starting with a 'clean slate'. The first attacks on Iraqi pipelines had initially been interpreted as signals

45

of resentment against this interruption of payments. By the middle of 2004, however, the insurgency had already been generalized to an extent that made it difficult to speculate about the motives or perpetrators of particular attacks. The so-called 'clean slate' policy has since been reviled by officialdom on both sides of the Atlantic, with an intensity that makes its original implementation even more curious. In any case, the ensuing struggle around the pipelines has since emerged as one major element of resistance to the occupation of Iraq.

Elsewhere, there are many more pipelines under military threat. The Khartoum–Port Sudan oil pipeline provides an outlet for one of the more recent countries to join the oil exporters club. The line[35] has been a repeated target of the Sudan People's Liberation Army (SPLA) guerrillas, who had vowed to deny the central government a source of income that would have helped them prosecute the civil war. Observers agree that the 20-year-old civil war intensified considerably when the country started producing oil in 1999. The fighting and attacks on the pipeline have died down since a US-sponsored agreement for a '50–50 split' of oil revenues between the government and the SPLA.

The Baku–Tblisi–Ceyhan line and its opponents

A similar 'militarization' argument has been used in discussing the construction of the BTC pipeline. There is a lengthy report entitled 'Some common concerns', prepared by a consortium of NGOs,[36] which makes a number of allegations against British Petroleum (BP), the operator and main shareholder of the BTC-pipeline. It claims that during the construction of the 837-km OCENSA oil pipeline in Colombia, the land compensation packages offered to the local peasants were intended to pay for a strip of 'right of way' for the pipeline through farmlands. The strip was just 12.5 m wide. However, the report continues

> The military imposed a civilian-free corridor and a curfew
> along parts of the pipeline, which blocked locals' access to their
> land and, for some, to their homes. As a result of the environmental damage and the security presence, a corridor of up to
> 200m wide has in fact been taken away from local people.

In a fascinating subsequent development, some 1,000 Colombian farmers sued BP for $28 million over claims of harassment they had suffered at the hands of far-right paramilitary groups as a result of their opposition to the OCENSA pipeline.[37] Lawyers for the farmers said they never accused BP of working with the paramilitaries: 'But the farmers' opposition to the pipeline put them in the paramilitaries' sights.' It was claimed, furthermore, that recent rulings enable British companies to be sued in British courts for what they do in the rest of the world. BP decided to pay undisclosed damages after the publication of two reports commissioned by environmental experts from Colombia's National University, detailing the extent of the damage to the zone.[38]

Returning to 'Some common concerns', the document suggests that, with an already sullied record, BP could not be trusted to behave well, within the framework of the BTC project, crossing through Azerbaijan, Georgia and Turkey. It states:

> the pipeline system would only skirt the predominantly
> Kurdish regions of south-eastern Turkey, [but] it would pass
> through areas of north-eastern Turkey where Kurds make up
> around 40 per cent of the population ... [and that] ...
> pipelines would require a continuous militarized corridor
> which would undoubtedly threaten the existing fragile cease-
> fire between Turkey and Kurdish groups.

Once again, there is a difficulty in distinguishing between reasonable, indeed urgent, concerns for the human rights of local populations and the debate on militarization *due* to pipelines. The record, however, presents a different picture.

At the end of the Second World War, in one of his less publicized blunders, Stalin had demanded that Turkey cede Kars, Ardahan and Artvin to the Soviet Union. These are three present-day Turkish provinces contiguous with the former Soviet frontier.[39] In response, the 'Truman doctrine' extended NATO's massive retaliation umbrella to cover Greece and Turkey. Meanwhile, NATO's and Turkey's military postures in the face of regional Soviet belligerence turned Eastern Anatolia into a heavily militarized zone. It was in the south of this zone that civil war erupted between the Turkish government and the Kurdish insurgency in the 1980s, well before the end of the Cold War. Some 30,000 people lost their lives. There has been a lull in fighting since the capture of the PKK leader Abdullah Öcalan, although everyone in the region seems to await developments with fingers on the trigger. It is difficult to see how a new pipeline or any other infrastructure project would lead to the *further* militarization of this area. In this context, the pipeline would appear to be no more or less provocative of war or insurgency than any other infrastructure project being carried out in the area.

Like much of the rest of the country, the Eastern and Southeastern parts of Turkey present a captivating mosaic of diverse ethnic and religious groups, who have not always been on the friendliest of terms with one another.[40] Historical enmities between Kurds and Armenians are legend. The point remains, however, that the manner in which local inhabitants are treated by the State during the settlement of land compensation claims and relocations due to major engineering projects is always a matter of concern. It is difficult to claim that citizens have confidence in the generosity of the Turkish State in settling compensation claims or that the relocation of local communities has ever been done with sensitivity. There are persistent problems in this region involving the protection of the legal rights of local populations during the execution of large engineering projects, whatever their ethnic origins. Confounding these very legitimate concerns with specious arguments in respect of possible militarization seems a needless diversion. It would make far more sense to tackle these problems as civic society and human rights issues.

In the next chapter, we will observe how 'geopolitical blockages' affect oil and gas transmission in the Middle East and how alternative transmission routes can perform a vital function in times of crisis.

Chapter III

Hostage pipelines of the Middle East

Nowadays it seems difficult to recall the age when Mosul, Baghdad and Basra were backwater provinces, existing calmly under the distant shadow of an impoverished Turkish Empire. In 1869, the Ottoman governor of Baghdad Province, Mithat Pasha, wrote to the Grand Vizier in Istanbul for permission to reclaim Turkish sovereignty over the al-Hasa strip. This was a patch of land a little further to the south, along the eastern edge of Arabia, between Kuwait and Qatar. The Governor explained that fighting between two sons of the Al-Saud in neighbouring Nejd had created an opportunity for installing a friendly notable in Riyadh, who would be willing to serve as the local Turkish subprefect. The move on Hasa was seen as part of an effort to counter British encroachment on the western shores of the Gulf and South Arabia. By 1870, the Trucial States, the once feared pirates of these dangerous waters, had fallen under the sway of British India, alongside Muscat and Oman and more recently Bahrain. Latterly, the British had landed fresh troops at Aden.

Mithat Pasha was an able man. He was aware that the cash-strapped Ottoman treasury could not meet the expenses of the new local administration. Furthermore, several battalions would be needed to preserve a semblance of order between the warlike tribes of the interior and the vulnerable farming communities of the coastal strip. The Governor assured his superiors that he had a plan to make the area pay for the new administration: 'The date groves roughly equalled the size of those in Baghdad... while exceeding them in productiveness ... .' In addition to agriculture, he had ' ... identified important sources of taxable income ... in pearls, trade, animal husbandry and fishing, centred on Hufuf, Qatif, Dammam, and Uqayr ...'. The Council of Ministers in Istanbul debated the matter and duly submitted to the Sovereign that an expedition to al-Hasa be undertaken. In May 1871, the Ottomans landed a force of 3,000 Turkish troops, supported by 1,500 Arab auxiliaries at Ras Tanura.[1]

The expedition failed, although the Turks managed to keep the Al-Saud clan out of Riyadh for another 30 years; but on a dusty morning in 1902, one young scion of the exiled family ambushed the rival al-Rashid governor of Riyadh by the city gates and stabbed him to death. His band then stealthily entered the city. They murdered everyone they could lay their hands on. At the time, Abdul-Aziz bin Abdul-Rahman bin Faisal al-Saud was just 22 years of age. After his success, he assumed the leadership of the clan, even though his father was still alive. In time, he expanded the kingdom to cover al-Hasa in the East, and in the mid-1920s, his warriors overran the Hejaz and Asir in the West. Such were the humble beginnings of the 'Saudi' Arabian kingdom.

When he died in 1953, King Ibn Saud left a very different Arabia behind. Nearly 70 years after the Turkish expedition, beneath the soil where Mithat Pasha had sought to tax date palms and plentiful goat's milk, Socal and Texaco found colossal oil wealth. By then, the Turks had long gone and the British, who had replaced them as the regional power, had already lost influence through a mixture of bad luck and ill-advised parsimony. However, Arabia is not where the amazing story of Middle Eastern oil actually began. Given the many accomplished accounts in print, however, it seems sensible to mention only briefly a few critical turning points of this formative period in the Middle East.

1 The Dusty Beginnings: The Temple of Fire and the 'Vilayet' of Mosul

Before the First World War, oil was first discovered in Iran. The earliest expedition had been funded by an Englishman, William Knox D'Arcy, who had made a fortune reworking a disused Australian gold mine. Success eluded the expedition at first. As expenses grew, the Burmah Oil Company was brought in to keep the venture alive. Yergin[2] describes how the leader of this difficult expedition, George Reynolds ('solid English oak'), kept the work going during long years of dry wells, managing to keep a step or two ahead of a letter from the managers in Glasgow, eager to close down the operation. In early 1908, *that* letter was finally in the post when the team struck oil, nearly seven years after their first attempt. It was near the site of a pre-Islamic temple of fire, 'Masjid-i Sulaiman', the Temple of Solomon, where rock formations were saturated with surface seepages of oil.

Despite his success, the dour Reynolds was suffered to keep his job for only another two years. He was fired unceremoniously, with a bonus of £1,000 'for his trouble'. Meanwhile, his discoveries led to the formation of the Anglo-Persian Oil Company in 1909, later renamed the Anglo-Iranian Oil Company and finally BP. The first pipeline in the Middle East was laid between Masjid-i Sulaiman and Abadan Island on the Shatt-el Arab waterway, where a refinery was quickly built and expanded in successive stages. Meanwhile, the age of oil-fired warships had dawned and the British Government needed to secure future supplies. Days before the general mobilizations of 1914, the Anglo-Persian Oil Company was effectively taken under the wing of the British Government. They bought a 51 per cent share in the company.

Meanwhile, in nearby Iraq, many potential oil deposits had been identified through surface seepages. Well before the War, place names such as Kirkuk, Tuz and Qaiyara had been carefully marked on maps drawn up for future exploration. In many of these localities, artisanal digging had already produced oil for local consumption. In Istanbul, a 'Turkish Petroleum Company' was constituted, which cautiously balanced British and German interests, and the Privy Purse of the Ottoman Sultan eagerly took a large share.

It has recently become widely known that Iraq is composed of three distinct provinces that do not easily graft together. The Ottomans had administered them through three separate governorships, answering directly to Istanbul. Mosul was the northernmost of the three, inhabited by a mixed population of Sunni Kurds, Turks and Arabs, alongside a rich mixture of Yezidis ('devil worshippers'), Nestorian Christians and Jews. Once the First World War had broken out, a hastily organized British–Indian force entered from the South but the venture ended in disaster. The invaders were encircled by the Turks at Kut and forced to surrender. In 1917, a larger and better-prepared second expedition landed from India, pushed the Turks back and took Baghdad. At the time of the armistice in 1918, much of the oil-rich province of Mosul was still behind Turkish army lines. After the armistice, British forces advanced and occupied the whole province.

By then, the potential oil wealth of the region had become the subject of lively debate between the victorious powers. The legal status of the various claims on Iraqi oil was established after lengthy negotiations. Before the War, Turkey had assigned a quarter share of the Turkish Petroleum Company concession to Deutsche Bank. In San Remo (1920), the British transferred that one-quarter share to France as part of their overall settlement for the Middle East. Claims by numerous other pretenders had to be weeded out, including the one from the defunct Ottoman royal house, by then in splendid European exile.

Meanwhile, the US Government came under pressure from Standard Oil of New Jersey (later Exxon) to seek the participation of American companies in Iraqi oil ventures. Lofty principles such as the 'open door policy' were invoked, under which the League of Nations' mandated territories (including Iraq) were expected to operate. Longrigg[3] gives a quintessentially English account of how American companies horned their way in for a share of the treasure, after a campaign that ' ... opened by a vigorous, but to some extent misinformed, letter by Ambassador Davis in May 1920'.

The final agreement gave 23.75 per cent each to Anglo-Persian (later BP), Royal Dutch Shell and the Compagnie Française du Petrole. The fourth 23.75 per cent was to be shared equally between Standard Oil of New Jersey and Socony-Vacuum (later renamed Mobil), 5 per cent famously going to the ubiquitous middleman, Calouste Gülbenkiyan, who, before the War, had helped negotiate the original Turkish Petroleum Company agreement. It made him a very rich man. The concession to the Turkish Petroleum Company covered the whole of Iraq for 75 years, with the exception of the 'Transferred Territories' (from Iran) and the province of Basra. The standard rate of royalty payable to the Iraqi government was fixed at 4 shillings (gold) per ton, with possible adjustment after 20 years.

Curiously, up to the clarification of the status of the 'Turkish Petroleum Company' and the signature of the treaty with the Turks in 1925, no major discovery of oil had actually taken place. From the outset, the new company had an unexpectedly complicated time. The British occupation had put Sunni Arabs of the central province of Baghdad in charge of the whole country. Furthermore, the Hejazi Prince Faisal, who was installed as 'king' by the British, had proved a far livelier client than had been anticipated. The new King was the son of Sherif Hussein of Mecca, whose power had recently been destroyed by ibn-Saud. Faisal strove to negotiate his own agreements with local tribes and looked to invite competing bids for the purchase of new oil exploration licences.

The company's troubles did not end there. The great depression of 1929 hit Europe and demand collapsed soon after engineers struck oil at Baba Gurgur (1927), on the giant Kirkuk 'structure'. By then, the company's name had been altered to 'Iraq Petroleum Company' (IPC). To fend off competing claims, they signed a convention with the government (March 1931). It committed them to build a pipeline to the Mediterranean, with a capacity of not less than 3 million tons p.a., to be completed before the end of 1935.[4]

2 The IPC Pipelines and the Interwar Years

Nothing is ever simple when it comes to deciding the trajectory of a pipeline. The French insisted it should cross from Iraq into French-mandated Syria and Lebanon, whilst 'British and Iraqi feeling' favoured a southern route through British-mandated 'Transjordan' and Palestine. Eventually, the justice of King

Solomon prevailed. Two 12-in diameter lines were constructed, each with a 2-million-ton capacity, running from Kirkuk to near Haditha, across the Euphrates in western Iraq. There, the lines bifurcated, the northern arm crossing Syrian territory to reach the coast near Tripoli in northern Lebanon, where a tanker terminal was constructed.[5] That was the 'French' line. The southern branch crossed Jordanian territory and Palestine to a terminal at Haifa.[6] Overall, the second line was some 150 km longer. It was an expensive Anglo-French compromise paid for by Iraqi oil. The two IPC lines were the first major cross-border crude oil pipelines constructed in the Middle East (Figure 3.1).

The arrangements with the host countries were to last for 70 years and gave the Company customs and tax exemption. ' ... in deference to the international convention to that effect and partly in anticipation of the general benefits to the transit countries' economy ... ',[7] *no charge* was made for the right of transit. Purchasing the right of way through heavily populated Palestine and Lebanon gave rise to problems of land acquisition ' ... which were successfully resolved'.[8] In retrospect, one is left wondering how long the two colonial powers really imagined they would be left in charge of these lands.

At the time, the IPC line was the greatest welded pipeline in existence and the last word in modernity. A road was built alongside the pipeline and telegraph communications established. The pumping stations were also connected by wireless telegraph and each had its own landing strip. More important, the completion of the project completely altered the commercial outlook for the IPC and the prospects for the development of the Iraqi oilfields. Production from the Kirkuk 'structure' jumped between 1933 and 1935 from less than 100,000 tons to above 3.5 million tons p.a. Much of the oil went to European refineries of IPC's constituent companies. A decision to double the capacity of the line was taken in 1938, but the beginning of the Second World War forced the postponement of the project. Nonetheless, business was good. In the run-up to 1939, the distillation unit of a 1-million-ton oil refinery was completed in the Bay of Acre, in Palestine. By the time the Second World War began, the £2 million paid in oil royalties made up one-quarter of all revenue to the State treasury of the Kingdom of Iraq.

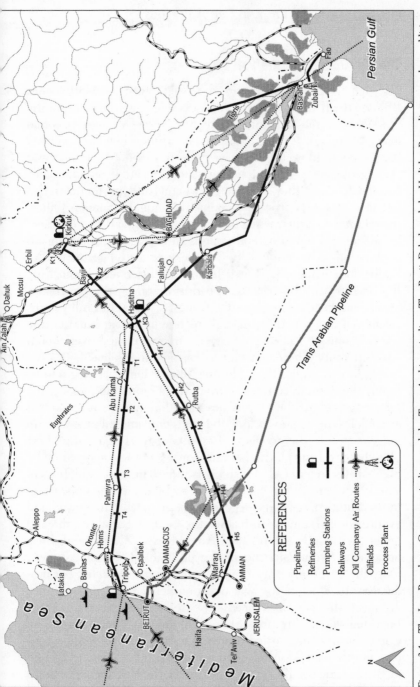

Figure 3.1 The Iraq Petroleum Company pipelines and the Trans-Arabian pipeline. The Bayji–Dahuk and the Haditha–Basra lines were later additions to the IPC-lines. Adapted from: (1) University of Texas Map Library, http://www.lib.utexas.edu/maps/index.html; (2) http://almashriq.hiof.no/lebanon/ 300/380/388/trapline/map.html; (3) http://www.iags.org/iraqpipelinewatch.htm

The British and the Arabian prize

Throughout these fateful years, the Anglo-Persian (APOC, later BP) and the IPC came tantalizingly close several times to winning the Arabian treasure hunt. In the 1920s, APOC geologists had made several quick visits to Arabia, at a time when the company had access to more oil in Persia than they could dispose of, and their geologists produced systematically negative reports. They famously claimed they would '*drink* whatever oil was found' in this forlorn country. Neither the companies, nor the Foreign Office, thought it worth their while to bail out the impoverished ibn Saud by spending a few thousand pounds to buy a concession for oil exploration. The story of how an exasperated Harry St John Philby, formerly of the British-Indian Civil Service,[9] urged King Ibn Saud to turn his back on the British and try the Americans instead has been told repeatedly. Almost a year after Philby's now celebrated lunch with a SOCAL representative in London, the princely sum of 35,000 gold sovereigns was turned over to Ibn Saud's treasury. The Americans had arrived in Arabia!

Anglo-Persian has the additional distinction of having refused to buy the Bahrain concession from Major Frank Holmes – going for a pittance just then.[10] Holmes was a lone prospector who had arrived in the region before the big companies, but could no longer afford the concession rents payable to the host Sheikhdoms. Instead, the Bahrain concession was snapped up by SOCAL (Standard Oil of California, now Chevron) and Texaco. The 1930s were also an exciting time for oil exploration elsewhere in the Middle East. Large deposits were discovered in Kuwait and eventually in Bahrain. Instead of the Gulf principalities directly under their hands, the IPC and Anglo-Persian elected to drill for oil all over Syria, Palestine and Egypt, with only modest success. Only the Egyptian excavations part-paid for themselves, but production there before the War never quite reached 1 million tons. To meet the country's needs, the refinery at Suez processed imported oil, mostly from Shell's East Indian concessions. The Canal, meanwhile, carried (south to north) nearly 4 million tons p.a., mostly bound for European refineries.

By the time the IPC arrived in Arabia, the al-Hasa concessions had all been made over to the California Arabian Standard

Oil Company (CASOC, offshoot of SOCAL, later enlarged to form ARAMCO). Apart from the daunting deserts of Nejd and the Rub Al-Khali ('The Empty Quarter'), all that was left to explore was the Western coastal strip of Arabia, comprising Hejaz and Asir, where no oil has ever been found. IPC test drilled in the Farasan Islands in 1937–8 and eventually abandoned the concession in 1941.[11] Meanwhile, the 'Basrah Petroleum Company', an IPC offshoot, began exploration work in Southern Iraq, where much of Iraq's oil wealth resides today.

In 1938, CASOC drilling teams struck oil in Eastern Arabia, beneath the lands where Ottoman Turks once eyed date palms as a source of revenue to pay for their fragile administration. However, war came soon afterwards and the astonishing oilfields of Arabia were left to be worked another day. During the Second World War, the Allies would be fuelled mostly by American and Mexican oil.

The death of King Faisal

Another poignant story of the inter-war years began with the untimely death of King Faisal of Iraq in 1933. In his eventful life, Faisal had left his comfortable life in Istanbul as guest-cum-hostage to lead the Hejazi rebellion against the Turks. His desert warriors fought as auxiliaries alongside the British, in return for a promise of kingship over Arab lands to be liberated from the Turks. After the war, Faisal was declared King of Syria by the British, only to be expelled by the French, to whom the British had also promised that much-coveted land. Honour was saved in 1921, however, when he was given the newly created Kingdom of Iraq by the then Colonial Secretary Winston Churchill. It was during the same spell that Faisal's brother Abdullah was given the 'Emirate of Transjordan' under British mandate, its borders quickly drawn with the help of a ruler on the map of the Middle East by Churchill's own hand. A foreigner in his new kingdom, the Hejazi Prince Abdullah was assassinated by a Palestinian in Jerusalem in 1951. However, Churchill's improvisation has survived to our day as the 'Hashemite Kingdom of Jordan'.

When he died in 1933, Faisal I of Iraq was succeeded by his 20-year-old son Ghazi, a young man with visions of uniting the Fertile

Crescent countries under his rule. He was to be the first of three Iraqi rulers to attempt the invasion of Kuwait. It is, nevertheless, not clear how the reported massing of Iraqi troops on the Kuwaiti border could have been undertaken without consent from London. On balance, the British were probably unlikely under the circumstances to have approved such an adventure. In the event, King Ghazi's addiction to high-speed driving turned out to be his undoing. With remarkable timing, he was killed in one of his fast cars, around the time that reports suggested the Kuwaiti frontier was due to be breached by Iraqi forces. He was succeeded by his four-year-old son, installed as King Faisal II. Ghazi's cousin, the loyally pro-British Prince Abdul Illah, was appointed as Regent and there were no more Kuwaiti expeditions . . . for a while. During the revolution of 1958, the young King Faisal II and Abdul Illah were both murdered, alongside Nouri Said Pasha, by then 14 times prime minister of Iraq.

3 The War Years: Rashid Ali and Plugging Up the Wells

During the early stages of the Second World War, several developments conspired to disrupt the activities of the Iraq Petroleum Company. Exports of crude oil and finished products from the terminals at Haifa and Tripoli were directly affected by naval warfare in the Mediterranean. In the late spring of 1940, the situation was further complicated by a short war in the area between British forces and the army of Iraq, under the leadership of Prime Minister Rashid Ali al-Gailani.

Limitations of space do not allow for tracing the evolution of Iraqi politics through this critical period.[12] It seems fair to say that there was clear dislike in Iraq for the British presence and for the regime they put in place to underpin indirect British control. Furthermore, the backdrop of Jewish encroachment in Palestine and apparent British tolerance for it created fertile ground for anti-Jewish and pro-Nazi propaganda. When war started, many in the region cheered on the Axis powers with hopes and expectations that still cause resentment in the West. In Iraq, these tensions erupted into open conflict, when Prime Minister Rashid Ali al-Gailani attempted to restrict British troop movements in the country (1940). He ' … refused to bow to British pressure to resign if he was not prepared to honour the clauses of the Anglo–Iraqi treaty giving landing and transit rights to British troops'.[13] The British-trained Iraqi Army supported its prime minister. When confrontation developed into fighting, British troops hastily reinforced from India gained the upper hand without great loss or difficulty. They reoccupied Iraq. Not unlike the Shah of Iran dethroned a year later, Rashid Ali appears to have harboured illusions of liberating his country from British control by encouraging an Axis presence. He was toppled and spent the war years in Nazi Germany.

Meanwhile, the capitulation of France in the summer of 1940 and the installation of the pro-Nazi Vichy Government in France brought new dangers. Under the Vichy-appointed high commissioner General Henri Dentz, Syria and Lebanon became 'enemy' territories. This necessitated cutting the flow of oil through Syria to Tripoli in Lebanon. The French shares in the IPC, alongside those of Gülbenkiyan who was still living in France, were transferred to the (British) Custodian of Enemy Property. However, Gülbenkiyan's rights as a British national were restored after he moved to Portugal. Later in 1941, Free French forces, assisted by British troops and the Transjordan Arab Legion, defeated the pro-Vichy forces in the area and established a Free French-dominated government in Syria and Lebanon.

Worse disruption to IPC operations in Iraq was to come in 1942 from the British military themselves. A series of 'denial' measures were taken against the prospect of a 'possible' German invasion of Iraq. In Kirkuk, all but six of the wells were plugged. The 'Ain Zala and Qaiyara fields lost all but one well to 'denial' activities. Much equipment and stores were moved to Basra, presumably with an eye to withdrawal towards India, in case of an invasion from the North. Eventually, none of these measures proved necessary and the Company was able to produce nearly 4 million tons a year throughout the war period.

One interesting footnote to the history of oil pipelines in Iraq comes from Longrigg's commendably loyal book *Oil in the Middle East*.[14] He explains that when the IPC took over a pair of concessions west of the Tigris, ' … The protection of the Company's camps and communications continued to be ensured by contract with the Chief of the Shammar tribe'. Later, in the days following the suppression of the Rashid Ali movement and the defeat of the Iraqi army, he explains that the facilities at Qaiyara were occupied by British troops: ' ... a footing was retained by the Mosul Company on a basis of care and maintenance ... . 'Ain Zala, which also quartered a military force, was not reoccupied by Company personnel. *Security arrangements with the sheikhs of the Shammar continued in force*' (my italics).

During the Saddam years, similar arrangements with local tribes were reinforced by two army divisions patrolling the pipelines. Against this background, it is difficult not to admire the self-assurance of the overseers of the occupation of 2003, who felt able to wipe the slate clean by cancelling all such agreements. We will briefly review the ensuing pipeline war later on in this chapter.

4 New Giant Pipelines: The Trans-Arabian and the IPC Line to Baniyas

It was clear from pre-war days that the production capability of the Kirkuk fields was far greater than could be conveyed using IPC's available export capabilities. Eager to expand sales, the company proceeded in 1946 to build a larger pipeline to the Mediterranean. In the aftermath of the War, however, steel was in short supply. The end of empire must have been keenly felt, when the IPC was constrained to purchasing 16-in lines by 'the inability of sterling-area manufacturers to produce larger pipe and the equal impossibility of obtaining dollars'.[15]

The new pair of pipelines was intended to boost the capacity of the two existing branches of the IPC pipeline by a little over 4 million tons p.a. each, bringing total exports from Kirkuk to about 13 million tons. Work on the southern branch to Haifa began first, in 1946, but that part of the world was rapidly changing for the worse. Construction was nearly completed, when on 17 April 1948, some ten days before the creation of the state of Israel, oil flows through the lines to Haifa were interrupted altogether. Both the 12-in and the 16-in lines have remained unused ever since (Figure 3.1).

This was the last anyone heard of the luckless southern IPC pipeline ... until 2003. In the early months of the latest occupation of Iraq, news agency wires were humming with apparently serious reports, suggesting that enquiries were being made about the state of the Kirkuk–Haifa pipelines and that pumping ' ... oil from newly conquered Iraq to Israel [were] being discussed between Washington, Tel Aviv and potential future government figures in Baghdad'.[16] The advantages of the move included ' ... cutting out Syria and solving Israel's energy crisis at a stroke ... It would also create an endless and easily accessible source of cheap Iraqi oil for the United States ...'.

In the heat of the moment, no one seems to have quite taken notice of the Jordanians, who as early as April 2003 were issuing frantic denials that they would allow a pipeline to Israel across their territory.[17] Meanwhile, 'Reuters quoted Israeli ministers as saying that restarting the pipeline could reduce Israel's fuel costs by 25 per cent'.[18] Not content with stirring up the tormented ghosts of the probably long-rusted IPC pipelines, Israel's National Infrastructure Ministry indicated that a new 42-in diameter line from Kirkuk would cost a remarkably affordable $400,000 per km. These subtle moves were soon engulfed, however, in the din and violence of the Iraqi insurgency.

Supplying Europe with Middle East oil

After the Second World War, an important shift took place in the way Europe was supplied. Whereas in 1946 nearly 80 per cent of Europe's oil was shipped from the western hemisphere, by the early 1950s, almost the same proportion was being imported from the Middle East. Much of this oil came from the Gulf and nearly two-thirds of Suez Canal traffic in 1955 was taken up by tankers.

Meanwhile, following the disruption of the Kirkuk–Haifa line, the IPC was even more anxious to transport its oil to the Mediterranean as quickly as possible. They moved rapidly to construct the northern branch of the 16-in line to Tripoli. Already partially usable in 1949, the line reached full capacity (6 million tons p.a.) in 1950. Shortly afterwards, the expanding needs of Europe, busy with post-war reconstruction, encouraged the IPC to build yet another and far larger line from the Kirkuk fields to the

Mediterranean coast. The new 30–32-in line was designed to carry 14 million tons p.a. It was constructed between 1950 and 1952, running from northern Iraq, through Syrian territory to Baniyas on the Mediterranean coast, some 55 km north of Tripoli. The entire project was completed in a remarkably short 17 months. This time, however, the job had been left to the Americans, who had just finished constructing the trans-Arabian pipeline ('Tapline'). The latter was constructed to carry 'Arabian light' from the Saudi super-giant Abqaiq field through Jordan and Syria to Sidon in Lebanon.

The trans-Arabian pipeline

In May 1943, Ibn Saud received a visit from a General Patrick Hurley, then President Roosevelt's personal representative in the Middle East. It was an auspicious time, with German armies having been turned back on the Russian Front and in North Africa. The visit went well. Several weeks later, the US Government floated the idea of acquiring an interest in CASOC (later ARAMCO), as well as helping to fund the construction of a refinery at Ras Tanura and build a pipeline to the Mediterranean coast. The move was not unlike Churchill's Admiralty in 1914 acquiring a controlling interest in the Anglo-Persian Oil Company. The need for the refinery and the pipeline were real enough, but the idea of the US Government actively participating in the oil business was received 'coolly' by the industry.[19]

For the producers of Saudi oil, the logic behind the construction of a pipeline to the Mediterranean was similar to that of the IPC pipelines. With modern tankers, the trip from Ras Tanura to the Mediterranean takes nine days. A pipeline across the deserts of Arabia to somewhere on the Mediterranean coast would have saved a journey of 5,600 km. With a barrel of oil selling at less than two dollars and passage through the Canal alone costing 18 cents, it was calculated that the cost of pumping the oil across the deserts to Lebanon was just half of that of the tanker journey.

Plans for the line were completed in December 1946 and construction started in 1947. Originally, the line was bound for Haifa but, as trouble developed over Palestine, the project was diverted through the Golan Heights in Syrian territory to Sidon in

Lebanon, where berths were constructed for simultaneously handling five large tankers. However, transit through Syria was no longer the simple matter it had once been.

After the war, Syrian independence was won at a high price, with some hard fighting against General de Gaulle's Free French, who had been extremely reluctant to relinquish 'their' colony. The elected Syrian government was not willing to concede free, or for that matter, cheap passage of oil to anyone. Led by President Quwwatly and Prime Minister Mardam, the Syrians not only opposed policies pursued by the USA in Palestine, but bargained hard for more favourable commercial terms to allow the passage of the line.

Neither Aramco, which owned part of the new installation, nor representatives of the newly formed company 'Tapline', a subsidiary of the four companies that owned Aramco, were willing to accede to Syrian demands: 'Syrian parliamentary objections necessitated the CIA-aided 1949 coup, in order to secure "right of way" over the Golan Heights.'[20] As told much later, in 1995, CIA agent Miles Copeland and Stephen Meade, the US military attache in Damascus, assisted Colonel Husni Za'im in seizing power on 30 March. Some bargaining appears to have been necessary over the amount of money needed to organize the coup. The elected president and prime minister of Syria were arrested. Za'im announced the suspension of the Constitution:

> According to former CIA agent Wilbur Eveland, the coup
> was carried out in order to obtain Syrian ratification of the
> Tapline agreement … In less than a month, the new Syrian
> regime was involved in negotiations with Israel, planning
> the resettlement of Palestinian refugees and, in mid May,
> approving the Tapline concession.[21]

Colonel Za'im was a Kurdish officer with a limited power base. In quick succession, he appointed himself prime minister and promoted himself to the rank of general. He urgently needed money to consolidate his tenuous hold on power and seems to have pressurized the nearly bankrupt Ibn Saud into raising a $6-million loan for him in the USA. When Za'im was toppled several months later and executed, Ibn Saud used $4.5 million of this money to settle his Palace's debts to various merchants, all the while keeping Colonel Hinnawi (Za'im's successor) committed to the Tapline deal by promising money. Eventually, a ' ... [$] 2 million and a 4 million tranche seemed to have been paid in two instalments, advanced successively by Aramco and Nederland Trading Society'.[22] The first tanker loaded at Zahrani, south of Saida (Sidon), in December of that year (Figure 3.1).

Originally designed to carry about 15 million tons p.a., additional pumping stations boosted the capacity of the 1,750 km Tapline to 25 million tons by 1957. In a world still licking its wounds after the Second World War and with steel pipe at a premium, the construction of the trans-Arabian pipeline ('Tapline') was considered 'among the greatest of all engineering achieve ments'.[23] Yergin suggests that independent oil producers in the USA attempted to block the allocation of the large diameter steel pipe, fearing that cheap oil imports would swamp the US market. The State Department regarded this enterprise as an essential component of post-war European reconstruction.[24]

In the early 1950s, many of the complications of inter-Arab politics that later proved so self-destructive had not yet taken definitive shape. The regularity of military coups in Damascus drew smiles from the uninformed and King Farouk's antics amused all who did not have to pay for them; but things were about to change. Soon, Egypt blew up in the faces of the British. The Anglo-French withdrawal forced by Washington after the Suez episode underlined the new world order that had emerged from the War. In 1958, General Kassem's revolution in Iraq ended British sponsored rule of that country. After 1958, in Egypt, Syria and Iraq, Arab nationalism missed the only opportunity it ever had to put its own house in order. What little momentum they had built-up was eventually broken by the war of 1967 with Israel.

5 Iraq's Pipeline Woes and the Death of Tapline

Returning to our pipelines, trouble for the northern IPC pipelines started as early as the 1956 Suez war. Syria damaged the line in protest against the British and French offensive on the Suez Canal. During the following two decades, Syrian demands for increasingly large transit fees dominated their relations with Iraq. The period is dotted with recurrent interruptions in the flow of oil through the pipeline. The nationalization of the IPC by the Iraqi wing of the Baath party in 1972 did not lead the Syrian Baath to moderate *their* demands. Instead, they nationalized IPC assets in Syria and doubled the transit fees. They also demanded preferential terms for oil lifted for domestic use. In the 1970s, political relations between Damascus and Baghdad were famously stormy. Between threats of interrupting the flow of oil and rising world prices, the Iraqis were mostly forced to accept Syrian demands.[25] Tariffs were raised in 1973 and again in 1976.

Seeing the trouble ahead, the Iraqis constructed a 'North–South strategic line', diverting Kirkuk oil southwards, to tanker terminals in the Gulf (Figure 3.1). The line opened in 1975 with an initial capacity of 15–20 million tons p.a., eventually expanded to about 70 million tons just before the Gulf War of 1991–2. This installation provided the Iraqis with the flexibility either to ship oil from the southern Rumaila fields towards the Mediterranean (Syrians permitting) or to pump oil from Mosul southwards, towards the Gulf. They also developed a deep-sea loading facility at Khor Al Khafji (renamed Mina al Bakr, 1975) in the south, with a yearly capacity of 120 million tons and the capacity to handle 350,000-ton tankers.[26,27] With most of Iraq's oil destined for Europe, the diversion necessitated the circumnavigation of the Arabian Peninsula and added to their costs. At vast expense, Iraq also constructed another line, far longer than the IPC lines, through Turkey's mountainous southeast to the Mediterranean. We will return to the Kirkuk–Ceyhan pipeline in the next section.

Meanwhile, disagreements between Syria and Iraq led to the suspension of operations of the IPC line between 1976 and 1979. The reopening was brief and lasted only until the Iraqi invasion of Iran. The Syrians declared support for Iran and closed the line once more. There was another short opening, during a brief rapprochement between the Syrian and Iraqi Baath Parties during 1981, but the Syrians again stopped the flow through the IPC-lines, when Iran promised to keep Syria supplied with oil instead.[28]

Strictly, the northern leg of the IPC line was never used again. However, following the 2003 invasion of Iraq, it became apparent that *some* oil had been pumped through to Syria, during the 1990s and later, in contravention of UN sanctions against Iraq. The Syrians appear to have refined this oil domestically, disguising the trade by exporting a greater part of their own domestic production. The total volume of these shipments is not known, although the US Energy Information Agency has claimed that the 50-year-old, 32-in line to Baniyas carried ' ... as much as 200,000 barrels per day of Iraqi oil (about 10 million tons p.a.), mainly from southern Iraq to Syrian refineries at Homs and Baniyas'.[29] The line was blown up by US forces soon after the 2003 invasion, probably at the level of the T1-pumping station west of Haditha in Iraq. But all is not lost! Reports have emerged in early 2007 suggesting that '... Iraqi and Syrian officials are in talks to reopen an oil pipeline sending Iraqi crude west to the Mediterranean Sea, though it could face Sunni attacks . . . '.[30]

Tapline's Syrian woes

After the first tankers loaded at Saida in December 1949, Tapline appears to have functioned according to plan until the Suez crisis of 1956. Following the Egyptian nationalization of the Canal and in the run-up to the invasion of Egypt, Syria had already interrupted Tapline for a day, as a general warning. When the Israeli land offensive began on 29 October, the Syrians sabotaged both Tapline and the IPC pipeline. The squeeze on European oil supplies was completed when traffic through the Canal was blocked by the Egyptians, who scuttled ships laden with rocks and concrete. This was never meant to have happened. Indeed, ensuring 'the security of the Canal' was to have been the pretext for the Anglo-French offensive. With the Egyptian army in full retreat across the Sinai, fortune of war, Anglo-French landings were delayed by several days due to Prime Minister Eden's illness.[31] Nasser used the time effectively. Suddenly, all oil supply routes from the Middle East to Europe were cut.

Recently, journalists drumming up Arab activism have recalled Nasser's victory in 1956. However, to draw the necessary lessons, it seems useful to review the posture adopted by the USA in 1956 and to compare it with the role she chose to play during subsequent phases of the Arab–Israeli conflict.

In 1956, Washington was furious at the Anglo–French–Israeli action. The Americans had been kept in the dark about Anglo–French operations, synchronized with a land invasion from Israel. The Eisenhower administration was intent on not angering the Arab world. In a rare example of post-war unity of action, the two superpowers jointly demanded the immediate withdrawal of the invading armies, although the Soviets went a little further and threatened nuclear war on Paris and London. Far from helping their European allies through the impending petroleum shortage, however, the Americans also threatened oil sanctions, unless a total withdrawal was immediately put in place. This was still a time when Europe relied primarily on coal for basic energy supplies, with only 20 per cent of energy resources relying on oil. Transport fuels and 'fuel-oil' were nevertheless crucial inputs for the functioning of the economy.

The troubles of British Prime Minister Anthony Eden did not end there. While the stunning effectiveness of the oil weapon took hold and threatened an energy crisis about a month down the line (December 1956), there was a run on the pound sterling. Whether the Americans actually triggered the run or simply watched it unfold has long been a matter of debate. In any case, the IMF refused to help the British 'under American prodding'.[32] From then on, the political defeat of the invasion was assured. Step by step, each move was undone. Israel withdrew from its first invasion of the Sinai. The Anglo–French paratroopers were withdrawn. By mid-March 1957, the Canal was cleared sufficiently to allow the first ships to go through. By the middle of May, British commercial shipping was ordered back into the now fully Egyptian-owned Suez Canal.

In terms strictly of volume, there is no doubt that the blocking of the Suez Canal represented a greater loss in supplies for the Europeans, compared with supplies from the IPC line and Tapline combined. Once the Americans had declared against the expedition, however, the combination was decisive. In retrospect, it is clear that the Anglo–French coalition blundered into the invasion with a total misconception of how the USA would react. Perhaps history should have viewed Eisenhower's legacy in more flattering terms after all, but that is another story.

Tapline's Saudi woes

In the 1950s, the price of a barrel of crude oil in the Mediterranean was calculated as the price charged at Ras Tanura (in the Gulf), plus the cost of transport around the Arabian Peninsula and passage through the Suez Canal. For the best part of a decade, crude oil carried by Tapline to Sidon fetched the same Mediterranean price and Aramco pocketed the difference. Meanwhile, Saudi royalties were paid on the basis of posted crude oil prices *at Ras Tanura*. Aramco thus made money both ways, until the fractious Abdullah Tariqi was appointed as the Kingdom's first Minister of Petroleum in 1960.

A nationalist and a reformist, Abdullah Tariqi was one of a new generation of Saudi commoners who had studied abroad. The constitutional monarchy he openly advocated was as distasteful to the profligate King Saud[33] (eldest surviving son and successor of the patriarch, Abdul Aziz al-Saud) as it was to the more sober Crown Prince (later King) Faisal. However, at the time, the King had been marginalized from active politics by the Crown Prince and was attempting a comeback. Tariqi was part of a group of would-be reformers whom King Saud drew to his side with, as it later turned out, false promises of reform. They were deluded into believing that isolating the strong-headed Faisal and restoring the 'weak' Saud to active power would help them achieve their goals.[34]

In the event, King Saud succeeded in sacking his younger brother and regaining power for another two years. Abdullah Tariqi, who until then headed the *Department* of Petroleum and Mineral Resources attached to the Ministry of Finance, was appointed *Minister* of Petroleum and Mineral Resources. During this period, Saudi production lingered between 1 and 2 million barrels per day, and small changes in the tax and royalty regime mattered desperately to the cash-strapped, spendthrift royal family.

Tariqi argued with the companies that, from the beginning, Saudi royalties for the crude exported through Tapline should have been calculated on the basis of the higher price charged by Aramco at Sidon. The companies resisted. They bided their time. In the end, Saud's powers failed and the royal family foisted

Crown Prince Faisal on him once again as prime-minister. Tariqi was replaced by Ahmad Zaki Yamani, then a respected but little-known lawyer, who had all the diplomatic charms his predecessor is said to have lacked. Yamani was successful in negotiating a retroactive settlement of the royalties issue.

Behind the scenes, however, the US Government, in its concern for the stability of the kingdom after the outbreak of the Yemen civil war, used its influence to persuade the Aramco partners to concede more. It brought a down payment of $160 million and better terms for the future.[35]

The end of Tapline

During the war of 1967, the flow of crude oil through Tapline was again interrupted when rumours spread that American and British planes had provided air cover for the Israeli air force as they hit Egypt's military airports. The embargo imposed on the USA, Britain and West Germany lasted only until August, however, after being considered as ineffective, even by President Nasser's close associate Heikal. It was practically impossible to implement.[36]

However, the fortunes of Tapline did not improve with time. In 1969, an attack attributed to the Popular Front for the Liberation of Palestine (PFLP) put the line out of action for nearly four months.[37] Several subsequent breaches in the line were repaired relatively quickly, leading P. Stevens to suggest that, given access for repairs, ' ... it is extremely difficult to sabotage pipelines effectively'.[38] Clearly, much depends on the overall security situation. At the end of this chapter, we will briefly review the pipeline war in Iraq.

In 1970, the Syrians claimed that the line had been 'accidentally' damaged by a bulldozer whilst laying telephone lines. When the Government failed to allow repairs to go ahead as 'too dangerous', however, the Saudis retaliated by barring the entry of Syrian goods and vehicles into Arabia. Syria riposted by banning flights and the passage of land cargo bound for the Saudi Kingdom. The impasse continued until Hafez al-Assad overthrew the left-leaning Baath leadership in a neatly executed coup, cutting telephone communications before moving tanks into Damascus. The flow to Sidon was resumed in January 1971,[39] although Assad insisted on doubling transit fees and a payment of $9 million ' ... to cover other claims'.[40] Similar terms had to be granted to Jordan and Lebanon. The Syrians thus gradually priced themselves out of rather lucrative transit fees. The increased costs eroded the economic advantages of pumping oil through Tapline, compared to shipping from Ras Tanura. Tapline throughput was further reduced when tanker rates collapsed during the 1973 war and its aftermath and Aramco opened a new terminal at Ju'aymah in the Gulf, with an additional capacity of 50 million tons p.a.

The timing of the 'bulldozer' incident in 1970, which resulted in the closure of Tapline, was nothing short of intriguing. It occurred at a time when Qaddafi was pressing the oil companies in Libya for higher posted prices. One of his actions was to limit their production quotas. As observed during the price hikes of 2004–5, relatively minor shortfalls when oil supplies are already tight can affect prices disproportionately. The Syrian action helped Qaddafi win his argument. Posted prices were increased by about 40 cents per barrel above what the companies had been prepared to pay. Although there was ' ... no evidence of collusion, in 1971 Libya made a substantial aid donation to Syria'.[41]

The outbreak of the Lebanese civil war finally put an end to the operation of Tapline. Definitive closure was announced in February 1975, although a reduced flow was maintained to the Zarqa refinery in Jordan and the Medreco refinery in Lebanon. The Israeli invasion of South Lebanon and repeated bombings of Sidon in 1982 again interrupted operations. Saudi deliveries to Zarqa nevertheless continued until 1990, when the usually cautious King Hussein unexpectedly declared support for Saddam's invasion of Kuwait.[42]

6 Saddam's Escape Routes and the Saudi Petroline

Since approximately the end of the First World War, the USA and Britain have rarely taken their eyes off the land of Iraq, and with good reason! According to the US Energy Information Agency:

Iraq contains 115 billion barrels of proven oil reserves, the third largest in the world (behind Saudi Arabia and Canada), concentrated overwhelmingly (65 per cent or more) in southern Iraq. Estimates of Iraq's oil reserves and resources vary widely, however, given that only about 10 per cent of the country has been explored.[43]

Iraq's oil deposits may be massive, but her access to the open seas is constrained by geography. In addition to the problems they (and everybody else) have had with Syria, the valuable Iraqi oil terminals at the mouths of the Shatt al-Arab are far too close to Iran for comfort. Even before Saddam attempted to invade that country in 1980, Iraq's relations with Iran had been strained. During the long decades of Saddam's power, Iraq adopted two parallel strategies for facilitating oil exports. The first was the Kirkuk–Ceyhan line constructed during the mid-1970s. This line runs north through Dahuk into Turkey and then westward, inside the Turkish border to the Mediterranean. Saddam's second route was the IPSA-I and IPSA-II lines, connecting the southern oilfields to the Saudi Red Sea ports of Yanbu and Mu'ajjiz, respectively. Both IPSA lines were constructed after the outbreak of hostilities with Iran in 1980 and were needed because of the Iranian interdiction of oil exports through southern Iraqi ports.

The Kirkuk–Ceyhan (Dörtyol) oil pipeline

The initial protocol for the construction of this line was signed in 1973, in the aftermath of Syrian–Iraqi difficulties over the IPC-line to Baniyas. The transit fee was fixed at 35 cents per barrel – later raised to 38 cents. The project triggered a barrage of invective from the Syrians against Iraq for 'betraying the masses' and 'delivering the Arabs' oil weapon into the hands of the imperialists and Zionists at a time when they most need to use it in the battle of destiny'.[44] The 965-km line was inaugurated in 1977, with a yearly capacity of 35 million tons. It was also agreed that the Turks could annually lift up to 10 million tons from the line, provided they paid for it. Despite occasional tussles about transit fees and delays in payment by Turkey, this arrangement has by and large worked reasonably well. A parallel ('looped') line was inaugurated in 1987 to boost total capacity to about 75 million tons p.a. By then, the transit fee had been raised to 65 cents and Turkish yearly revenue from the line rose to some $350–360 million.

The Kirkuk–Ceyhan dual pipeline was the largest of Iraq's crude oil export lines. However, the Iraqis had learned their lessons and made sure they had yet another alternative export route. In the late 1980s, they announced plans to construct a second north–south strategic line carrying 900,000 barrels per day.[45] Nevertheless, the Kirkuk–Ceyhan line operated regularly until Saddam's invasion of Kuwait and subsequent UN-imposed sanctions against Iraq interrupted the flow. After 1995, much of the later notorious 'Oil for food' was in fact pumped to and sold from Ceyhan.

Estimates of Turkish loss of trade and transit fees, arising from UN sanctions on Iraq, vary widely. It is rumoured that local Turkish traders and trucking outfits did a lively business carrying foodstuffs and consumer items across to Iraq, returning with contraband oil. Meanwhile, throughout the 1990s, successive Turkish governments complained bitterly about the cost to the Turkish treasury of interrupting nearly all trade with their once cash-rich neighbour. These economic losses may well have contributed to the eventual Turkish refusal to allow the US Fourth Infantry division safe passage across Turkish territory in 2003. One interesting detail about those negotiations was the a-priori refusal of the Turkish General Staff to allow *any* British troops at all through Turkish territory.

After UN sanctions were lifted in May 2003, pumping oil from Kirkuk to Ceyhan was no longer illegal. However, according to the US Energy Information Agency, the Al Fatha Bridge over the Tigris (near Bayji), which was destroyed in bombing raids by US planes, partially blocked the pipeline tunnel crossing the river. These facilities have not been repaired. Meanwhile, the IT-1 and IT-2 pumping stations have been damaged; the first can still be operated manually, whilst the second has been destroyed.[46]

Shunting oil away from the Gulf?

The Straits of Hormuz provide a sensitive gateway between western Asia and the Indian Ocean. In the sixteenth century, the Turks lost a fleet in these waters while trying to counter Portuguese penetration. The area has since fallen under the sway of a succession of aspiring world powers, from the Portuguese and Spaniards to the Dutch and finally the British, who in the nineteenth century successfully corralled the various tribes of warlike locals into the 'Trucial States', convincing them, with a little help from the Admiralty, to renounce their traditional income from piracy. After the Second World War and the British withdrawal from 'East of Suez', the task of keeping order in these turbulent waters was taken on by the US Fifth Fleet, with headquarters in Bahrain and major regional air bases over a wide arc from Incirlik in Turkey to the Island base of Diego Garcia far out in the Indian Ocean, and with several bases sprinkled over the Gulf area itself.

The volume of oil that needs to be seen safely through the Straits of Hormuz is large. In 2004, a daily average of nearly 17 million barrels of oil (14.8 million in 1996), representing a little over 20 per cent of total world production, passed through the Straits, much of it bound for East Asia.[47]

For Iraq, their narrow opening to the Gulf, squeezed between Kuwait and Iran, has proved enormously problematic. During the Iran–Iraq war, Iran was able to interdict tanker traffic from Iraqi ports that were often within artillery range. With Iran's ally Syria blocking the IPC line to Baniyas, the only export route left operating was the Kirkuk–Ceyhan line, plus whatever could be sold by proxy through Kuwaiti outlets.

Iraq attempted to counter by damaging Iranian oil exports and unleashed the 'Tanker War' in the Gulf, during which hundreds of craft were sunk or damaged. With Iran attacking Kuwaiti tankers, some of which were carrying Iraqi oil, the US Navy was drawn into the fighting. They initially destroyed two Iranian oil platforms and several warships. One of the lasting images from the tanker war, however, was that of the stricken US warship Stark. The incident took place shortly after Kuwait had persuaded the USA to offer protection to its tanker fleet and the US Navy began patrolling the Gulf. On 17 May 1987, a French-made *Iraqi* super-Etandard fired two air-to-ship Exocet missiles at the Stark, whose defences appear not to have functioned adequately. The level of US–Iraqi understanding at the time is underscored by the earnest Iraqi apology for the incident. This was closely followed by a US, Iraqi and Saudi coordination agreement, to make sure such incidents were not repeated. The US Navy also 'accidentally' downed an Iranian airliner carrying nearly 300 innocent passengers. There were no apologies. When, however, the US warship Samuel B. Roberts hit a mine, probably sown by the Iranians, the US retaliated by sinking several Iranian warships and patrol boats.[48]

From the beginning of the Iran–Iraq war, it was obvious that increasing difficulties for shipping in the Gulf would alter the pipeline map of the area. In 1981, the Saudis constructed an east–west oil pipeline dubbed 'Petroline', connecting the Abqaiq oilfields in eastern Arabia to the newly opened Red Sea port of Yanbu, equipped with three berths for tankers up to 550,000 dead weight tons (each). The move was announced as part of a policy to revive the economy of the Western Seaboard, although the timing suggested concern about the freedom of movement in the Gulf and through the Straits of Hormuz. The first 48-in line had a capacity of 1.85 million barrels per day (over 90 million tons p.a.). This line was 'looped' in 1987 with a parallel 52-in line, following the intensification of the 'tanker war', to 3.2 million barrels per day. Despite the drop in volumes bound for Europe and the expansion of sales to East Asian markets, the capacity of the east–west Petroline was expanded again in 1993 to 5 million barrels per day,[49] about 250 million tons p.a.

Iraqi pipelines across Saudi Arabia (IPSA-1 and IPSA-2)

Once the Iran–Iraq war got underway, the only operational route left to Iraq for oil exports was the Kirkuk–Ceyhan line. To supplement this capacity, the IPSA-1 line was agreed with the Saudis as early as 1981. This was a 630 km tie-line from the southern Iraqi Rumaila fields into Petroline, pumping oil to Yanbu, partly by using the Saudi facility. However, progress was slow and the first Iraqi oil shipped through this line was exported in September 1985, during a period of slack oil prices and excess capacity on world markets.

The Saudis would not have wanted to pump much Iraqi oil just then. In October 1986, Iraqi exports ceased for additional construction work. Soon afterwards, in February 1987, the Saudis restricted Iraqi exports to 250,000 barrels per day, to Iraq's 'bafflement and frustration'.[50] This seems typical of what happens to export capacity through the territory (and in this case the facilities) of a competing producer at times of excess oil on the market.

IPSA-2 was constructed to run parallel to the Petroline, ending at the export terminal of Ras al-Mu'ajjiz, just south of Yanbu. It had a design capacity of 1.65 million barrels per day (about 83 million tons annually). Soon after opening in 1989–90, however, the line was closed by the Saudis, in protest against Iraq's invasion of Kuwait. A decade later, in 2001, the Saudis formally expropriated the line despite protests from Iraq. They claimed that continued threats and aggression from Iraq had destroyed the rationale for maintaining the pipeline on its behalf. In 2002, Iraq wrote to the United Nations demanding that Saudi Arabia should be held accountable for any damage to the $2.2 billion pipeline. By October 2003, the Al-Jazeera news agency was quoting unnamed Saudi officials as saying: 'It is not an Iraqi pipeline any more.'[51]

Whilst Saudi Aramco officials have suggested that corrosion would have rendered the long and 'suddenly abandoned' line unusable,[52] the US EIA has suggested that the Saudis have ' ... converted the line to carry natural gas to the Red Sea industrial city of Yanbu for domestic use'.[53] In any case, with much of the export from Gulf ports bound for East Asia, loading at Yanbu would add about five days to a tanker's journey, say to Singapore or Yokohama. In the absence of danger to shipping in the Gulf, exporting oil from Red Sea ports is not an attractive option. At present, Petroline is pumping at slightly less than 2 million barrels per day, over half of it for export.

What if Iran...?

In the Gulf, western security scenarios mostly assign the role of potential regional villain to Iran. On the face of it, it is not clear why the government in Tehran would want to block Hormuz, since the passageway carries *all* Iranian oil exports. Nonetheless, a pipeline system bypassing the straits has periodically been contemplated by the United Arab Emirates (UAE), the latest running from Habshan, in Abu Dhabi, to Fujairah on the Indian Ocean, just north of the Omani frontier.[54] However, the distance of this port from the presumed aggressor's potential bases of operation seems relatively modest and any improvement in the level of security for tankers operating out of Fujairah appears marginal.

Ewell and co-workers[55] have suggested that, 'in case of danger' to passage through Hormuz, Petroline throughput could be approximately doubled yet again, to shift the bulk of Saudi exports to Red Sea ports. The calculation was based on using both Petroline and IPSA-II. Technically, flowrates through a pipe can be speeded up by injecting drag-reducing agents (DRAs) into the flowing fluid.[56] However, since pumping action destroys DRAs, these chemicals need to be injected into the crude oil downstream of each of the 11 pumping stations, at fairly low concentration (70 parts per million). The cost for speeding up the oil flow to Yanbu was thus calculated at about one-dollar per barrel on top of a fixed investment of about $600 million at 1996 prices, not a great deal of money when required for shifting an extra 5 million barrels per day (approximately another 250 million tons p.a.). These authors have described their vision as ' ... an opportunity to buy strategic insurance at bargain rates'.

7 Pipelines of the Middle East today

We could be forgiven for viewing the transnational pipelines of the Middle East as so many carcasses of once-wondrous engineering projects. Mercifully, many of the inland pipelines are functioning more or less as intended. These include the Syrian oil and gas lines, carrying the country's modest but significant hydrocarbon resources to market, with 10–15 million tons of oil exported annually through Tartus and Baniyas. Similarly, the Saudi internal networks have been growing in complexity and penetration. It was said in the 1970s and 1980s that gas flares in Eastern Arabia were among the few features discernible from space. These were the flares incinerating the vast amount of natural gas released during the production of crude oil that, unbelievably, simply went to waste for many long decades. In the meantime, domestic fuel needs have caught up and the Saudis have finally stopped squandering at least some of this huge resource. Natural gas is now pumped around the country, notably for power generation, water desalination, fertilizer manufacture and domestic consumption.

Several other regional pipelines are operating successfully and deserve honourable mentions.

The SuMed line; peaceful but is it transnational?

This is an important pipeline operated on Egyptian territory, between the Gulf of Suez and the Mediterranean (hence 'SuMed') near Alexandria, effectively bypassing and competing with the Suez Canal. The Canal Zone is listed by the US Energy Information Agency as one of the world's critical choke-points for oil flows: closure of the Suez Canal and/or SuMed Pipeline would divert tankers around the southern tip of Africa (the Cape of Good Hope), adding greatly to transit time and cost, and effectively tying up much tanker capacity.[57] Partly, the SuMed line was meant to sidestep the relatively modest 'Suezmax' tanker tonnage limit of up to 180,000 tons. The Gulf of Suez terminal can accommodate up to four 500,000-ton vessels, while Sidi Kerir on the Mediterranean can take vessels of up to 350,000 tons.

The 320-km-long pipeline is jointly owned by Egypt, Saudi Arabia, Kuwait, UAE and Qatar, and has a capacity of 2.5 million barrels per day.[58] In June 1997, Saudi Aramco assumed Petromin's 15 per cent share in SuMed:[59] 'In 2000, it is estimated that SuMed transported 2.2 million barrels per day northbound, largely from Saudi Arabia. This compares favourably with the 700,000 barrels per day shipped through the Suez Canal.'[60] Finding the competition difficult to handle, the Canal Administration has suggested that vessels under the Suezmax limit should not be serviced by SuMed facilities.

Egypt–Jordan gas pipeline ('Arabline')

The one relatively recent development in the Middle East has been the line pumping Egyptian gas to Jordan, with plans eventually to extend the service to Syria and Lebanon. From modest beginnings in the 1970s, Egypt has become a middle-rank

hydrocarbon producer. Oil production approached 1 million barrels per day (~50 million tons p.a.) in the mid-1990s, about half
of it bound for export. The balance sheet has somewhat deterio-
rated since those peak years, with production gradually dropping
towards 700,000 barrels per day, whilst consumption has been
steadily rising towards 600,000 barrels. Meanwhile, gas production
in the Delta and the Western Desert has picked up from about 8
billion cubic metres p.a. in 1990 to nearly 32 billion in 2004.
Confirmed Egyptian reserves appear to be of the order of 2 trillion
cubic metres, with probable reserves of approximately double that
figure, comparable with those of Turkmenistan and Bangladesh.
Not surprisingly, Egypt has begun exporting gas, in the first
instance to Jordan (2003).

Construction to install a 278-km-long gas pipeline from the
Egyptian border town of Al-Arish to the Jordanian port city of
Aqaba started in Autumn 2001, extending 18 km in waters as
deep as 850 metres and giving Israeli territorial waters a wide
berth.[61] The enterprise cost an estimated $330 million. The far
easier project to pump gas from Al Arish to Israel has been abandoned following the onset of the second Intifada. Interestingly,
Egypt and Jordan have been offered incentives by the USA to do
business with Israel. Some categories of merchandise may be
exported *duty-free* to the USA 'provided they contain a stipulated
minimum content of Israeli input'.[62] It would seem, however, that
the current political price of cooperating with Israel on energy
issues is judged to be greater by the Egyptian administration than
its potential commercial benefits.

Initially, Egyptian gas was landed at Aqaba in Jordan, intended
for use at the local power station. From Aqaba, a 390 -km pipeline
has now been completed, connecting to the Samra and Rehab
Power Stations in northern Jordan.[63] The contract was awarded
in January 2004 and completion of construction announced in
January 2006.[64] The throughput of the line is being raised from an
initial annual 1 billion cubic metres to about 10 billion. Furthermore, Rehab is only 24 km from the Syrian border. In a third
phase of the project, it was planned to extend the 36-in diameter
line from Rehab to Homs in central Syria and eventually to supply Tripoli in Lebanon through a secondary pipeline extended
from Homs.[65] How the latest tensions between the USA and Syria

and the Israeli devastation of South Lebanon in 2006 will affect that part of the plan remains to be seen.

The pipeline war in Iraq

In the early months of the occupation of Iraq, Washington-appointed administrators dismissed *en masse* the army officer corps, police and intelligence apparatus of the former Iraqi regime. This move is now widely acknowledged to have been an error, which possibly gave shape to and certainly provided impetus for the ongoing insurgency. A related but less publicized lapse in judgement led to the cutting of subsidies to the Northern Beni Shammar tribesmen, who since the distant days of the IPC were paid to 'protect' the pipelines. These subsidies were meticulously adhered to even in the days of the once all-powerful Saddam, *even during times of internal peace*, but for good measure, Saddam had thrown in a couple of army divisions to guard his pipelines. In 2003, the consequences of this ill-judged thrift by the US occupation authorities were not slow in exploding under Iraq's oil and gas infrastructure.

Briefly, there were 35 major attacks on Iraqi pipelines, oil installations and oil personnel in the second half of 2003. Another 148 major attacks have been recorded in 2004, and about a hundred each in 2005 and 2006. Operations and security personnel including ordinary guards have been systematically targeted, as have wells, pumping installations, stabilizing plants and sections of actual pipelines.[66] The trend has evolved towards fewer but more destructive attacks. In one particularly murderous incident during August 2006, some 34 people lost their lives in an explosion and ensuing fire. Nor can repair, routine maintenance and replacement work proceed at pace. The Special Inspector General for Iraq Reconstruction, a US federal agency monitoring how Iraqi reconstruction money is spent, has reported that work on a 50-km stretch of the Kirkuk–Bayji pipeline is ' ... years behind schedule'.[67]

Whilst it seems difficult to be precise, Iraq's gross oil production appears to have been oscillating around an average of 1.5 million barrels a day during the first three and a half years of the occupation, depending on the security situation. This is half the 3 million barrels that US officials had envisaged, at the outset of the war, that they would have had access to without significant additional investment.[68]

The statistics provide interesting pointers for military and insurgency analysts. The attacks appear to come mostly in clusters of three or four in a given area before moving on, suggesting that marauding explosives teams are constantly on the move. The majority of attacks have taken place along the Kirkuk–Bayji–Baghdad axis and in the Kirkuk–Bayji–Dahuk (north, towards Turkey and Ceyhan) direction. Particular effort appears to have been made by insurgents to disrupt supplies reaching the Bayji and al-Dawrah (Baghdad) refineries, suggesting a focus on internal disruption. During 2006, the lines leading to the Turkish port of Ceyhan have also been systematically bombed – apparently successfully interrupting exports through that route. The regional distribution of attacks would point to a concentration of activity in the ethnically mixed Mosul-Kirkuk, Bayji and Baghdad regions, possibly due to the greater possibility of assistance to insurgents from elements of the local population. The pattern of violent incidents during 2005 and 2006 was more focused on the northern and central pipelines and associated facilities, with far fewer incidents in the south. Indeed, reports suggest much of the oil produced for export is coming from the southern Rumaila oilfields.

Oil pipelines have thus taken central stage in a conflict where the stakes at national and regional level could not be higher. At issue is the nature of the post-occupation settlement in Iraq, including the control of the country's immensely important untapped oil *reserves*, strategically far more significant than current volumes of production. One version of the draft law governing Iraq's oil resources would distribute revenues through the federal government, giving it wide powers in exploration, development and awarding major international contracts. Meanwhile, what appears to interest the international oil companies far more is the widening of access to so many known, confirmed oil reservoirs, many of them classed as supergiants. The administration in Washington has demanded the passage of an 'oil law' as a condition for continued military support to the government in Baghdad. '[British] Foreign Office minister Kim Howells has admitted that the government has discussed the wording of the Iraqi law with Britain's oil giants',[69] whilst Iraqi nationalist opinion appears sanguine that such a law could not be enforced in peacetime.[70] Immediately, however, the insurgency is targeting existing production, transmission and distribution facilities, as well as personnel associated with these activities. The two realities appear to exist in parallel.

Calculating on the basis of a nominal price of, say, $60 per barrel, the loss of income (between producing 3 or 1.5 million barrels per day) was about $90 million per day, or a little above $32 *billion* annually. These are the sums of which post-Saddam Iraqi administrations could have made use to stabilize their hold on power and of which the insurgents are trying to deprive them. To make matters worse, the almost daily attacks have been taking place under the anxious eyes of jittery oil markets, with prices edging up in the aftermath of every significant attack. By late summer of 2006, officially reported figures had talked up production to nearly 2.3 million barrels.[71] Whilst this would have indicated increasing exports from the south, the optimistic figures contrasted sharply with increasingly grim news coming out of Iraq during that period. Some months later, the authorities had gone back to admitting the figure of 1.5 million barrels a day with a frequency, suggesting they might not even be doing that well.

Commenting on the sporadic misfortunes of Tapline during the early 1970s, Stevens wrote: 'Contrary to popular opinion, if access is possible for repair it is extremely difficult to sabotage pipelines effectively.'[72] The Iraqi experience suggests otherwise. With thousands of defenders constantly in action, daily attacks and breaches followed by rapid repairs, this could fairly be called the first ever full-scale pipeline war. As with shipping in the Atlantic during both World Wars, much cargo seems to make it, but at great cost in men and materials. The outcome of this struggle will no doubt be shaped by the wider war. However, like the Battle of the Atlantic, the 'battle of the pipelines' has become one of the components of a war, the outcome of which will undoubtedly influence the result of the struggle at the national and the wider regional levels.

8 Concluding Remarks

Not surprisingly, the history of pipelines in the Middle East closely follows the region's recent turbulent political history. The emerging picture is not just one of Arab–Israeli enmity, although the devastation brought on by that conflict has been disastrous for the region as a whole. The general picture also shows, however, at times quite vicious inter-Arab rivalries with immense loss in treasure and much else, for nearly all the countries of the region. Alongside the almost palpable mutual dislike between kings and sheikhs on the one hand and presidents and generals on the other, the rivalries between nominally similar political formations in Iraq and Syria have caused much damage in this unhappy region.

Looking beyond the heat and dust of proliferating struggles and regional wars, we can observe seismic shifts in production levels and sale destinations for Middle Eastern crude oil. Production in the region has increased by more than 45 per cent since 1971, from 810 million tons to 1,180 million tons in 2004.[73] Saudi production alone has more than doubled in the same period to 492 million tons. Secondly, the bulk of Middle Eastern oil is no longer destined for Europe; much of the exports from the Gulf are now bound for East and North-east Asia, through the vulnerable Straits of Hormuz and Malacca. In Chapter VII, we will discuss how China, with nearly half of its oil imports coming from the Middle East, is striving to diversify her oil imports and how Japan and Korea are in an even worse predicament, importing as they do over 80 per cent of their oil from this region.

In terms of oil and gas transmission lines, Israel is effectively cut off from its neighbours, although we saw how tantalizingly close they came to receiving a proportion of Egypt's growing natural gas exports. Recently, there has been discussion about using the Eilat–Ashkelon oil pipeline, in the north–south direction, to transmit Caspian oil to India. The overall configuration of this particular installation is not dissimilar to that of the SuMed line, in the sense of bypassing the Suez Canal and enabling large ships to load and unload at either end. However, the oil supply from the Black Sea and the Caspian will need to increase substantially before the present south–north oil flow is reversed, and oil from the Mediterranean is pumped towards the South and East.

The reader may well ask why Iran has not occupied a greater place than it already has in our discussion. Although Iran has been intimately involved in the affairs and indeed the wars of the region, her role in shaping the Middle East's transnational pipelines and pipeline politics has been marginal. Instead, Iran's confrontations over oil transmission have taken place at sea, notably during the 'Tanker War' with Iraq. There has been relatively little hydrocarbon transmission between Iran and her Arab neighbours. The one major link since the 2003 invasion of Iraq has been cross-border contraband shipments of subsidized, refined Iraqi oil products to Iran. Iraqi and Iranian officials have discussed building a short pipeline link from the southern Iraqi oilfields to nearby Iranian refineries – notably the one in Abadan, meticulously flattened by Iraqi shelling during the Iran–Iraq war and since rebuilt.

Iran's geographical position makes her an important player in the Caspian Basin and in Central Asia. In Chapter VI, we will discuss Iran's critical position in relation to Caspian oil and gas transmission and her potentially complementary role for Central Asia's existing pipeline networks. Iran will also figure prominently in the next chapter on South Asia, where India and Pakistan have been drawing closer over the prospect of sharing a gas pipeline from Iran's South Pars field. The strategic implications of these developments have been focusing minds not just in the region's capitals, but as far afield as Washington, Moscow and Beijing.

Chapter IV

South Asia's long-awaited pipelines

1 Oil and Gas Transmission in South Asia

For our purposes, we will define South Asia as a broad arc from Iran in the West, running through Pakistan, India and Bangladesh to Myanmar in the East (Figure 4.1). To some extent, our definition is arbitrary but useful in relation to the proposed rather problematic regional transnational gas pipelines. The other pipeline axis of immediate concern broadly traces a north-west–south-east line, from Turkmenistan through Afghanistan to Pakistan and India.

In outline, the region's hydrocarbon transmission needs can be described relatively simply. India and Pakistan require more oil and gas than they produce. Both countries have plenty of coastline and adequate infrastructure to land imported crude oil, and convey it through internal pipelines to their own refineries and beyond. At present, the region has no need of cross-border *oil* pipelines.

Projected natural gas demand in India and Pakistan is also greater than amounts likely to be extracted locally. The good news is that most of their neighbours have natural gas to sell. Iran is home to the second-largest gas reserve in the world after Russia and is keen to export to the subcontinent. In the north,

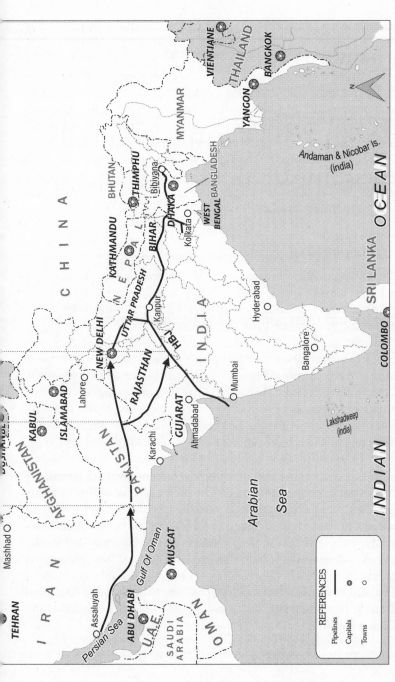

Figure 4.1 The proposed Iran to Pakistan & India overland gas pipeline, and the Bibiyana to Delhi gas pipeline connection proposed by UNOCAL. Adapted from: (1) India Oil & Gas Conference, http://www.bhpbilliton.com/bb/investorsAndMedia/investmentPresentation.jsp?id=Presentations%2FP_BHPBilliton170102.html; (2) http://www.acdis.uiuc.edu/Research/OPs/Samrina/SamrinaOP.pdf

Turkmenistan, with over 2 trillion cubic metres of reserves, has been trying to find a way through turbulent Afghanistan to sell natural gas to Pakistan and India. In the east, estimated natural gas reserves in Bangladesh are of comparable magnitude to those of Turkmenistan. To date, this gas has only been used for domestic consumption. Initially, Bangladesh had no immediate plans to exploit the Bibiyana fields in the north-east, and the Indians had been examining its possibilities with interest. Those fields have since been connected to the Bangladesh national grid.[1] Further to the south, Myanmar also has gas to sell and, again, the Indians are interested. The key question is: how to convey all this gas to the subcontinent at affordable prices?

LNG or pipelines?

We have already observed that shipping natural gas as LNG requires larger initial capital outlays than transmission by pipeline. Over distances of up to several thousand kilometres, transmission of natural gas by pipelines is usually advantageous. However, in South Asia, each of the likely overland routes for importing gas raises fierce diplomatic and security concerns. During the past several years, the advantages of sharing pipelines seem to have toned down some of the region's political tensions. Might pipelines serve as harbingers of peace, just this once? The potential benefits of these projects are enormous and interest in these negotiations has been near-universal – well beyond the frontiers of the parties that are directly involved.

In this chapter, we will examine the fortunes of some seemingly very attractive pipeline projects. In each case, we will review the geopolitical and economic circumstances that bar the way to actual implementation. Indeed, not all the protagonists and certainly not all the out-of-area observers are backing favourable outcomes. Meanwhile, LNG can be brought in by refrigerated tanker-ships, and nuclear energy is always a possible alternative. The latter has the advantage of bypassing irritable neighbours and difficult gas producers, but usually turns out to be significantly more expensive.

2 The Jewels in the Crown: Natural Gas Needs of India and Pakistan

Powering India

In the centre of the region, India's population topped 1 billion in 2000, and her economic growth during much of the past decade has exceeded the 5–6 per cent mark. She has the greatest energy needs and potential market for oil and gas. On the other hand, per capita gross domestic product (GDP) is still around $500 and India's *total* GDP of over $500 billion is comparable in magnitude with the US defence budget. As in the case of China, however, these overall figures partly mask the dynamism of rapidly growing industrial and service sectors, against a background of stagnation in the immensely populated and perennially underfunded agricultural sector.

Already a large producer of coal in colonial days and up to independence, India also hoped to become self-sufficient in hydrocarbon production. As early as 1889, prospectors in Upper Assam had not been very disappointed when the Digboi Well No 1 gave a modest 200 gallons of crude oil per day. It was hoped that a little perseverance would yield much more. There had been stories of wild elephants with oil-soaked legs leading men to a salt lick, where seepages from the ground suggested the presence of petroleum deposits nearby. Some of the engineers had described how the ground near their campfire had suddenly burst into flames. Visvanath[2] describes elephants being used to drag machinery on sleighs through leach-infested forest paths, in a region where 'the heavy smell of oil discouraged habitation'. However, Digboi Well No 2 turned out to be dry, and Well No 3 was almost abandoned when ' … [the work master's] brother … not having anything else to do … decided to drill a few feet deeper … oil gushed 40 feet'.

Over its 100-year-long history, the Digboi field produced some 14 million tons of crude oil. Not a negligible amount perhaps, but Assam never became an oil Eldorado. During the First World War, the Royal Navy and the British-Indian Army's steadily expanding motor transport corps were supplied by Shell from the Dutch East Indies, while the Western Front was mainly supplied from the USA and Mexico. However, production continued during the

Second World War, when the Digboi field was given the only anti-aircraft battery in India, the Bofors guns being dragged to the hilltops by the all-conquering elephants of the Assam Railway and Trading Company Ltd.

After the war, considerably more oil was found in Cambay and Ankleshwar in Gujarat. Offshore fields near Mumbai now represent a large fraction of India's domestic hydrocarbon production. New fields have also been developed in Andra Pradesh.[3] Nevertheless, India's oil and gas reserves match neither her past wealth in diamonds,[4] nor her increasing energy needs.[5] With imports exceeding 90 million tons and domestic production stagnant at around the 40-million-ton level, India will be a net importer of hydrocarbons for the foreseeable future. Meanwhile, refinery capacity has nearly doubled in the five years after 1998 and the country has been positioned as a major regional *exporter* of finished oil products, with over 14 million tons shipped in 2003 and 17 million tons in 2004.

The picture for gas is different. Between 1980–1 and 1994–5, the share of gas in energy utilization increased from a meagre 2 per cent to approximately 8 per cent, corresponding to about 17 billion cubic metres. Since then, offshore gas fields near Mumbai (Bassein and Tapti) and in Rajasthan have been expanded. By 2004, when imported LNG began coming in, annual domestic production had stabilized at nearer the 28 billion cubic metres mark.

The Gas Authority of India Ltd (later renamed 'GAIL (India) Ltd') was established in 1984 by the Indian Government as the country's principal gas transmission and marketing company. Among other large projects, GAIL undertook the construction of north-west India's backbone gas transmission system, the Hazira–Bijaipur–Jagdishpur (HBJ) natural gas pipeline, first commissioned in 1997. The 2,800-km line runs from the western offshore fields to Hazira on the coast and serves parts of Gujarat, Madhya Pradesh and Rajasthan, before ending in Uttar Pradesh with links to the Delhi area. The line supplies seven power stations, six fertilizer plants and a number of smaller installations. Its capacity has been increased from an initial 6.5 to 12 billion cubic metres p.a.[6] and it presently takes up the entire western offshore gas production.[7]

Despite these developments and several recent new discoveries,[8] game-changing step increases in Indian gas production are not expected and there is a need to decide how to power the country's future economic growth. Next door, Iran is looking to sell gas from her vast reserves. Despite the evident dangers, until the recent flare-up in fighting, the possibility of piping gas from Turkmenistan across Afghanistan had also been kept under review. India is likewise looking for ways of importing gas from Myanmar through Bangladesh. Not everybody thinks, however, that these contacts will bear fruit quickly. The IEA Gas Information Book (2005) expects new developments through Iran on a timescale no shorter than 2030 and from Myanmar not before about 2010.[9] Furthermore, the routes from Iran and Turkmenistan pass through Pakistan, requiring a significant Indo-Pakistani accommodation.

While India considered her gas-transmission options via pipelines, increasing electricity demand (and shortages) has convinced several multinationals that there are profits to be made in selling gas to power generators, whatever the state of affairs in talks with Iran and Pakistan. One obvious way to circumvent difficulties across India's international borders is to make use of her vast seaboard. At present, there are nine major LNG projects on the drawing-board, involving nearly 45 billion cubic metres of gas imports annually. Three of these projects have actually been initiated and one has already been completed. Mostly, the new gas is intended for gas-fired power stations constructed near the regasification plants, alongside small amounts piped to other consumers.

However, selling gas in India is subject to an added complication. In the past, the Government has subsidized domestically sold natural gas and the treasury is wary of more gas coming on the market that would require similar subsidies. That is one reason why they have been reluctant to boost domestic gas supplies with imported LNG during the past two decades.

'Petronet' was the first group to complete the construction of LNG landing facilities and a degasification plant in Dahej, 300 km north of Mumbai. The consortium is composed of several Indian state-owned energy companies, who have contracted to buy 7 billion cubic metres of gas from Qatar on a take-or-pay basis, with an acceptably low 'fixed' price of $3.86 per million BTU[10] (about $139 per 1,000 cubic metres). Imports began in April 2004. There are plans to double project capacity by 2010–11, that will probably involve some tough negotiations on the gas price.

The second project in Hazira involves Shell. The terminal was laid out for about 7 billion cubic metres, although initially it was to function at about half this capacity. Shell itself has no long-term gas supply agreements, having earlier elected to buy LNG 'just in time'. It seems they had banked on low gas prices and a slack market. These decisions would have been taken before 2002, when gas was relatively cheap and the New York City 'gate' price hovered between $2 and $3 per million BTU[11] ($72–105 per 1,000 cubic metres). According to reports,[12] Shell has been finding it difficult to market gas at current high world prices to its sole customer, the Gujarat State Petronet Corporation, which lifts gas 'when there is demand from customers in the state'.

The elusive price of gas

Any attempt to summarize the movement of gas prices will only help to reveal the chaotic nature of this market. Some of the difficulties are structural. Once completed, natural gas transmission infrastructure is fixed. The complexity and cost of the hardware creates a partial barrier to the movement of natural gas to receivers other than those originally intended. Gas supply contracts are therefore signed for relatively long periods, usually before pipelines are constructed, and such contracts have a tendency to limit price movements. As a result, natural gas price differentials between regions cannot be equilibrated as readily as crude oil price differentials. Unlike the global trade in crude oil, therefore, spot markets for natural gas tend to be more localized.

Despite the risk of confusion, quoting a few benchmark prices might nevertheless help us to appreciate some of the problems that have recently emerged in relation to Indian LNG imports. The discussion below is submitted with a note of caution; the prices quoted are merely intended as snapshots of some short-term trends, during 2005–6. Gas prices have been volatile during this period and more of the same may be expected in the medium-term future.

During the first half of 2005, continental US gas prices were reasonably high but stable, between $6 and $8 per million BTU.[13] Multiplying by the conversion factor of (approximately) 36, this price corresponds to between $216 and $288 *per 1,000 cubic metres*. From July 2005 onwards, production shortfalls due to hurricane damage to installations in the Gulf of Mexico[14] and the approaching winter (from October) combined to push prices as high as $15 per million BTU (about $540 per 1,000 m^3). That was a very high price! During this period, the average European wholesale purchase price for Russian natural gas was about $135 per 1,000 cubic metres (approximately $3.75 per million BTU), a little above half the *usual* New York City 'gate' price during that period.

However, in December 2005, the NYC 'gate' spot price hit highs of $540 per 1,000 cubic metres for the second time in two months. Gazprom then forced up the natural gas price for Western Europe from $135 to $255 dollars. However, the very high prices in the USA during November–December 2005 were due to exceptional circumstances. As production recovered, in mid-February 2006, the New York City 'gate' spot price drifted back to oscillating around $7–8 per million BTU ($252–88 per 1,000 cubic metres), around $5–5.50 in late summer 2006 ($180–200 per 1,000 cubic metres) and back to between $7–8 during winter 2006–7.

To summarize, before the wild price fluctuations in the USA, Russian gas for Europe cost about half the NYC 'gate' spot price. After the price fluctuations of October–December 2005, the 2006–7 price of Russian gas to Europe was raised into the same price-band as the New York City 'gate' spot price.[15]

Selling LNG to India

Returning to the Shell Hazira project, following the completion of the degasification plant, and with no long-term gas supply contracts in hand, the company was constrained to picking up floating cargoes of LNG (as originally planned!). However, with spot prices fluctuating wildly and Indian utilities desperately anxious to keep electricity prices low, the Hazira plant was left in difficulty. In early 2006, there were suggestions that the state-owned Oil and Natural Gas Corporation Limited (ONGC),[16] one of the members of the Petronet consortium, might make a bid to buy the Hazira plant from its present owners. In early 2007, Shell was still looking to double its gas imports to 'roughly 56 per cent of the terminal capacity … as long as customers agree to pay international prices …'.[17]

The trials of the now defunct Dabhol Power Company (DPC), India's third LNG project, similarly underscore the narrow price margins within which energy companies must work in India. The project near Ratnagiri, some 240 km south of Mumbai, was undertaken by General Electric who supplied the equipment, Bechtel who designed and constructed the plant, and Enron who undertook to develop and run the project. Phase-I was designed to burn naphtha (a light-medium petroleum distillate), to provide 740 MW of electric power to the Maharashtra State Electricity Board (MSEB).[18] In the second stage, the plant was to regasify 7 billion cubic metres of natural gas annually, with total power deliveries eventually rising to a sizeable 2,200 MW. In view of the cost of importing LNG relative to Indian domestic energy prices, the World Bank had raised questions as early as 1993, regarding the economic viability of the project. The problem has not gone away.[19]

Following the collapse of Enron with far-reaching financial and legal consequences, construction at Dabhol was stopped in June 2001.[20] A second difficulty arose from disagreements, yet again, on the price of gas, between Dabhol Power Company and its principal buyer, MSEB. However, power shortages have provided a strong incentive to get the project moving. In late 2005, the plant changed hands. Ratnagiri Gas and Power Ltd, a joint venture between NTPC[21] and GAIL, was formed with the aim of taking the project forward. Since then, the LNG regasification and storage facilities have been completed. There is capacity to generate an additional 1,440 MW.[22] However, concerns over the price of natural gas have persisted. Problems were also encountered in naphtha procurement. The LNG terminal at Dabhol requires 7 billion cubic metres of natural gas to be viable. Of this, about 3 billion cubic metres would be utilized by the power plant, while the remainder would be sold to other users. Far from assisting Dabhol with gas contracts, however, Petronet has suggested that Ratnagiri themselves ' … should directly enter into … gas deals'.[23]

What price signed contracts?

In the course of negotiations during 2004–6, the Indians would readily admit that they had been calculating on an ex-ship LNG price of between $3.65 and $4.15 per million BTU. Meanwhile, RasGas of Qatar offered gas to the Dabhol Phase II power plant at $7.50. In other words, India needed to buy the gas at between $130 and $150 per 1,000 cubic metres, to avoid subsidies, whilst the Qatari offer for Dabhol stood at $250–70.

Meanwhile, Indian officials could have been excused for thinking they had a signed and sealed supply of LNG at a lower price from Iran. The signed agreement announced in January 2005 was for 7.5 million tons of LNG (~10 billion cubic metres) p.a., starting in 2009 and over a period of 25 years. The agreed price formula fixed the price at $2.97 per million BTU for the first three years. This would make the price competitive compared to the Qatar price, then selling to India at $3.86 for five years up to 2008. Depending on the oil price, the Iranian price formula eventually allowed the price to drift to an upper limit of $3.21 dollars per million BTU (about $115 per 1,000 cubic metres). The total LNG deal between the two countries worked out at around $35–$40 billion.[24]

However, following Mr Ahmadinejad's election as president (Summer 2005), Iran's Supreme Economic Council refused to clear the already signed deal on the grounds that the previous regime had 'undersold' the gas. It was probably this deal that had originally encouraged the Indian Government to show interest in the Shell-Hazira and the Ratnagiri-Dabhol projects. Iranian Foreign Minister Manouchehr Mottaki was quoted as saying that the pipeline situation was ' … a little bit complicated because of the changing of circumstances from the time when the contract and agreement was signed'.[25]

Indian sources have naturally greeted 'Iranian unwillingness to honour its commitment'[26] with disdain. Apart from putting the Indian LNG-import programme in jeopardy, Iranian prevarication over the LNG price changed the atmosphere during talks about the construction of the Iran–Pakistan–India gas pipeline (see below). The new Indian Petroleum Minister Murli Deora, already rumoured to be lukewarm to the pipeline project, has been quoted as saying 'India will not be rushed into any pipeline deal unless the LNG contract was honoured'.[27]

Rumours of multiple Iranian refusals to honour signed contracts following the election of Mr Ahmadinejad have been legion, some of these contracts involving production-sharing agreements

with Russian and Chinese partners. The latter have not gone public on these delicate matters. Instead, they have visibly and publicly vacillated during discussions on United Nations sanctions
against Iran, in relation to Iran's uranium enrichment programme.
For the Ahmadinejad administration, on the other hand, this is
not *just* a matter of money. It also relates to his direct criticism of
the previous administration during the election campaign, and his
promises to 'eradicate corruption'. Apparently, the tearing up of so
many contracts was intended to project an image of cleaning up
the mythical stables.

The shift in the Iranian position during the Indian gas sale
negotiations carried distant echoes of actions by the revolutionary
governments of 1978–9, which had effectively scuttled the IGAT-1
and IGAT-2 projects with the Soviets. The initial (IGAT-1) project
was conceived in the mid-1960s, to supply gas to Iran's northern
cities and to export gas to the Soviet Union.[28] The line was intended
to pump 6 billion cubic metres of Iranian natural gas p.a. by 1970
and 10 billion cubic metres from 1973. An additional agreement,
negotiated in 1967 with a view to increasing gas supplies to 20 billion cubic metres by 1980, was never finalized.[29] The reluctance of
the revolutionary Iranian regime of the late 1970s to continue deliveries was variously attributed to a tendency to conserve resources and
slow down rates of depletion, an intended shift from domestic oil
consumption to gas, as well as to general ill will against 'Western-
style materialistic ambitions'. At the time, Soviet capacity for producing gas for export to Europe was limited, and the shortfall affected
both Western Europe and Warsaw Pact member Czechoslovakia.

India's energy subsidies

As already signalled, India's troubles have their roots in the low
purchase price of natural gas in the country as a whole. In
February 2005, the price of gas paid *to* ONGC by the local power
and fertilizer plants was about $43–4 per 1,000 cubic metres
($1.22 per million BTU), compared to the then reigning price of
$180–220 NYC 'gate'. In 2004–5, the loss to the Union treasury
through natural gas subsidies alone was of the order of $4–5
billion. Analogous government subsidies were costing about $1.5
billion for LPG[30] and $3 billion for diesel fuel.[31]

Keeping energy prices low is a policy instrument of debatable value. The Congress Party-led government views cheap energy as a lifeline for the poor, a politically sensitive subject for the voting public. The Government also entertains hopes that low energy prices will help to stimulate the economy. However, subsidies are not politically neutral. They favour the energy-utilizing sectors of the economy. Furthermore, keeping energy prices low squeezes the profit margins of energy-related investments. It has been suggested that *state-owned* ONGC themselves are shutting in supplies in the Tripura gas fields of Assam, because of the low price of gas. Similar suggestions have been made regarding the lack of investment in the state-owned coal industry, with the shortfall in supplies being made up by imports from Australia.

In addition to impeding investment and costing the Government enormous sums of money – through state-owned corporations – the cheap energy policy in India has also worked against improvements in technology and energy efficiency. We will see in the next few sections that the effort to keep gas prices low is also limiting the Government's options in their negotiations to import natural gas by pipeline.

Powering Pakistan

Pakistan produces about 3 million tons of crude oil and imports about 15 million more. Nearly *half* the country's energy requirements are met by locally produced natural gas and 13 per cent by hydroelectric power. Pakistan ranks third in the world, behind Brazil and Argentina, for using natural gas as a motor fuel, and is looking to make natural gas the fuel of choice for future electric power generation projects.[32] Unlike India, Pakistan has not made extensive use of available coal reserves in the past, although there appears to be new political will to mobilize some of these resources, in collaboration with China.[33] The overall economic picture is one of relative underdevelopment, albeit with some hopefully large GDP increases from a low base.

The recoverable gas reserves of Pakistan are estimated at a relatively modest 750 billion cubic metres, while production was 32 billion cubic metres in 2004 and nearly reached 36 billion cubic metres in 2005.[34] At current rates of consumption, the country has

30 years' worth of gas reserves. Rapid economic development would require importing significant quantities of gas. The reasoning is thus not significantly different from that in India. Furthermore, economies of scale require Indian participation for pipelines from Iran and/or from Turkmenistan to be economically (more?) attractive.

3 Devil in the Pipeline; Gas from Iran

Iran's 'proven' recoverable crude oil reserves of 126 billion barrels make up nearly 10 per cent of the world's known petroleum deposits. In 2005, the country produced nearly 205 million tons of oil and condensate. It derives upwards of 80 per cent of its foreign earnings from oil. With prices surging since mid-2004, the economy has been able to maintain a growth rate of about 5 per cent. In addition to its stupendous oil wealth, Iran's natural gas reserves, estimated at 27 trillion cubic metres, are the second largest in the world after Russia.

More recently, Iran has been considering a project involving the construction of a natural gas pipeline to Pakistan and, across Pakistan, to India (Figure 4.1). If successful, the project would exploit Iran's advantageous geographic position to develop the vast untouched hydrocarbon potential on the Gulf seabed and derive a large income, whilst enhancing her international legitimacy and influence as a peacemaker between Pakistan and India. With a little luck she might also win the cooperation of Pakistan to help stabilize next-door Afghanistan.

India expects to lift about 60 billion cubic metres per year, if the pipeline enters service in 2010. This is expected to rise to 90 billion cubic metres in several years. Pakistan's needs are smaller: the initial 30 billion cubic metres would be expected to double by 2013. The value of involving both India and Pakistan turns on the economies of scale: 'doubling the diameter of a pipe allows for about six times the gas flow'.[35] The total length of the line is estimated at 2,775 km and the cost at about $7 billion. However, that is only where the problems begin.

The odd couple – U.S. and Iran

Ever since the overthrow of the Shah, successive US governments have been hostile to Iran and towards anybody remotely interested in doing business with Iran. Latterly, US attitudes to the Iran–Pakistan–India gas pipeline project have been couched in terms of opposition to Iran's ambitions to develop nuclear weapons. In fact, US resistance to this or any other project involving Iran predates this latter phase of their confrontation. At present, the USA is also accusing Iran, probably rightly, of funding anti-Israeli militias and stirring up militant attacks against US and British forces in Iraq.

There are, however, other concerns. Differences have persisted between India, Pakistan and Iran over issues no less vital than the future of Kashmir and of Afghanistan. Writhing in poverty and the ravages of near permanent war, exporting narcotics and importing arms, and more recently with American and other NATO troops rushing around, Afghanistan has been a constant source of worry for Iran. Meanwhile, widespread collusion between elements of the Pakistani state and the post-Taliban insurgency in Afghanistan (and in Pakistan) is causing alarm in both Tehran and Washington.

Nor can it be said that either the Indian or the Pakistani establishment were uniformly in favour of the IPI-gas pipeline project. In a February 2003 despatch, India's (since replaced) Petroleum Minister Ram Naik was quoted as saying there was ' ... no question of speaking with Pakistan on the proposed Indo–Iran gas pipeline'. The minister instead suggested that Tehran and New Delhi had decided to undertake a feasibility study for an offshore pipeline outside Pakistan's exclusive economic zone.[36] Until the thaw at the top between India and Pakistan during 2004–6, few observers seriously believed the talks were likely to translate into an actual project.

After the elections that brought a Congress-led coalition to power, Mani Shankar Aiyar replaced Naik as Indian petroleum minister. Initially, he appeared to be a lone voice in the Congress-led government. He was opposed by the usual lobby of analysts, intelligence officials and diplomats who had made their careers during the decades of the old enmity. They rejected the idea of engaging Pakistan in an overland pipeline project. It would have broken all the old rules. In those early stages, the news from Pakistan mirrored these long-held attitudes, with a tri-nation pipeline nowhere near the line of sight of officials in Islamabad.[37]

However, Aiyar linked up with the Prime Minister's office and sidestepped opposition by the Ministry of External Affairs. In a parallel move, the Prime Minister's office appointed another official (S. K. Lamba) as the PM's personal go-between in relations with Pakistan.[38] Serious discussions were undertaken from late 2003 between Iran, Pakistan and India. Meanwhile, US diplomacy has been trying to help bring the old enemies together – all the while vehemently opposing the gas pipeline project with Iran. According to the US Energy Information Agency:

In March 2004, President Bush extended sanctions originally imposed in 1995 by President Clinton for another year, citing the 'unusual and extraordinary threat' to US national security posed by Iran. The 1995 executive orders prohibit US companies and their foreign subsidiaries from conducting business with Iran, while banning any 'contract for the financing of the development of petroleum resources located in Iran'. In addition, the US Iran–Libya Sanctions Act (ILSA) of 1996 (renewed for 5 more years in July 2001) imposes mandatory and discretionary sanctions on non-US companies investing more than $20 million annually in the Iranian oil and natural gas sectors.[39]

Instead, the USA has been expounding the virtues of a gas pipeline from Turkmenistan, crossing Afghanistan, to serve both Pakistan and India. As we will see below, this is a project long cherished in Washington. It suffers from several fatal flaws.

Throughout 2004–5, officials in Iran, Pakistan and India issued weekly declarations to the effect that US opposition would not impede the development of this project. The involvement of Russia and China were sought, to provide some diplomatic counterweight against opposition by the USA. The Russians fielded energy minister Victor Khristenko to indicate interest in the pipeline.[40] A visit by Gazprom chairman Alexey Miller to Islamabad in early October 2005 was concluded with the signing of a memorandum of understanding.[41]

The idea of Chinese participation was a little more creative. It involved sending gas across the Myanmar–China border to southern China. We will see below that India is looking for ways to import gas from Myanmar into Assam, which would then be piped *across* Bangladesh, east–west through north India, to link up with the gas-ring around Delhi. Chinese involvement would imply reversing this flow, sending gas from Myanmar to China, *supplemented by* Iranian gas, pumped from Delhi *eastward*. While technically complicated, the proposal had the advantage of being inclusive, keeping the Chinese on-side, interested and supportive.

Meanwhile, in the face of US opposition, Pakistani officials at all levels know they are walking a tightrope. During her visit to South Asia in April 2005, the US Secretary of State reiterated Washington's 'strong' opposition to the construction of the Iran–Pakistan–India gas pipeline. Islamabad has been taking delivery of 77 F-16 combat aircraft, part paid for by the Benazir Bhutto government over a decade ago. The deal has been supplemented by 20 Cobra helicopters – probably intended for anti-insurgency operations. It may be recalled that delivery of the F-16s had originally been held up because of Pakistan's development of nuclear weapons. They are now being released[42] to reward President Musharraf's efforts to cashier the more active Taliban supporters within Inter Service Intelligence (allegedly, his erstwhile allies) and scatter some of the more fanatical local religious groups. His opponents have returned the courtesy by trying to assassinate him, twice.

Washington could hurt Pakistan, simply by limiting armament sales, or even by delaying the delivery of spare parts. Pakistani officials visiting Washington during April 2005, and since, have been constrained to give conflicting signals. S. Shah, advisor to Pakistan's Prime Minister, was quoted as saying, ' ... for example, were the gas to be delivered to Pakistan at its borders, it might not involve any investment on Pakistan's part ... ',[43] meaning investment *in Iran*. Whether such refined exegesis would let the Pakistani Government off the hook in the eyes of the US Department of Defence remains to be seen. In 2005–6, Washington seemed to be fighting a vigorous and reasonably successful delaying action, despite the attractions of the project.

4 Problems in Baluchistan

Apart from the price issue, there are unresolved 'technical' problems still under discussion between Iran and India. Tehran would like a (usual) 'take-or-pay' contract, requiring India to pay for contracted gas even if it does not take delivery. Meanwhile, Indian misgivings about the security of the pipeline and about the continuity of gas deliveries have led to suggestions that India and Iran should sign a contract for deliveries at the *Indian* frontier. Their officials have been asking for a 'supply-or-pay' contract, making Iran responsible for the delivery of the gas through Pakistan, so that Iran would have to pay India for undelivered gas.[44] They would also like Pakistan to commit to making good the losses in case of interruption of supplies and that large buffer tanks be built on the Indian side to compensate for short-term interruptions, as a result of action by 'third' parties.

Among others, the latter concern was inspired by acts of sabotage by Beluchi tribesmen against existing domestic Pakistani natural gas pipelines and equipment. The instances of violence by the tribesmen have multiplied since disagreements with the Pakistani Government came to a head after 2003–4. The Government has refused to come to terms with the region's demands. Instead, the leader of the movement, Nawab Akbar Bugti, a former provincial governor, was killed by the army in August 2006. From wanting a greater share of the revenue, the 6-million population of the mineral-rich province is gradually passing into a state of rebellion and insurgency.

'For Pakistan the project of enabling pipelines through its territory also means a crucial domestic undertaking, namely bringing under municipal law, areas that have until now been only nominally under its control.' This sounds like code for extending central government control to Baluchistan, which Pakistan has signally failed to do in over half a century.[45] The Iran–Pakistan–India pipeline would have to cross this same territory.

Iran's nuclear games

With the pipeline not even on the drawing boards, Iran made at least one concerted effort to use it as inducement to gain Indian diplomatic support at the IAEA negotiations. With the global superpower having unleashed its armed forces both east and west of Iran (in Afghanistan and Iraq, respectively), it is understandable that Iran's nervous political cadres should scramble to make the only weapon that *may* guarantee a level of safety from attack. It is also obvious that acquisition of these terrible weapons by Iran would further destabilize the region.

In September 2005, India supported an IAEA resolution for the agency to consider reporting Iran to the UN Security Council if it did not meet its nuclear obligations. In Autumn 2005, the Iranians asked Delhi to 'compensate the past default by supporting Iran in the next meeting of the IAEA board of governors in November [2005]'. The Indians appear to have balked at the Iranian suggestion to change their policy on Iran's nuclear activity. In the end, 'Tehran has removed the political hurdle it created by taking out nuclear politics from the Iran–Pakistan–India gas pipeline project …'.[46]

The burning question: the price of natural gas

As already signalled, the government of India is determined to reduce budget expenditure on gas subsidies, while Iran would like to sell at the highest price it can muster. As their opening position, the Iranians proposed that India pay the same price as that for the gas lifted from the degasification plants in Gujarat. The new Iranian stance set the negotiations back from the position reached in 2005 (before the election of Ahmadinejad), when the Indian Petroleum Ministry considered it was ready to seek Cabinet approval to enter into the final stage of negotiations.[47]

The two positions seemed to be a good hundred dollars (per 1,000 cubic metres) apart. Every trader knows that bargaining is an advanced stage in the life of a sale. However, one year later, respective positions had not shifted. As late as August 2006, Iran proposed a formula linked to the price of Brent crude oil with an escalating cost component that translated to a price of $7.20 per million BTU ($260 per 1,000 cubic metres), with a 3 per cent p.a. escalator.[48] This was higher than the price Western Europeans were paying for Russian natural gas at that time.

Many Indian decisions underpinning the importation of gas from Iran (or from anywhere else) had been made in the days when gas was cheaper. During the peaks of about $15 reached (in New York) in mid-December 2005, the $4–4.15 that Indian negotiators were seeking seemed a little forlorn. Two months later, however, continental US prices had dropped back to about half those peaks (around $8 per million BTU), and by late Summer 2006 they had slipped back further to about $5. India's proposed price thus occasionally re-enters the plausible target zone.

In early 2007, just as difficulties appeared insurmountable, a surprise announcement of an actual agreement was made, followed ten days later with outlines of the price formula.[49] For a Japanese crude oil 'cocktail' price of $60 per barrel, the price of gas comes to $4.93 per million BTU ($177 per 1,000 cubic metres). It is lower than the European price for Russian gas ($255), but not as low as the earlier LNG formula agreed between Iran and India.

Until the very last minute, it did not seem out of the question that India and Pakistan would walk away from this project. Despite the political capital already invested, a politically unacceptable gas price would have been a decisive show-stopper. However, it is not yet clear whether the pipeline is quite safe. Deora had earlier made the honouring by Iran of the LNG contract signed in 2005 a precondition for pursuing the IPI-pipeline project.[50] It will be recalled that the price formula of *that* contract was rejected by the incoming Ahmadinejad administration. No announcement has been made about a resolution of Iran's take-or-pay and India's deliver-or-pay formulas – although the two are not mutually exclusive. There are many more details to be ironed out. Reports have suggested that India had asked Pakistan for the waiver of their transit fee, likely to amount to about $125 million.[51] Finally, there is implacable opposition by the USA that must somehow be resolved. It seems possible, just, that the pipeline may turn up as a bargaining chip during negotiations over Iran's uranium enrichment programme.

The subcontinent's gas utilization projects

There are added complications. In both India and Pakistan, the uncertainties about gas imports naturally hook onto the timing of downstream investment decisions, involving the construction of new power and fertilizer plants. These installations involve substantial amounts of capital. Clearly, decisions to construct them depend on economic viability, which in turn depends on the price of the gas, the *sale* price of electricity and the magnitude of possible government subsidies.[52] The alternative to constructing the pipeline from Iran is either to use more LNG, which is expensive, or to go short or to turn to locally available coal. The latter causes far more pollution, but would be far cheaper if gas prices climb again to $15 in New York or Iran moves away from this latest price formula. On the other hand, coal-fired power stations and associated fertilizer complexes normally take twice as long to build and require more investment capital. Either way, South Asia appears on the eve of some very costly throws of the dice.

Within this complicated matrix, it is not clear whether a slowdown in pipeline negotiations had caused the demotion of Indian Petroleum Minister Aiyar in January 2006, or was a consequence of that demotion. His successor, Mr Murli Deora, was said to have 'deep contacts' in the US Congress and to have been offered technical assistance in further developing nuclear power in India. The Indian Government now appears committed to the Iran–Pakistan–India pipeline. Despite the agreement on the gas price, however, the pipeline is far from being out in the clear: 'The US has told the Indian government that it is opposed to plans to build a natural gas pipeline from Iran to India through Pakistan, US Energy Secretary Samuel Bodman said in New Delhi today.'[53]

Furthermore, India is not entirely devoid of alternative sources of natural gas.

5 Gas from Myanmar Through Bangladesh to India?

Myanmar was invaded by the British in three waves, between 1824 and 1885, by which date they gained control of the whole country. Until 1937, the country, then called Burma, was run as part of British India, after which date she was administered as a separate colony. It is a large country with a population of nearly 42 million. It is also home to some of the world's oldest oil-wells, operated by the 'Burmah Oil Company Ltd' (BOC) from the 1880s until 1963. The Ychaugyaung field, discovered in 1887, and the Chauk field (1902) are among those developed by the 'Burmah' engineers in those far-off days and are still in production.[54]

Myanmar gained its independence in 1948 following the evacuation of the colonial administration from the subcontinent. In

1962, the country passed under a military administration led by General Ne Win, who partly relinquished power to his younger fellow officers in the mid-1990s, after more than 30 years of stagnation. Elections held in 1990 yielded a large majority for civilian rule and have been ignored. The leader of the opposition, Nobel Peace Prize winner Aung San Suu Kyl, is at present under house arrest.

Myanmar's hydrocarbon production is not enormous. In 2003, the country produced about 1 million tons of oil, but reserves are estimated at a respectable 3.2 billion barrels. Natural gas reserves are estimated at an again respectable 2.5 trillion cubic metres, about as much as Turkmenistan. In 2005, production exceeded 12 billion cubic metres, with nearly 80 per cent going for export as LNG. The country has suffered from deficient infrastructure, international opprobrium and some reticence to invest, in view of the repressive nature of its regime. The discovery of new natural gas fields has, however, attracted the interest of India's state-owned ONGC and GAIL,[55] who retain about 30 per cent equity in Myanmar's offshore gas reserves. Their initial plan involves pumping up to 5 billion cubic metres of natural gas from Myanmar to India.

There are two basic routes for a gas pipeline to pass through the intricate borders of the region and end up in India. The simplest is a 950-km pipeline running through Arakan State (Burma), and the Indian states of Mizoram and Tripura – south of Assam. It is possible to add gas from the Tripura fields to the line, which would then travel west through Bangladeshi territory back into Indian West Bengal (Figure 4.1).

The second, longer and less economic route would bypass Bangladeshi territory. This route would involve running north, then west, parallel to the Bangladeshi border, passing through the narrow Indian land corridor between northern Bangladesh (in the south) and Bhutan and Nepal in the north, to end up in Indian West Bengal. Had Bangladesh been disposed to sell, the Indians would have wanted to buy natural gas from the Bibiyana gas fields in Bangladesh as well. In early 2007, that basin entered production at about 2 billion cubic metres and is intended to help ward off potential gas shortages in Bangladesh.[56]

The Burmese have been willing to sell, but this particular project has been bogged down for nearly a decade due to prevarication by Bangladesh. Let us take a closer look.

Gas through Bangladesh? Gas from Bangladesh?

Bangladesh is a crowded country where some 145 million people squeeze into a small land mass, at a density of over 1,000 people per km². Every year, during the monsoon rains, nearly a third of the country floods. At partition in 1947, the territory was awarded by the British to the then Republic of Pakistan. It was named East Pakistan and was run mostly by West Pakistanis, with somewhat less than due care and attention. During the elections of 1971, the Awami League of East Pakistan won plurality in the national parliament in Islamabad. The results went unrecognized by the (then) Prime Minister Zulfikar Ali Bhutto. He was supported by the army.[57] In East Pakistan, events escalated into rebellion against the central power. Extreme force was used by troops under General Tikka Khan, dubbed the 'Butcher of Bangladesh'. The emerging Bengali insurgency was assisted by Indian forces. When, in response, the Pakistani air force bombed Amritsar, Srinagar and targets in the Kashmir valley, the Indian Eastern Command invaded East Pakistan. Tikka Khan's forces surrendered less than a fortnight later. East Pakistan declared its independence as Bangladesh soon afterwards.

The state that emerged from these tragedies was secular, Bengali-nationalist and probably more prone to dialogue with India than with Pakistan. It did not have auspicious beginnings. The administration of national hero and elected Prime Minister Mujib-ur Rahman was unable to alleviate poverty or fight endemic corruption. The famine of 1974 was handled badly. Externally, forces opposed to the formation of the new state included the USA, China and Saudi Arabia. They are alleged to have conspired (probably separately) for the overthrow of the regime. Shortly after declaring himself president for life (1975), Mujib-ur Rahman was murdered by the military and his family was massacred at his home. In outline, the military regime that replaced the elected Awami League government was more right-wing, anti-secessionist (from Pakistan), anti-secular and hostile to 'Indian influence in Bengal'.[58] They tended to promote political Islam and clearly wished to explore its possibilities to further their popularity. These moves were openly supported by the USA, which at the time viewed and assisted Islamic political movements as so many defensive shields 'against communism'.

One of the prominent initiators and exponents of these Islamizing policies was a General Zia-ur Rahman, the military commander behind the coup of 1975 and president of the republic after 1977. To this day, *his* assassination in 1981 is blamed by his partisans on Indian security services. The regime that developed under Zia and his successor, General Ershad, was virulently anti-secular and famously corrupt. Successive elections since Ershad was forced out of office in 1990 have been fought between two political formations. The first is the secular coalition aligned behind Mujib-ur Rahman's daughter, who survived the massacre because she was abroad, Sheikh Hassina of the Awami League. Continuity with the succession of military regimes is maintained by General Zia-ur Rahman's widow, Khaleda Zia, leading a coalition of the Bangladesh Nationalist Party and various religious formations that have since been recast as political parties. The general election held on 1 October 2001 was won by a four-party alliance, led by Khaleda Zia, and included the Jamaat e-Islami. She was sworn in on 10 October 2001 as the Prime Minister for the third time and served until Autumn 2006, when she handed over to a caretaker government, charged with preparing new parliamentary elections.

Against this political backdrop, it would have been surprising to see the governments of Khaleda Zia easily coming to amicable arrangements with Delhi on pipelines or, indeed, on any other problem. There are several other unresolved problems between the two countries. The first is active deforestation on the Indian side, which is plausibly claimed to worsen the floods in Bangladesh during the rainy season. The second is the multiple dam system constructed by the Indians on the tributaries of the Ganges running into East Bengal. The system tends severely to limit the water received in Bangladesh during the dry season. India claims to have agreed this with general Ayub Khan in the 1960s, during the negotiations over the waters of the Indus in 'West Pakistan'. It looks much like a compromise by (West) Pakistanis at the expense of the land then known as 'East Pakistan'.

India and Bangladesh have also been blaming each other for tolerating cross-border insurgency. The Indians claim that over 2 million illegal immigrants from Bangladesh live in their border provinces, a proposition flatly rejected by the other side. To the immense displeasure of the government in Dhaka, the Indians have been constructing a 'fence' to stop more people from crossing over. Fire fights between border guards take place at regular intervals and occasionally someone loses his life. On the face of it, none of this seems too difficult to fix with a little give and take. It is not clear, however, that internal political conditions in Bangladesh are conducive to normal neighbourly relations with India. The level of exchanges may be judged from press reports emanating from fellow travellers in Pakistan:

A majority of the Bengalis ... expressed their helplessness over the harassment and bullying being inflicted by India over Bangladesh.[59]

In this context, the signing of a memorandum of understanding in January 2005 between Myanmar, Bangladesh and India about gas transmission might have been considered a small victory for common sense. The 'memorandum' is about the passage of a gas pipeline carrying possibly 5 billion cubic metres of Myanmar gas to Tripura and through Bangladesh into India. The sting in the tail, however, comes in the form of three pre-conditions put forward by Bangladesh. The first is a customs-free right of passage through a land corridor to and from Nepal and Bhutan. The second is for a customs-free passage of (hydro-)electricity transmission lines from Nepal and Bhutan. The third condition is more interesting. It puts the onus on India to redress the trade imbalance between the two countries – at present in favour of India.[60]

Meanwhile, Union Oil of California (Unocal, bought by Chevron in 2005) have completed the development of the gas deposits in the Bibiyana region, in the east of the country, which Bangladesh had not previously included in their gas utilization plans. Unocal claims to have discovered 67 billion cubic metres of gas, and initially presented plans for constructing a pipeline for exporting gas to India at a rate of 5 or 10 billion cubic metres per year. The fields have since been connected to the Bangladesh national grid, with expected production in Bibiyana eventually rising to 5 billion cubic metres annually.

The Indian government had previously pointed out that importing this gas into India would go a long way to redressing the trade imbalance between the two countries. However, Dhaka has been unwilling to contemplate the export of a 'national resource', while periodically reiterating its demand throughout 2005–6 that India needs to redress the trade imbalance. For good measure, Bangladesh also rejected an Indian proposal to establish a new cross-border railway line to improve communications.[61]

Until Khaleda Zia resigned her post at the end of her five-year term in October 2006, the negotiators clearly had a great deal of time on their hands. However, the interim government charged with preparing fresh elections during January 2007 has postponed the elections, which are to be held 'as soon as possible'. They have also undertaken some conspicuously medium-term commitments, including an anti-corruption drive which saw the arrest of Begum Khaleda Zia's son. The revival of the pipeline project in fresh talks with India has been put back on the agenda.

5 Turkmen Gas Via Afghanistan?

With seven gas fields developed during Soviet times and reserves of nearly 2.5 trillion cubic metres, Turkmenistan is a significant player in natural gas extraction.[62] After 1991, the country has been largely hemmed in by her geographic situation and by the regional political configuration that emerged following the fall of the Soviets. First, the USA pressured the Niyazov administration away from doing business with Iran. Secondly, disagreements over some offshore fields in the Caspian have precluded a trans-Caspian option for exporting gas through Azerbaijan. Turkmenistan has since been resigned to selling gas to the Russians, much as before. As we shall see in Chapter VI, this is not a lucrative business. Her only other option is to export the gas across Afghan territory to Pakistan and India.

Since the mid-1990s, Unocal has also been proposing to construct a pipeline from the Daulatabad and/or Yashlar fields in the south-west of the country that would cross into Herat in Afghanistan. It would then probably follow the Herat–Kandahar highway on relatively flat country along the Farah–Delaram axis, passing south of Kandahar and then climbing to nearly 1850 m across the mountains through to Quetta in Pakistan, and through the Bolan Pass down to the flats, probably closely shadowing the railway and then turning north-east on Punjabi flat ground to reach the gas pipeline hub at Multan. The 1,600-km line is proposed to carry 30 billion cubic metres of natural gas annually. In 2003, the line was estimated to cost $2.5 billion, revised upward to $3.3 billion in late 2005.

This project was originally proposed by Bridas, a relatively small Argentinean outfit who managed to sign a contract with Niyazov's government and opened negotiations with the Taliban, then in charge of most of Afghanistan. In his fascinating study 'Taliban',[63] Ahmed Rashid describes how Unocal nuzzled Bridas out of the way and proceeded to encourage the Clinton administration to make a treaty with the Taliban in Kabul. The project was temporarily abandoned after the bombings of two US Embassies in East Africa (1998) were traced to the Al Qaida operation based in Afghanistan.

Following the 11 September attacks on the USA in 2001 and the subsequent destruction of Taliban power in Afghanistan, Unocal and the US Government have tried to revive the trans-Afghan project. For the USA, keeping alive the *discussion* of this project carried several advantages. It cut across Iran's lines of communications to Pakistan and India. It offered the newly established Afghan central government an (albeit hypothetical) source of income, lending it much-needed political credibility. It was also an inexpensive way for the USA to present itself as a benevolent contributor to Afghanistan's infrastructure and to its future wellbeing. It was also rumoured at the time that, after 'September 11', some of the more prominent backers of the Taliban within Pakistan's Inter Service Intelligence (ISI) agency were being weeded out. In December 2002, Turkmenistan, Afghanistan and Pakistan signed an agreement to go ahead with the construction of the pipeline from Dauletabad to Multan. Should India decide to join the project, an extension of the line from Multan would have crossed into India and connected to the Indian distribution system near Delhi. Afghan President Karzai has repeatedly gone public to encourage potential participants to commit to what has been dubbed the trans-Afghan pipeline (TAP) project.[64]

In Afghanistan, however, the situation on the ground never looked favourable for conducting anything approaching large engineering projects, even before the flare-up in 2006–7. During 2002–5, which may now be looked upon as more peaceful times, construction workers who were engaged on projects funded by foreign governments were being specifically targeted. Taliban leader Mullah Omar and Hizb-e-Islami leader Gulbuddin Hekmatyar were (and are) still at large, and they are waging low-level war. Furthermore, Afghanistan currently produces nearly 90 per cent of the world's opium, accounting for a little over 50 per cent of its gross domestic product.[65] The spread of opium cultivation has made it difficult to bring many areas under central government control. It transpires that nearly half the opium produced in the country is grown in Farah, Helmand and Kandahar provinces. All three are on the projected pipeline route. Not surprisingly, the arrival of fresh NATO forces in Helmand province during 2006 has led to the intensification of fighting. The situation is showing all the signs of blowing up into yet another full-scale Afghan guerrilla war.

Normally, the security situation along the trajectory of the pipeline would been sufficient to scupper the project. However, the venture turns out to have still another fatal flaw. In 2003, Turkmenistan signed a contract with Gazprom to deliver 90 billion cubic metres p.a. for 25 years. Questions have been raised by the Russians, by Pakistan and by India about the ability of the Turkmen fields to deliver the expected 30 billion cubic metres to the TAP project, after delivering the gas committed to the Russians under *their* contract. Indeed, a study by the Asian Development Bank (ADB) showed lower-than-expected gas deliverability at the Daulatabad fields, with gross reserves of 1.4 trillion cubic metres. Given the commitment to Gazprom, the known reserves of Turkmenistan would not, on their own, be sufficient to provide gas for the trans-Afghan pipeline as well. According to the ADB report: 'They will need to find gas from other fields to meet [the TAP] pipeline design targets.'[66]

Many decisions seem to have gone back into the melting pot since the demise of the flamboyantly autocratic President Niyazov in late 2006. However, it is difficult to see how Niyazov's own people, who are still in power, could change course abruptly. In the matter of gas exports, they still need to contend with the US interdiction to send gas to and through Iran, and they still need to desist from attempting the impossible through war-torn Afghanistan.

6 Overview – Pipeline Engineering too is the Art of the Possible!

While India and Pakistan can import petroleum through their own ports as a matter of routine, natural gas transmission is dependent on a more complicated set of parameters. There are concerns over the price of the gas, as well as geopolitical show-stoppers on each of the possible pipeline routes. Importing gas as LNG through purpose-built port facilities and regasification plants would sidestep difficulties with neighbouring countries. This solution is geopolitically (relatively) neutral and possibly affordable, but certainly expensive in terms of the purchasing power of the customer base of the subcontinent.

Three options

The Iran–Pakistan–India project is probably the most feasible in terms of economic outlook and emerging regional geopolitical reaccommodations. However, after the election of a new administration in 2005, Iran adopted what appear to be intractable pricing policies and she has already reneged on one major agreement signed with India. In addition, this project is facing stiff opposition from the USA, which is fighting hard to isolate Iran. The more recent agreement on a pricing formula has not yet stood the test of time.

Technically, the Myanmar–Bangladesh–India project appears as feasible as the Iran–Pakistan–India project. In purely economic terms, it has benefits and nearly no costs for Bangladesh. However, the ideological posture adopted by the Khaleda Zia Government did not, to date, allow a sensible agreement with India and Myanmar to be reached. In view of India's expanding demand for gas, the smaller-scale Myanmar–Bangladesh–India project and the Iran–Pakistan–India pipeline are probably not mutually exclusive. In the (probably unlikely) event of both projects going ahead, however, the timing of Indian gas purchases would need to be carefully synchronized with the completion of installations intended to *utilize* the imported gas.

The likelihood of realizing the third alternative, the pipeline from Turkmenistan, seems remote. Here, there are not one but *two*

111

major show-stoppers. The obvious one is the deteriorating security situation in Afghanistan, where even road construction has become dangerous, let alone constructing and operating pipelines full of high-pressure, explosive and flammable gases. The second show-stopper is the size of Turkmenistan's gas reserves. On present evaluation, once the gas contracted to Russia is accounted for, Turkmenistan would be unable to supply the necessary 30 billion cubic metres of gas required for the TAP pipeline for the lifetime of the project.

One major alternative – not mentioned so far – would have involved importing gas from Oman directly into India by pipeline. However, the underwater line would have had to traverse rugged underwater terrain at depths of nearly 3,500 m. By a wide margin, this would have been the deepest pipeline ever built. The daunting technical challenges and the estimated high cost of around $10–12 billion led to the abandonment of this project in the mid-1990s.

Surveying the overall position, each of the possible pipeline routes appears to be hostage to one or more of the region's 'geopolitical blockages'. However, something significant has already begun to emerge from all the comings and goings. It may be optimistic and too early to ascribe the developing exchanges between Pakistan and India to anything but the pulling power of pipelines. However, it is clear that the economic advantages of cooperation on pipeline projects has acted as a catalyst at a time when the old (dare we call them 'former') enemies appear to be developing more sophisticated, multi-layered relationships.

Another seismic shift in the making involves the tri-cornered relationship developing between the USA, Japan and India. The joint naval exercises of April 2007 provide a milestone in this newly emerging axis, with which the Indians will no doubt wish to balance their increasingly active three-cornered relations involving Russia and China. And the Iran–Pakistan–India pipeline, which the USA opposes and Russia supports, has to fit in there somewhere. We will touch upon these developments again, in Chapters VII and VIII.

Chapter V

The Russian nexus: Ruptured links and flying sparks in Eastern Europe

The most durable of the eighteenth-century empires, Russia exploited servile labour well into the nineteenth century and was ruled by Czars until as late as 1917. After the Revolution, it was painfully transformed by the Bolsheviks, but the succeeding Soviet state retained the land masses conquered in the age of Catherine the Great (d. 1796) to which Central Asiatic possessions were added in the nineteenth century. At the dissolution of the Soviet Union, the tired old empire covered nearly a sixth of the planet's land mass.

Everything about the 'Commonwealth of Independent States' (CIS), which emerged in its place, showed aspects of hasty improvisation. We do not really know what Yeltsin and his entourage really meant to achieve by dissolving the Soviet Union. There are straws in the wind but no real answers. Certainly, the act of dissolution has spared the expense of subsidizing Byelorussia and the Central Asian republics, which were costing already impoverished Russia a great deal of money. It appears, despite the act of formal dissolution, that the Kremlin expected to keep over-arching control over former Soviet lands. Certainly, the Russian military and the KGB put up no overt resistance to the impending loss of territory, of strategic depth and of diminished Russian hegemony that was, in fact, bound to follow. Crucially, they do not

113

appear to have calculated that Ukraine under Leonid Kravchuk might refuse to join the new three-way union contemplated with Belarus and Russia. We might also ask why it took the KGB (re-branded as FSB) nearly ten years to take matters in hand and steady the ship.

In the event, dissolution created its own realities and Russia was forced to disgorge some of Empress Catherine's cherished conquests. The three Baltic republics, still smarting from nearly two centuries of 'foreign' occupation, quickly cut their ties and went over to NATO. Never truly willing members of the Union, Georgia and Azerbaijan have also drifted away from the Russian security orbit. To differing extents, the trans-Caspian states also experimented with alliances involving western powers. Mostly, the imperial reach of the other global superpower was found wanting and they drifted back into the fold. The crucial shift, however, took place in Ukraine, one of the pillars of the old Empire. In Soviet times, political Russia never really regarded Ukraine, or, for that matter, Belarus, as distinct entities. For the Russians, Ukraine is not expendable. In vital issues concerning energy supplies, armaments and other industrial production, the selection of political and military elites, Russia and Ukraine were, and in some respects still are, parts of a long-united whole. No one really expected Ukraine to exchange all that for a breath of fresh air. Having resolved the problems of the 2004 presidential elections, the country has continued to debate her momentous options.

Meanwhile, the Russian Federation itself is still an empire, exercising power and authority over some very unfamiliar peoples across an enormous land mass, including notably Chechnya, Daghestan, Bashkiria, Tatarstan and parts of Siberia inhabited by Buryats, Yakuts and others. Nevertheless, the Soviet Union was a far more inclusive place than the Romanov Empire and it turned out to be an unexpectedly resilient edifice. When Yeltsin colossally blundered into the dismemberment of the Union, most of the republics had not seriously contemplated, let alone demanded, independence.

One essential component of integration within the Soviet Union was interdependence in oil and gas production and transmission. The gigantic pipeline network constructed during Soviet times was designed to serve the Union very much as a single unit. For instance, Kazakhstan's major oil production centres lie close to the western (Caspian) rim of the country, while the main population centres are in the east. Within the framework of the Union, no connecting lines were ever contemplated between the two regions, nearly 2,000 km apart. Instead, refineries were constructed in Eastern Kazakhstan and supplied from western Siberian oilfields (today in Russia). It appears that Yeltsin's Kremlin at best underestimated, at worst never even imagined, the damage that would be caused to economic life by rupturing the innumerable links that held the vast machinery of Soviet industry together. After 1991, the new republics took ownership of installations on their own territories, including segments of oil and gas transmission networks. More worrying for the Russians, their own gas and oil export corridors toward the West now cross into the territories of independent Ukraine and somewhat less independent Belarus. Since the break-up of the Union, the Russians have had immense problems with both governments over energy supplies and transit fees.

In the next two chapters, we will review how the territorial break-up of the Soviet Union has led to discontinuities in oil and gas transmission, and to friction and discord between the old centre and the new republics. In Eastern Europe, the Caucasus and Central Asia, the new political geography has thrown up a multitude of contradictions between Russian security and economic interests and those of the newly independent states.

1 Soviet Pipelines, End of Empire and the Collapse of Oil Production

Before 1914, the Russian Empire was one of the world's largest oil producers and for a spell *the* largest. Production in Baku and Grozny peaked early, in 1901, at 12 million tons and then declined slowly. After the Revolution, these resources were rapidly taken in hand and developed by the Soviets. By 1940, production had risen to a little over 31 million tons.[1]

In the years following the Second World War, all regions of the Union were explored for oil and gas. Of the 15 Soviet republics, only four (Armenia, Estonia, Latvia and Moldova) failed to yield commercially significant amounts of oil. By far the largest fields, however, were discovered on what is now Russian Federation territory: the Urals, the Volga and Tyumen basins and Western Siberia. The new finds were spectacularly large. During these exciting times, investments were inevitably channelled away from Azerbaijan, where the major onshore fields had already been largely depleted. Also partly neglected were Kazakhstan and Turkmenistan, where significant but less gigantic quantities of oil had been discovered. Baku retained its central role, however, as the major centre for the manufacture of equipment for oil exploration and production.

The newly discovered fields were developed rapidly. By the late 1980s, the Soviet Union had become the world's largest oil producer, with total annual crude oil and condensates output reaching nearly 600 million tons, about 12 million barrels per day.[2] This is larger than present-day Saudi oil production, which hovers around the 9–10 million barrel level. At the time, it was claimed that the Soviets could produce 10 per cent of the world's total crude oil for decades to come. The Union also turned out to be home to one-third of the world's proven natural gas reserves.[3]

The land mass over which these resources are distributed is vast and the reserves mostly landlocked. The Soviets constructed a network that was 84,000 km long and almost entirely interconnected. It was the largest single trunk pipeline network in the world.[4] The average distance for oil transmission was between 1,500 km and 2,000 km, compared to 470 km in the USA.[5] The size and extent of the grid made Soviet oil transmission both flexible and reliable. Crude oil could be shunted around to cope with production shortfalls at particular fields. The system could also accommodate changing uptake volumes by individual refineries. It was operated by the state-owned oil pipeline monopoly, Glavtransneft, which also functioned as the 'buyer' of the crude oil from individual production units.

Glavtransneft's tentacles extended early on into the territories of the Warsaw Pact allies. The Druzhba (Friendship) network came into operation during 1962–3 and was designed to supply crude oil to Poland, East Germany, Czechoslovakia and Hungary[6] (Figure 5.1). The system consisted of some 4,700 km of trunk

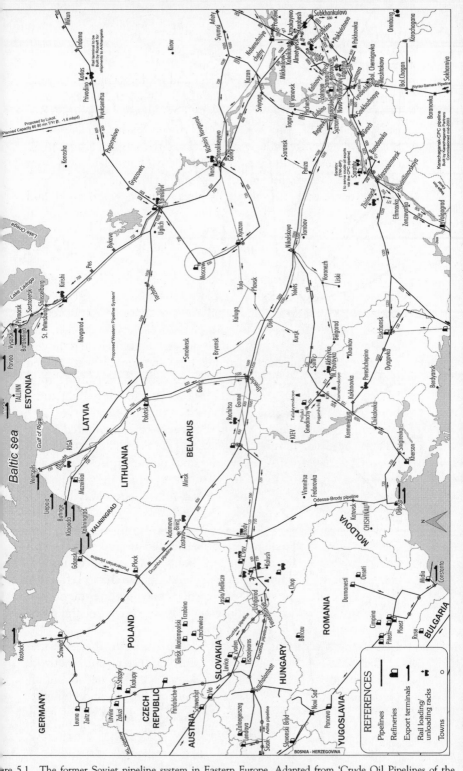

Figure 5.1   The former Soviet pipeline system in Eastern Europe. Adapted from 'Crude Oil Pipelines of the former Soviet Union', Centre for Global Energy Studies, UK London, 2006, http://www.cges.co.uk

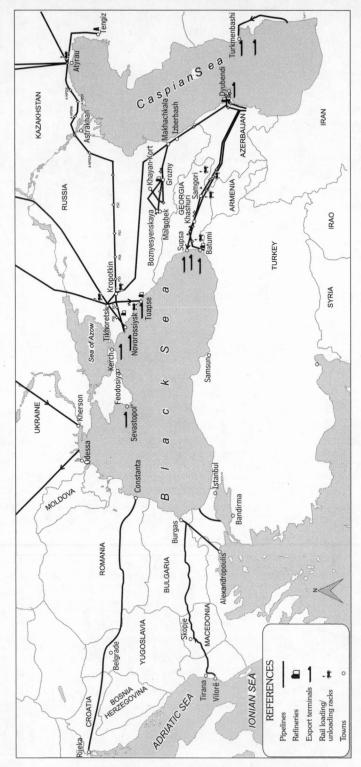

Figure 5.2 Black Sea and Caspian Sea oil export terminals. Adapted from 'Crude Oil Pipelines of the Former Soviet Union', Centre for Global Energy Studies, UK London, 2005, http://www.cges.co.uk

pipeline, with a total carrying capacity of 1.2 million barrels per day (some 60 million tons p.a.).[7] Spurs were constructed for supplying Soviet Lithuania and a major pipeline was built to the tanker terminal at Ventspils in Soviet Latvia, with a capacity of about 18 million tons per year. Other export outlets of the Union were on the Black Sea coast: Odessa (now in Ukraine), Novorossiysk, Tuapse and several other smaller terminals had a combined export capacity of nearly 90 million tons (Figure 5.2). At its peak, the *Soviet Union* exported about 100 million tons of crude oil per annum from all outlets, and depended on the income to finance her investment programmes and grain purchases.

Oil spills and rust

Not all Russian pipelines are the rust buckets everybody thinks them to be. Nevertheless, the Russians are not yet rich enough to worry too much about pollution. Maintenance standards can be low and general anxiety over environmental matters relatively less intense. Consider the story of an oil leak some 1,200 km north east of Moscow, told in charming Russo-English:

'NARYAN-MAR, May 24 (Itar-Tass) – Experts learnt about a rupture at an oil pipeline in the Nenets Autonomous Area only two months after ... at the Musyurshor-Sandivei 150-mm oil pipeline owned by the Severnoye Siyanie (Polar Lights) company. A Nenets reindeer-breeder informed about the emergency. A special commission confirmed information about oil leakage at the pipeline section in the area of the Khorei-Ver village (215 km from Naryan-Mar), through which the company pumps oil from well No. 60 of the Musyurshor oil field ... local residents conveyed information about the incident to the president of the Association of the Nenets People Yasavei, Vladislav Peskov who for some unknown reason concealed this information. The leadership of Severnoye Siyanie also concealed the fact of the incident from executive power bodies and control structures of the republic and is currently continuing the pumping of oil ... A rupture had already taken place at this oil pipeline last summer when the Sandivei and Kolva rivers were polluted by oil. The oil slick reached the Komi republic then. The incident inflicted damage worth over 19 million roubles.'[8]

The leak was reported to have released 'just' 150 cubic metres of crude oil, approximately 150 metric tons. A quick calculation suggests northern Russian territory must be cheaper to pollute than most places on Earth. Nevertheless, the leak

> has already heavily contaminated local water sources...
> An extensive area of the treeless tundra and its frail vegeta-
> tion ... were polluted by the spill ... the spread of the oil
> slick on the Kolva River near the town of Khariaga – about
> 80 km from the point of the leak ...[9]

Some of the pipeline failures in Russia are also related to increasing poverty, leading to Nigerian-style pipeline vandalism and crude-oil poaching.[10] A joint UN Development Programme (UNDP)–World Bank report[11] on Soviet and Russian spillages between 1986 and 1996 makes worrying reading: 113 major spills were reported in this period, but the report estimates that several hundred more (possibly smaller) spillages went unreported. The overall evaluation focuses on the poor state of maintenance of the system and 'erratic operating procedures'. It was also suggested that oil spills, not publicly reported in the former Soviet Union, are also not widely publicized in the post-Soviet Russian Federation.

According to the same report, pipelines in the tundra (frozen steppe) region were more susceptible to ruptures than pipelines in the more temperate belt. In over two-thirds of recorded accidents, no estimate had been provided of levels of environmental damage caused by the spills. Legal and regulatory frameworks were said to focus more on punishing offenders than on providing guidance. Procedures were found to be old and 'obsolete'. Pollution from oil pipelines is not exclusively a Russian problem. On any given day, collected dispatches reveal several major leaks at widely separated points of the planet. Post-Soviet statistics admit, however, a nearly seven times greater rate of pipeline-related accidents compared to their European counterparts.[12] This is consistent with the hurried construction of the pipeline grid during the rapid expansion of Soviet oil production in the 1950s and 1960s.

In the wealthier parts of Europe and the USA, improved pollution prevention and health-and-safety are twin goals that are enforced by law, at least in spirit. This implies spending money to improve equipment quality and standards of maintenance, to reduce the number of incidents. In this context, the apparently wilful neglect by BP of the Alaskan facilities provides a pointer to the likely consequences of cost-cutting combined with lax public scrutiny. A close second to spending money to reduce risk, however, is the *culture* of safety, allied to a legal regime that makes injury and loss of life more costly than prevention. In these respects, Russian attitudes appear similar to those found in less industrialized countries such as Turkey or China.

After the dissolution of the Soviet Union

Nearly 90 per cent of oil and condensate production of Soviet times and nearly 85 per cent of confirmed reserves are found on Russian Federation territory.[13] To answer these greater transmission needs, a large fraction of all pipelines had been constructed in Russia proper. After 1991, a new company named Transneft was created to run the nearly 50,000 km of pipeline that remained within the Russian Federation.

The dissolution of the Soviet Union and the accompanying wholesale collapse of economic activity were disastrous for the oil industry. Total production drifted downward to nearly half the peak volume recorded in Soviet times. Clearly, some production had shifted to the new republics (notably Azerbaijan and Kazakhstan) and was no longer counted as 'Russian', but over two-thirds of the decline in Russia was due to natural depletion and lack of new investment, coupled to poor maintenance. Production eventually picked up, increasing from 303 million tons in 1999[14] to about 460 million tons in 2004,[15] an increase of about 50 per cent in five years. In 2005 and 2006, the rate of increase fell back to about 2.4–2.6 per cent (year on year), a development that will be discussed below.

Compared to Soviet times, one fundamental change is the increased volume of exports, both in absolute terms and as a proportion of total production. This is clearly a worrying statistic in terms of Russian industrial recovery. The 253 million tons exported in 2004[16] is more than double the exports of the 1980s. These figures are slightly skewed, since before 1991, purchases of

Russian oil by, say, Ukraine or Belarus would not have counted as 'exports'. On the other hand, compared to Soviet times, the capacity of former Soviet republics to absorb oil imports has diminished significantly. In 2004, only 40.3 million tons of total Russian exports were destined for CIS countries.

This level of oil exports provides an interesting perspective on the state of the economy in the Russian Federation. Russia has kept internal energy prices artificially low, in order to mitigate the effects of the de-industrialization that took place after 1991 and the transition to new forms of ownership. The measure has in part been successful in maintaining consumption at higher levels than would otherwise have been the case. The total drop in internal consumption is nevertheless large, approximately 200 million tons on an annual basis,[17] giving some idea of the magnitude of the industrial contraction that has taken place. Nor has there been an industrial revival that parallels the growth in oil production since 1999. Relatively suddenly and a little unexpectedly, Russia is being transformed into an economy entirely dominated by primary commodity production. Growth is now being driven mainly by the oil and gas sectors.[18]

It is useful to put these developments in some sort of context. In the 1980s, the Soviet Union exported on average less than 20 per cent of its production of nearly 600 million tons. At that time, the USA was producing somewhat more than 500 million tons and *importing about as much again*. If energy consumption is taken as a broad indicator of economic activity, the gap between the two giants has evidently grown. In 2003, when oil production in Russia expanded by a healthy 10 per cent, domestic oil demand rose by only 0.1–0.3 per cent.[19] Space does permit a detailed discussion of the shift in the Russian economy signalled by these figures. However, the degree to which oil and gas exports have taken centre-stage in Russian economic thinking suggests a slide towards the status of a *rentier*-state, increasingly dependent on world commodity prices. The upward movement in oil prices since mid-2004 has done nothing to deflect the Russian leadership from this path. What they will do with their newly acquired wealth, however, is another matter. There is a growing body of evidence to suggest that ploughshares are fast being turned into swords. These developments make Russia's policy-makers more sensitive than ever before to the security of their oil and gas export pipelines towards the West.

In the past, Russian export corridors would run from Soviet territory into the lands of the Warsaw Pact allies. Instead, the Russian Federation now ships nearly 20 per cent of its oil production and most of its lucrative gas exports through pipelines running across the territories of the sovereign republics of Belarus and Ukraine. Just beyond the former Soviet border, they run into Poland, Hungary and the Czech and Slovak republics, all of them new members of NATO. A little further to the north-west, the one-time outermost shield of the Soviet European defence system, the German Democratic Republic, has now become a part of core NATO member, the Federal Republic of Germany.

2 Russia's Retreat and the Silent Reconquest of Eastern Europe

It must be said that Eastern Europe was never quite resigned to Soviet domination. The Hungarians rebelled in 1956 and the Czechoslovaks in 1968. The Poles went through major periods of unrest during 1956–8, 1968–70 and again in the late 1970s. By the end of the 1980s, when Gorbachev began his troop withdrawals from Eastern Europe, no one was surprised to see local Communist parties lose power to a whole spectrum of new political formations. The disintegration of the Communist Party of the Soviet Union followed soon afterwards.

Since the dissolution of the Union, furthermore, long-buried antagonisms have been bubbling up all around the rim of the Russian Federation. Old enmities between local nationalities have erupted into violent conflict. In the Caucasus, there is evidence that the Russians actually fanned the flames of war, aiming to assume the role of arbiter and to keep an element of control over the fate of the region. In Eastern Europe, however, the dissolution of the Warsaw Pact and of the Soviet Union has cost Russia heavily, in terms of territory, power and prestige. These vast changes have also led to conflict and partial loss of control over their energy export corridors, with economically detrimental and often irrational consequences.

Strategies of a cold peace

During the chaotic Yeltsin years, European and US negotiators found little difficulty in persuading their Russian counterparts to accept some very forward strategic moves by the West. The eastward expansion of NATO and the EU were viewed in Russia initially with surprising equanimity. Partly, this may be explained by economic disruption in the Russian Federation and neglect by a weak leadership. Crucially, however, at the time, important sections of the Russian foreign policy establishment fully expected a succession of moves by the West that would tend to integrate Russia more closely into the European framework. There was hope that such a coming together would gradually make NATO irrelevant. Indeed, there were slow moves to advance Russia's bid for membership to the World Trade Organization (together with Ukraine, Saudi Arabia and Vietnam). Russia was given a seat at the G7 meetings, but only in separate 'G8-sessions'.

Nevertheless, it must have been galling for the Russians to watch celebrations of the end of the Cold War run parallel with the eastward advancement of NATO, the essential Cold War security instrument of the Western powers. The second Clinton administration reversed early decisions to stay out of 'Russia's backyard'. Hungary, Poland and the Czech Republic formally joined NATO in 1999, followed by Lithuania, Bulgaria, Estonia, Latvia, Romania, Slovakia and Slovenia in March 2004. Considerable Western political and economic penetration has since taken place in the Caucasus and Central Asia, the latter partly under the aegis of the 'war on terror'. The Russians have carefully overseen the subsequent reversal of much Western penetration in Central Asia. The new leadership cadres that have emerged in Georgia and Ukraine, however, have been viewed in Russia with immense suspicion. Gazing at the crystal ball, Georgia and Azerbaijan appear to have nearly totally extricated themselves from the post-Soviet Russian orbit, while it seems difficult to imagine how Russia would let go of Ukraine.

Russia's strategic depth

It is well known that Russian generals are accustomed to thinking in terms of strategic depth provided by land masses. With the

124

self-inflicted creation of sovereign Belarus and Ukraine added to the dissolution of the Warsaw Pact, the Russian line of defence has been moved eastward, in places by over 1,200 km. Conversely, the border crossings for *westbound* oil and gas export pipelines have been moved *east* by similar distances. Kursk, site of the last great German offensive in 1943, is now *just inside* the Russian border with Ukraine. Their military may be considered as outmoded. Nevertheless, Russia does not forget that she has been invaded from the West twice in two centuries; three times, counting the German invasion during the First World War. (In fairness, there have also been several Russian invasions westwards and, the last time, it took them nearly 45 years to pull out from Central and Eastern Europe.)

For the Russians, the break-up of the Soviet Union and the Warsaw Pact has created two distinct sets of problems in terms of exporting oil and gas towards the West. First, economic disintegration in Eastern Europe followed soon after the political collapse, weakening demand for oil. That is now behind them. Secondly, however, Russian export corridors crossing independent Belarus and Ukraine have led to an unexpected and turbulent chapter in relations between Russia and the two former Soviet republics.

3 Russia's Pipeline Woes in the West

The transition economies that emerged in Eastern Europe during the 1990s were unable initially to sustain previous levels of oil purchases. Meanwhile, as NATO's new recruits, former Warsaw Pact members were encouraged to reduce their hitherto total dependence on 'Russian' oil. Supplies permitting, East Germany's crude-oil imports can now be met from western sources through the port of Rostock on the North Sea, or through eastward extensions of the West German pipeline network. As early as the 1980s, Poland had completed the construction of an oil-import terminal at Gdansk. Similarly, in the early 1990s, the Czechs built an oil terminal connecting the refinery in Litvinov with the German supply system. There is also a new line for pumping oil to Hungary from the Croatian tanker terminal at Omisalj. Not surprisingly, Russian oil sales suffered and for long stretches of the 1990s the Druzhba network functioned at nearly half its design capacity.[20]

Most 'experts' usually forget that most matters associated with the energy trade often change quite quickly. During the lean years of large oil surpluses and low prices of the 1990s, observers queued up to lecture the Russians about the former Soviet Union having had '... big pipelines where they are no longer needed and small lines where they [now] need big ones...'.[21] During these difficult times, the Russians severely rationed the transit of Kazakh crude towards the West, to stifle a little of the competition in contracting markets. However, the end of the decade saw reviving demand and resurgent levels of Russian oil exports, even as far west as Germany. From the middle of 1998 onwards, the load on the Druzhba system gradually increased, reaching nearly full capacity in 2001–2. Since then, oil supplies have been tight and a barrel of oil has fetched, at times, as much as $97. Even the newly hatched NATO members appeared to have lost their scruples about overdependence on 'Russian' oil and are buying crude wherever they can, not least through the Druzhba line. In 2006, the system's throughput was reported to have risen to 80 million tons.[22]

Vulnerable export corridors

Even before the oil price hikes of mid-2004, oil and gas exports represented over 20 per cent of Russia's gross domestic product (GDP) and over 50 per cent of her total hard currency earnings. The oil sector alone provided over a quarter of the country's tax intake.[23] Not surprisingly, the Russian Federation views the long-term security of her energy transmission corridors to the west as a vital concern. In addition to oil exports through the Druzhba line, Russia also exports to Europe nearly 140 billion cubic metres of natural gas, which represents as much as 40 per cent of Europe's gas imports. Germany, Poland and Italy are large customers; so is France.[24] The gas is produced in the immense fields of the Yamalo-Nenetsk Autonomous Region in the north of Western Siberia. It is pumped west along two main axes. The 'Northern Lights' splits at Smolensk (in Russia), one leg continuing as the 'Yamal-Europe' line through Minsk (Belarus), entering Poland at Kondratki, running on to Poznan and entering Germany at Frankfurt-an-der-Oder. The second axis runs through Kursk (Russia) into Ukraine at Sumy, running near Kiev onto Uzhgorod on the Slovakian border. From there, the lines split into the 'Transgas' and 'Brotherhood' lines, both of which cross the length of the Czech Republic and link up with the German network.

In addition, the Russians have begun constructing a new line to supply another 60 billion cubic metres of natural gas directly to Germany. Initially, the new line was intended to cross Belarus, Latvia and Poland into Germany. However, the trajectory of the 'North European Pipeline' has now been changed to run over the Baltic seabed and avoid all border crossings. The decision has been greeted with dismay in the countries that will be bypassed. It appears that the Russians have tired of former friends and allies, using their strategic position to exercise rights as gatekeepers to Russian oil and gas exports. There is no shortage of such examples.

Oil pipelines run foul of politics

After the dissolution of the Soviet Union, one major problem quickly arose regarding crude oil exports through Ventspils (Latvia), the large Soviet-era tanker terminal on the Baltic. Apart from adding to Moscow's security concerns by expressing undisguised enthusiasm for NATO membership, the Latvians clearly irked the Russians by demanding a ton-km rate of nearly 2.5 times the charge paid by Transneft in Russia, effectively for traversing erstwhile 'home' territory!

In 2002, Transneft completed the construction of an alternative pipeline to a new and far larger tanker terminal at Primorsk, some 110 km north-west of St Petersburg. The port operates with icebreakers for about five months of the year, which adds to the cost of the oil. Nevertheless, Transneft stopped crude oil deliveries to Ventspils in late 2002. The Russians are expanding the capacity of Primorsk from 48 to about 62 million tons.[25] To the consternation of the Latvians, all previous arrangements involving Ventspils have now been cancelled, saddling the country with a rather large and mostly unused pipeline leading to an oil terminal that is fed by railcars, and operating at a little more than half its normal capacity.[26]

Not unlike Latvia, Ukrainian transit fees for oil transport to Eastern Europe are higher than those paid by Transneft in Russia, by a factor of between 1.8 and 3 on a metric-ton/km basis. This amounts to an added cost of about $5.20 per ton for oil conveyed in the direction of Eastern Europe and $4.40 per ton for oil shipped to Odessa. Russian attempts to persuade the Ukrainians to lower these fees have been unsuccessful and Transneft has constructed the Sukhodolnaya–Rodionovska bypass, which came into operation in 2001. This 260-km line was aimed specifically at avoiding Ukrainian territory and using the old network in Belarus. A little brazenly, the Ukrainians proposed to reduce tariffs, if construction were stopped. Since 2002, Transneft has had no *new* crude oil export pipeline plans involving Ukraine.[27] In response, the Ukrainian parliament has refused to participate in the interconnection of the Druzhba and Adria pipelines, through which Russian oil would have been exported towards the Croatian port of Omisalj (see below). All this occurred during the tenure of President Leonid Kuchma, whose administration was widely considered to be friendlier to the Russians than the previous administration under Leonid Kravchuk.

The Odessa–Brody–Plock line

In an attempt to raise income and reduce their dependence on Russian oil, the Ukrainians also constructed a 30-million-ton capacity pipeline from Odessa to Brody. The latter is a pipeline hub in northern Ukraine, 85 km from Lvov, feeding into a segment of the former Druzhba line now owned by Ukraine. The Odessa–Brody line was intended to carry Caspian oil shipped from Georgian ports on the Black Sea into East-Central Europe, to supplant Russian oil in the region. As a general rule, however, pipelines can be constructed far more quickly than oilfields can be developed. Production rates in Azeri and Kazakh fields are still rising, but, to date, there has been little demand to ship oil northbound through the Odessa–Brody line. In Russia, the construction of this line has been perceived as a hostile move to cut out Russian oil from western markets. Once again, many Russian worries were alleviated when oil supplies tightened, prices began to rise and consumers bought oil where they could.

For the time being, the Odessa–Brody line is carrying small amounts of Russian oil *southwards* to Odessa. However, Ukraine intends to extend the line from Brody, through the pipeline hub at Plock in Poland, to the port of Gdansk on the Baltic Sea. Thus the Odessa–Brody line extension to Gdansk is intended to carry Azeri and Kazakh oil to the Baltic Sea.[28] It is indeed likely that, with expanding production at Tengiz, Karachaganak and Kashagan, Kazakh oil reaching the Black Sea[29] will in the future need outlets other than the Turkish Straits (see below).[30] The Ukrainians are also considering building an oil refinery in Brody, a project well in tune with the present world shortage of refining capacity, but one which would cost in the region of $3.5 billion and probably come on stream in three to five years' time.

Gas to Ukraine? Gas through Ukraine?

Ukraine consumes about 80 billion cubic metres of natural gas. The country has a domestic production of about 18 billion cubic metres and, before the contract of January 2006, received 30 billion cubic metres as a transit fee for Russian gas exported through Ukrainian territory into East-central Europe. In theory, Ukraine was contracted to pay for any additional gas lifted from the pipeline system. According to the Russians, in 2003 Ukraine owed about $2 billion in unpaid gas bills. The figure, however, is imprecise, as *usually* part payment was made through barter agreements involving Ukrainian goods and services, with each side proposing its own valuation.[31]

Meanwhile, 'unsanctioned' diversion of natural gas from the pipeline system has been a major source of frustration for the Russians. As early as autumn 2000, Putin declared that Russia was not prepared 'to tolerate Ukraine's uncivilized behaviour', whilst the then Ukrainian president Kuchma simply issued a 'categorical prohibition against unsanctioned diversion' of Russian gas.[32] No one denied there had been large-scale gas theft. The Kremlin has claimed that, in 1999–2000 alone, Ukraine stole 15 billion cubic metres of transit gas, worth $900 million (at $60 per 1,000 cubic metres). On the other hand, Gazprom felt that it was constrained to continue pumping gas into the pipeline, for fear of losing earnings from the higher prices charged to the Europeans, further down the line. In retrospect, it seems a wiser policy than that they adopted in early 2006, which is discussed below.

In any case, it is no accident that Gazprom announced an agreement with Germany about the latest incarnation of the North European Pipeline, bypassing Belarus, Lithuania and Poland as well as Ukraine. The $4.7 billion pipeline will have an initial capacity of 27 billion cubic metres and will run from newly developed fields in the Yamal peninsula to Potovaya Bay near Vyborg, north of St Petersburg. It will then run along the seabed and land in Greifswald in Germany, after 1,160 km on the Baltic seabed.[33] The three countries (Belarus, Lithuania and Poland) expecting to benefit through transit fees and access to gas have voiced strong objections. The Estonian Prime Minister has rushed in, with suggestions of a regional environmental threat: 'After World War II ... about 300,000 metric tons ... chemical weapons ... 50,000 metric tons of toxic agents were buried on the Baltic floor ... The pipeline will inevitably encounter and damage the containers ... whose exact whereabouts are not known.'[34]

According to the same dispatch, the Prime Minister of Latvia announced that in concert with Lithuania, Estonia and Poland, they were 'still' trying to persuade relevant EU bodies that the project must be dropped. Meanwhile, the Latvian Foreign Ministry has issued a statement to the effect that *all* EU countries needed to be engaged in such a large-scale project. The minister would press for a revision of the project to include Latvia's natural gas terminal on the Baltic coast. Polish President Alexander Kwasniewski also criticized Russia and Germany ' ... for ignoring their European partners' economic interest in such a large-scale project'. Initial estimates for the cost of the overland pipeline had been put at a little more than half the projected cost of the undersea pipeline, in the vicinity of $2.6 billion.

The incident is interesting, showing, first, the desirability of having a large gas pipeline transit through one's own territory; secondly, the lengths to which serious men of state will go to try and deflect such a project in their own direction; and thirdly, the lengths to which pipeline operators might go to avoid crossing into third countries. Only the official reaction from Belarus was relatively muted, although they took care to explain the advantages of an onshore line as opposed to the difficult project the

Germans and Russians are about to undertake. However, Russia and Belarus have had their differences in the past. A *Moscow Times* dispatch of Friday, February 2004 reported that Gazprom had asked for an improved price of $50 per 1,000 cubic metres and had reduced gas deliveries by 30 per cent[35] in the face of Byelorussian intransigence: '... the dispute may disrupt deliveries ... to Germany and Poland'. In March of the same year, talks were stalled over disagreements regarding the gas transit price from Russia to the West. Worst was to follow.

A kingdom for the price of gas

Whilst economically damaging, the inability of her customers to pay has been useful for Russia in another respect. Moscow has demanded and obtained, as payments in kind, numerous industrial assets in Belarus, in Ukraine and in the Caucasus (Armenia and Georgia). In Ukraine, this process has led to the sale of over '... 50 per cent of the country's "strategic industries"...' .[36] A large part of Ukraine's refinery capacity has passed into Russian hands. Among others, Lukoil obtained a controlling interest in the Odessa refinery, whilst Tiumen Oil obtained majority shares in Ukraine's largest refinery, Linos, situated in Lysychans'k. Smolansky enumerates a long list of Ukrainian industrial assets that have passed under Russian control:

> The Alliance Group, Alfa-Nafta, and Tatnafta participated in the privatization of the Kherson, Nadvirna, and Kremenchuk refineries, respectively ... it was also expected that over 90 per cent of the shares in the Oriana complex would be put on the market and that Tiumen' Oil Company would emerge as the new owner ... Russian companies have also been active in the post-Soviet markets for petroleum products. In Ukraine, the Tiumen' Oil Company and Lukoil control 45 per cent of the market, while Alfa-Nafta (part of the Lukoil holding) controls another 20 per cent.

> ... Russian companies have taken over Ukraine's aluminium industry, as the Siberia Aluminium Company acquired the Mykolayiv Aluminous Industrial Complex and the Avtovaz

131

Investment Company bought the Zaporizhya Aluminous Industrial Complex. Some inroads have also been made into ferrous metallurgy ... Investment Company acquired the Donets'k Metallurgical Industrial Complex ... Finally, as for financial and banking enterprises which, throughout the 1990s, were regarded as a pro-Western sector of the economy, 'the Ukrainian market was inundated with Russian capital'. Consequently, some 'powerful Ukrainian commercial banks are now fully or partially controlled by . . . [Russian] financial-industrial groups . . .'.[37]

The strategy of acquiring energy-related assets in CIS countries for geopolitical dominance appears to have been adopted as a coherent policy early in the Putin presidency (2000). Anatoly Chubais, an architect of the privatizations of the Yeltsin years, described this policy as a new Russian 'liberal empire'. It is being implemented chiefly through state-controlled energy giants RAO-UES, Gazprom, Rosneft and Transneft.

New Russian methods for acquiring energy infrastructure have also been visited on the Baltic States. In May 2006, with Russian giant Lukoil and Anglo-Russian TNK-BP in the bidding, majority shares in the large Mazeikiu Nafta refinery in Lithuania were sold to a Polish company. Moscow was probably justified in suggesting that the decision had been politically motivated. However, the Druzhba line soon ceased pumping oil to the refinery due to 'a leak', which has not been repaired for a good nine months. Semyon Vainshtok of Transneft explained that the 42-year-old pipeline would have to be rebuilt completely, but that the company had other priorities.[38] The emerging picture is of giant Russian corporations acting as component parts of a larger, single unit.

Meanwhile, Gazprom has been increasing the gas price all across Eastern Europe and, when customers are unable to pay, demanding pipelines or other installations in part payment. In Ukraine, however, not all was as it seemed. The story is well worth telling.

Gazprom's deafening pipeline rattles

For some years, Ukraine had bought Russian gas for $50 per 1,000 cubic metres. For Georgia, the equivalent price was $63, while

Armenia bought at a slightly concessionary $54. During this period, the average European price for Russian gas was about $135 and, in the USA, the Henry Hub spot price oscillated mostly between $210 and $250 per 1,000 cubic metres ($5.8–7 per million BTU).

'Just why Gazprom agreed to sell Ukraine gas at rock-bottom rates has never been fully explained.'[39] There is, in fact, a rather simple explanation. Since the dissolution of the Union, successive Russian governments have used concessionary energy prices as one way of binding the CIS together. In this sense, the policies of Gazprom and of the Russian government appear indistinguishable. In Kiev, the Kuchma administration had initially given the Russians a rocky ride. However, Ukraine began edging back towards Moscow when questions appeared in the Western press about the nature of governance in Ukraine and suggestions regarding the need for more open government.

From Moscow's perspective, maintaining low energy prices was a small price to pay for a growing *rapprochement* with Kiev, and greater 'geopolitical loyalty'[40] on the part of the second Kuchma administration. To Moscow's intense disappointment, however, Victor Yushchenko has since been elected president. Initially, the new regime in Kiev had listed membership of NATO and of the EU among its policy objectives. Irrespective of how realistic these aims might eventually turn out to be, Moscow saw no reason to ease the path of the new administration in Kiev. Gas prices were soon on the rise.

It is useful to recall that Ukraine has not been an ideal customer in the past. There had been the notorious 'unauthorized withdrawals' of transit gas. Trouble had also flared up when, exasperated by Ukraine's growing debts, Gazprom had passed a few of the unpaid gas bills to Turkmenistan in lieu of payment for the gas *Gazprom* had been buying from Turkmenistan.

Throughout most of 2005, negotiations dragged on about Ukrainian gas purchases from Russia for the year 2006. Gazprom demanded an increase from $50 to $160 per 1,000 cubic metres. Meanwhile, Georgia and Armenia were asked to pay $110. Tiny Moldova, of politically suspect loyalties (and still under partial occupation by Russia's 14th Army), was also asked to pay $160; they eventually agreed to pay $110.[41]

The already impoverished former Soviet republics were deeply shaken by these demands. In any case, they had never been able to pay their bills at the far lower 'old' price. They had all fallen into arrears and had had to 'sell' their domestic industrial installations to the Russians to cover part of the debt. On one item of hardware, however, the Ukrainians were unmovable. Throughout 2005, dispatches suggested Gazprom had offered some flexibility on the price of gas, if Ukraine would put 50 per cent ownership of the pipeline network on the table.[42] The offer was cordially rejected by the wary Ukrainians. Neither the Ukrainian political establishment nor the public found it acceptable to sell what is considered a vital national asset.[43] The Russian strategy was more successful in Belarus, where part-ownership of the transit pipeline was transferred to Gazprom; the land on which it was built has been leased to Russia on a long-term basis.[44] In return, Belarus continued to pay Gazprom $47 for 1,000 cubic metres of gas *in 2006*.

Meanwhile, the Ukrainian pipeline system appears to be in urgent need of repair. Ukraine has not been able to carry out proper maintenance and has resisted Russia's demand for (hazard a guess?) part-ownership of the system, in return for carrying out the required maintenance work. Russian claims on the network have indeed taken some astonishing forms: in October 2003, President Putin declared it was Russia's 'prerogative' to maintain pipelines constructed by the Soviet Union 'in order to protect its national interests and parts of the system that are beyond Russia's borders'.[45]

No gas for Ukraine?

Retracing our steps to the summer of 2005, US gas prices were reasonably settled at quite a high level, before several hurricanes caused mayhem, among others, on gas production platforms and transmission infrastructure in the Gulf of Mexico. The Henry Hub[46] spot price climbed sharply from a reasonably stable price between $210 and $250 (in July–August), to between $468 and $540 in October–November 2005.[47] Probably mentally shadowing these price series, on 14 December 2005 the Russian asking price for gas to Ukraine was raised from $160 to $230.[48] In the same dispatch, Novosti quoted Deputy Gazprom Chairman Alexander Medvedev: 'Ukraine has virtually missed the moment with its negotiating tactics, and today there can be no talk of [delivering gas at] $160 [per 1,000 cubic metres].' To drive the point home, President Putin personally showed up at the negotiations!

Finding the old price of $50 difficult to pay and appalled at the prospect of paying $160 per 1,000 cubic metres, Ukraine flatly refused the new price of $230. Russia claimed with some justification that theirs was a 'fair market price' at that point in time. Indeed, it was still lower than the $255 the West Europeans had just been asked to pay. Ukrainian negotiators also rejected the Russian offer of a $3 billion loan facility; there seemed to be no point going further into debt. On 30 December, under the headline 'Russia rattles the pipeline', Moscow's Kommersant announced: 'It was already clear last night that Gazprom would not reach any agreement and the gas supply would be shut off on January 1 ... .'[49]

In the last few hours of 2005 that most mundane of household fuels suddenly grabbed banner headlines across Europe. On 31 December, the Ukrainian President rejected a direct offer from President Putin to delay the price increase by three months, on condition the Ukrainians signed up to the new price of $230. In turn, Yushchenko offered to pay $90 per 1,000 cubic metres. On 1 January 2006, in the middle of a very cold winter, Gazprom cut the pressure of natural gas pumped into their westbound pipelines, by apparently just the amount that would have been destined for Ukraine. However, there were immediate reports of reduced gas supplies further down the line, in the Czech Republic, Hungary, Austria, Germany, Italy and in France.[50]

There are many versions of what happened next. The Russians, who seem to have momentarily confused business practice with coercion, claimed Ukraine had stolen the gas intended for Russia's European customers. The Ukrainians denied the claim, but made no attempt to explain where the missing gas had gone. In the absence of sufficient gas to pump, there were red faces all around. The APX Gas Exchange wholesale gas price in the United Kingdom rose above $500 per 1,000 cubic metres.[51] Somehow, the Ukrainians appeared to have successfully deflected the opprobrium of the West towards the Russians, who were accused, among other things, of being unreliable suppliers. For the world outside, there was less gas to go around and Russia had confessed to deliberately restricting supplies. That was all that mattered.

For the best part of a quarter-of-a-century, Gazprom had been cultivating an image of respectability in the West. They probably never meant their strictly commercial posture in Europe to be confused with the Kremlin's carrot-and-stick (mostly stick) approach towards former Soviet republics. On 4 January, it was announced that Gazprom would restore the flow to normal levels. It was also announced that the 'friendly' Russian and Ukrainian nations had agreed on a price of $95 per 1,000 cubic metres. This was very near the price the Ukrainian Presidency had mooted in the days leading up to the interruption of supplies on 1 January. Both sides claimed victory. Suddenly the problem was solved. Or was it? We may never know what really happened, but some straws in the wind are certainly intriguing.

The agreement between Russia and Ukraine made a little-known Swiss-based company, RosUkrEnergo, 'sole provider' of gas to Ukraine. It was also announced that Russia would get the $230 it had demanded from RosUkrEnergo and Ukraine would get the gas cheaper, at $95, from RosUkrEnergo. Inevitably, there were questions. Furthermore, it was not clear why Russia had allowed its long-cultivated reputation as a reliable supplier to be tarnished, only to agree to a far lower price that could probably have been agreed on 31 December.

One aspect of the agreement seemed straightforward. Gazprom would pay a higher transit fee, fixed for five years, for gas crossing Ukrainian territory into Eastern Europe.[52] Similarly, Ukraine would pay cash for all the gas it buys, ending the barter system that had so confused matters in the past. It also finally emerged that RosUkrEnergo would buy gas from Turkmenistan (and from Uzbekistan and Kazakhstan) at $58 per 1,000 cubic metres and 'blend with Russian gas'.[53] There was no suggestion that anybody pay a 'fair market price' to the Central Asian republics for *their* gas. Under the relatively little-publicized terms of the Ukrainian agreement with Gazprom, RosUkrEnergo was appointed as the *exclusive distributor* of all gas imported into Ukraine. Effectively, the agreement reallocated a large chunk of Ukrainian Government revenue from gas distribution to RosUkrEnergo, which additionally was to absorb some of Gazprom's profit margin from the sale of cheaply bought Turkmen gas.

Who is RosUkrEnergo?

With a little ferreting, it emerged that the Swiss-based company was a 'joint' venture, owned by a Gazprom-run bank and the Swiss subsidiary of Austria's Raiffeisen Zentralbank. In turn, Raiffeisen Invest and another outfit called Centragas were acting as custodians for 'a group of international investors in the gas business', rumoured to be some of Gazprom's own executives. Incredibly, RosUkrEnergo's offices in Zug, Switzerland appeared to be empty.[54] Cynics have suggested that the company had been created with the purpose of skimming off profits from *Gazprom*. One Moscow source suggested that this was '... more or less private business ... ' operating in the interests of Gazprom senior management.[55] On the other hand, Global Witness, a Washington-based NGO, has alleged that shareholders of RosUkrEnergo are Ukrainian officials linked to Naftogaz Ukrainy, the state-owned oil and gas concern.[56] It is always difficult to decide what to think in these situations.

It soon emerged that both RosUkrEnergo and state-owned Naftogaz Ukrainy had already been investigated by Ukraine's state security agency. As a result, both Prime Minister Yulia Tymoshenko and her ally Oleksandr Turchinov, the then head of the security agency, had been sacked by none other than President Yushchenko. After parliamentary elections in 2006, Yushchenko initially appeared ready to reappoint Ms Tymoshenko as prime minister. However, some months of negotiations later, the *baton* of office went instead to Yushchenko's erstwhile presidential rival Viktor Yanukovych! In 2004, Yanukovych had run against Yushchenko and had been declared the winner (duly congratulated by President Putin), before the elections were annulled as 'fraudulent' by the Ukrainian judiciary. His appointment as prime minister in the summer of 2006 by Yushchenko provides Ukraine with interesting geopolitical options. Meanwhile, it seems improbable that the investigation at Naftogaz Ukrainy will go any further or that many more questions will be asked of RosUkrEnergo.

Looking beyond Yushchenko's media-made 'pro-NATO' and Yanukovych's 'pro-Moscow' labels, it is not unlikely that the two protagonists are conversant with similar interest groups inside

Ukraine. After all, they had both previously served as Leonid Kuchma's prime ministers. It was always doubtful, furthermore, that Yanukovych would have found it any easier than his predecessors to negotiate a lower gas price with his friends at Gazprom, particularly after Alexey Miller accepted to pay the higher price of $100 for Turkmen gas in September 2006 (see Chapter VI)![57] In the event, Yanukovych meekly signed for $135 per 1,000 cubic metres, for purchases during 2007 – much to the displeasure of Ms Tymoshenko and her parliamentary associates. Meanwhile, in late February 2007, President Viktor Yushchenko signed a law prohibiting the privatization of the country's natural gas transportation system – just in case!

4 Russian Crude Oil Production Figures

We have already seen Russian annual production rise steeply from just over 300 to nearly 460 million tons during 1999–2004. About 40 million tons go to the CIS and a little over 200 million tons to the world beyond. These are record figures. They show, incidentally, that repeated warnings over the years that Russian oil exports were being limited by pipeline and port capacity were mistaken. More generally, predicting *any* trends connected with the energy business has traditionally been a dangerous occupation.[58] We nevertheless need to formulate *some* views about near-term oil production trends in Russia.

Russia's Economic Development and Trade Ministry has forecast a total oil output rise to 530 million tons during 2005–8, from 458.8 million tons in 2004.[59] This is a relatively modest increase of over 13 per cent in four years. The estimates assume only marginal increases in Russian oil *consumption* and suggest that most increased production would be available for export. The production increase announced by the Russian Industry and Energy Ministry for 2005 is 2.4 per cent, with total production standing at 470.2 million tons for the year, of which 251 million tons were exported.[60] A similar increase (2.3 per cent) was recorded for 2006.[61] The latter figures support the expectation of slower growth after 2004. A period of consolidation in the Russian oil industry thus appears reasonable to expect. During 1999–2004,

Russia surpassed expectations (estimates) on both the produc-tion front and in respect of export infrastructure capacity. Nevertheless, it is probable that significant further increases in production, by say another 50 – 100 million tons after 2008, will require large new investment for field development (i.e. for production) and proba-bly also for additional port and pipeline infrastructure.

Meanwhile, Western observers have been questioning whether present levels of Russian oil production are sustainable. The Soviets had often been suspected of working their oilfields too hard, to achieve the desired rapid increases in production. Western observers have consistently viewed Russian methods of water injection as wasteful. In simple terms, 'overproducing' a field is generally thought to leave behind more and larger pockets of unrecovered oil. On the other hand, Soviet engineers have argued that their reservoir recovery rates (in Soviet times) approached and occasionally exceeded 35 per cent. These per-centages refer to the proportion of oil in any particular reservoir, which can be extracted economically. The present state of the art does not allow profitable recovery of the rest, which is left behind. The Russians are thus claiming to have performed better (in Soviet times) than the best Western averages.

It is not always possible to verify whether such comparative sta-tistics use the same baseline. In any case, it seems reasonable to expect that large injections of capital will be required in the Russian Federation, for keeping levels of production steady, let alone stepping up production from the already high present levels. At the anecdotal level, information filtering through suggests, first, that new field development is not being undertaken at nec-essary rates and, secondly, that Yukos, Lukoil and the other semi-private Russian companies were concentrating on the most productive fields. In Russian oil company parlance, this is called 'selective production': '... associated natural gas is flared off and low yield wells are simply shut down. At the beginning of 2003, more than 34 per cent of oil wells under Yukos control stood inac-tive; some 51 per cent of Sibneft wells were inactive ... .'[62] All this is impossible to verify, but tends to suggest a systematic squan-dering of resources, possibly on a massive scale. One interesting facet of oil production in the USA has been the milking of low capacity wells by small private companies, making a decent income for individuals, where giant oil firms would not have bothered. There are many such wells and production totals are moderately impressive. The Kremlin does not appear interested in this mode of extraction, which would have made a solid contribution to production figures without requiring much additional investment.

5 Oil Exports from The Black Sea: Polluting the Bosporus

Meanwhile, the Russians have been considering their options regarding the consolidation and possible expansion of their oil export routes. They repeatedly discussed with the Ukrainians the use of the Odessa–Brody line in the reverse direction (north–south) than the one originally intended (i.e. south–north). This would mean exporting Western Siberian oil through the northern arm of the Druzhba line to Brody and pumping the crude south, to the Odessa tanker port. Of the three major Soviet-era tanker terminals, Tuapse and Novorossiysk (and its satellite port of Yuznaya Ozerevka) remain on Russian territory, and despite Russian reticence about dealing with Ukraine, the port of Odessa can be fed through already existing pipelines, even without using the Brody–Odessa spur. The present combined capacity of the three ports adds up to a little over 100 million tons and there has been expansion activity at Novorossiysk in 2004–5.

Traffic in the Turkish straits

The problem lies with the limits imposed by the only maritime route from the Black Sea, running through the straits of Istanbul and Çanakkale. According to the 1936 Treaty of Montreux, the straits operate as international waterways, allowing free passage for 'innocent' shipping. Currently, nearly 50,000 pieces of commercial shipping move up and down these narrow waterways. Annually, 5,500 tankers of all sizes carry an estimated 90–100 million tons of crude oil.[63]

In fact, tanker traffic through the straits has nearly doubled in less than a decade. The ships move up and down the Bosporus between two halves of Istanbul, a city with a population of nearly 12 million. It is the commercial and industrial heart of the country. The area has often been the scene of collisions and fires, as well as routine discharges of bilge water and occasional massive pollution due to oil spills by the heavy tanker traffic. In one notorious incident during 1979, a small Greek freighter, the *Euriali*, struck the Romanian tanker *Independenta*. The tanker drifted into the port area, ran aground and caught fire, spilling some 95,000 tons of crude oil into the inland Sea of Marmara.[64] She smouldered for many months after the main fire had died down, causing further untold environmental damage.

More recently, the Turks have acquired a $45 million radar-controlled 'Vessel Traffic and Management System', similar to an air-traffic control centre, to monitor ship movements through the straits, to improve safety and regulate the flow of traffic. The largest tankers able to pass through the Turkish Straits are the Suezmax class (120,000–200,000 dead weight tons). Since 2002, Turkey has forbidden tankers longer than 200 m from entering the straits, except during daylight hours, on grounds of safety. Effectively, this covers most long-haul oil tankers operating in the area. The move has led to costly delays for tankers queuing up at the approaches to the straits and intensely annoyed the Russians, who claimed these measures violate the Montreux Treaty.

Whatever the rights and wrongs of the case, a step increase in tanker traffic through the Turkish Straits does not now appear to be a realistic prospect. Initially, the Russians accused the Turks of restricting access through the Bosporus in order to channel the flow of oil through the Baku–Tblisi–Ceyhan pipeline. Early discussions have not been short of acrimony. Furthermore, all proposed alternative pipeline routes involve transit fees, while tanker transport through the straits does not incur a charge, making it theoretically more competitive. However, oil companies have complained that the delays are costing them nearly $1 billion annually in tankerage fees. The costly tanker queues at either end of the waterways thus appear to have concentrated minds. During 2005–6, discussions were all about the construction of large pipelines that would bypass the Turkish Straits.

Alternative Bosporus bypass routes

At present, there are several options on the drawing board. Any one of these *could* be made available over a three-to-five-year time horizon, which is consistent with the likely speed of expanding export volumes from the Black Sea. The first of these was proposed by a consortium known as 'Thrace Development', aiming to build a 50-million-ton p.a. trans-Thracian pipeline running parallel to the Bosporus, to the west of Istanbul. The line would have connected the Turkish Black Sea coast with the Bay of Saros in the Northern Aegean (Figure 5.2).

Together with tanker terminals constructed at both ends, this installation would have cost a relatively modest $500 million.[65] It seemed to fit in with the energy partnership developing between Russia and Turkey in the first few years of the new century. This partnership involved large-scale gas imports by Turkey and the construction of the Blue Stream gas pipeline (see below). At one stage, there was talk of 'Blue Stream II', for supplying gas through Turkey to Southern and Central Europe – a sort of Russian Nabucco (Chapter VI) – and to Israel, although the latter always seemed a little far-fetched.

At another level, however, it would have been surprising for the Russians to commit to yet another export corridor through Turkish territory. The lively business climate between the two countries has gone a long way to attenuate traditional enmities, which had been directly transposed onto the Cold War in the 1950s and beyond. However, we will see in Chapter VI that Turkey presently serves as a crucial strategic partner to the regimes in Tblisi and Baku and plays host to the Baku–Tblisi–Ceyhan oil pipeline, which the Russians consider as a thorn in their strategic and commercial flank.

Later developments indicated that the Turkish Government itself might be less than enthusiastic about the trans-Thracian route – perhaps because it was too close to Istanbul. Instead, they proposed a trajectory running from the Black Sea port of Samsun to the increasingly busy tanker port near Ceyhan, with a good 475 km of the Central Anatolian plateau to cross. During a ceremony for the 'opening' of the Blue Stream gas pipeline (see below), President Putin and the prime ministers of Italy and Turkey appeared to have agreed that they would favour this route. At first glance, the nature of the terrain makes the choice of trajectory seem a little peculiar. The Anatolian plateau rises to an average altitude of 800–1,000 m above sea level. Perhaps the planners expected to use terrain and routes already opened for the Blue Stream gas pipeline, which extends from Samsun to Ankara near the centre of the country.

The Russians eventually distanced themselves from this project. Nevertheless, in November 2005, ENI of Italy and Turkish contractors Çalik signed a preliminary agreement to plan the construction of the pipeline along the Samsun–Ceyhan axis.[66] It would cost an estimated $1.5-2 billion for an annual capacity of 1.5 million barrels per day (~75 million tons p.a.).[67] This is a throughput that cannot be easily achieved unless the Russians decide to export some Western Siberian crude through the line, alongside Kazakh crude from Tengiz, Karachaganak and eventually from Kashagan. We will better acquaint ourselves with these localities in Chapter VI. In the meantime, Shell signed a preliminary agreement to study the feasibility of joining the Samsun–Ceyhan consortium.[68]

Several other pipeline routes bypassing the Turkish straits have been considered during the past decade. The favourite, the Bourgas–Alexandroupolis route, would start with a tanker terminal at Bourgas, on the Bulgarian sector of the Black Sea coast. The 286-km line would run south-west into Northern Greece and reach the Aegean Sea at Alexandroupolis (Figure 5.2). Both Bulgaria and Greece are eager for a share of the oil wealth that has so far passed them by. For the Russians, a whiff of natural affinity for Greece and Bulgaria might have been expected. According to semi-official Novosti: ' … the Burgas-Alexandroupolis project seems a good option with regard to its economic, political and even religious [Bulgaria and Greece are Orthodox countries, like Russia] aspects.'[69]

Initially, however, not all was as it seemed. In late 2004, the Russian government expressed its preference for the Bourgas–Alexandroupolis route. Optimistic reports emanated from Greek ministers of a possible signing by 15 March 2005, which were promptly countered by Transneft and Lukoil spokesmen, who denied any knowledge. It turned out that the two companies considered they would have had better control of oil pumped through the trans-Thracian (Turkish) route, which, they said, was the more profitable.[70] The manner in which the Russian decision-making machinery stalled around this issue during 2003–4 was not unlike the chaotic Yeltsin years; but that was before President Putin showed his hand.

Some ten days before the announcement of the ENI-Çalik (Samsun–Ceyhan) agreement on 15 September 2006, a meeting was held in Athens between Presidents Putin (Russia), Parvanov (Bulgaria) and Prime Minister Karamanlis of Greece, reaffirming their will to sign an agreement to proceed with the construction of the Bourgas–Alexandroupolis oil pipeline.[71] The project had first been mooted in the mid-1990s and repeatedly delayed, over disagreements about transit tariffs and the structure of ownership. Greece and Bulgaria wanted equal shares with Russia. Furthermore, the Russian state-owned energy giants had each pulled in different directions. Putin imposed a 51–49 split, with state-owned Rosneft, Transneft and GazpromNeft being offered 17 per cent each, which they probably could not refuse. Bulgaria and Greece were offered 24.5 per cent, each. In the face of further delays, Putin suggested they might take it or leave it. The agreement was signed on 15 March 2007; the line is expected to cost $1.2 billion and to carry initially 35 million tons, rising to 50 million: 'Financing has yet to be lined up on international credit markets; the Russian side will not finance this project, at least not directly.'[72]

In reaction to the signing in Athens, Ankara signalled the cancellation of plans for the second Blue Stream line.[73] Semi-official Russian sources spoke of ' … Moscow's … pipeline confrontation with Turkey …'.[74] Apart from a ' … slowdown in energy cooperation between Ankara and Moscow … ',[75] these developments suggest it will be increasingly difficult for smaller states to steer a middle course within the increasingly competitive relationship between the USA and Russia.

Another proposed trans-Balkan route would start, again, at Bourgas, run nearly due west into Macedonia, and reach the lower Adriatic at Vlore in Albania. Led by a US-based company, AMBO, the 35-million-ton p.a. project is for an 850-km pipeline. In March 2007, the construction start date was announced for 2008, with operations expected to start in early 2011, although the line has not yet secured oil commitments or the necessary finance. After the signing in Athens, the consortium conceded that the Bourgas–Alexandroupolis project 'now has an advantage'.[76]

The third and northernmost route would run west, from the Romanian port of Constanta through Serbia into Croatia and Slovenia, reaching the sea at the top of the Adriatic Sea near Trieste. The 'Pan-European Oil Pipeline' would connect to the trans-Alpine line, which distributes oil to northern Italy and connects to users in Austria, the Czech Republic and Germany. Various pipeline capacities up to about 50 million tons per year have been discussed. This seems to be the capacity of installation that would make a significant difference in export strategies.

For the Russians, one final Adriatic option involves the Adria line, originally designed to pump crude oil to Hungary as part of the strategy to reduce her dependence on Russian oil. The Russian alternative would be to reverse the originally intended direction of flow (shore to land), to carry Russian crude oil from the Hungarian end of the Druzhba line onto the Adriatic coast at Omisalj. This port can accommodate tankers up to 350,000 tons and would – in this variant – serve to export Russian oil by tanker through the Adriatic, out to the Mediterranean and beyond. Originally considered by Yukos, the plan has been adopted by Transneft. However, this option requires pumping oil through the southern leg of the Druzhba line through Ukraine, which requires approval by the parliament in Kiev. One of the last acts of parliament during the Kuchma presidency was the formal rejection of this project.

The flurry of agreements and ceremonial handshakes over the multiplicity of trans-Balkan alternatives suggests final decisions have not yet been taken. In a region where the Odessa–Brody line is still running nearly dry, it is possible that none of these schemes will succeed, and it seems wise to wait a little longer before reading the tea leaves. However, with Russian (read Putin's) political will firmly committed, the Bourgas–Alexandroupolis line must be considered a likely front runner.

6 Blue-Stream: The Sulking American

Blue-Stream is the pipeline that carries Russian natural gas across the Black Sea to Turkey. The difficulties overcome during its construction rank this pipeline among significant achievements of modern engineering. However, between Gazprom's zeal for selling gas and the profligacy of past Turkish governments in signing for more take-or-pay gas contracts than appears needed, the line's commercial prospects have been mired in controversy and accusations of corruption.

In Turkey, some 30 million tons of crude oil are consumed annually, 90 per cent of which is imported from the Middle East and Russia. The share of oil in the country's energy mix is about 40 per cent. In 1986, Turkey also began importing natural gas, to satisfy energy needs and to begin reducing the appalling levels of pollution in its large cities. From a low base of about 4 billion cubic metres in the early 1990s, consumption gradually climbed to 18 billion cubic metres in 2002, with the power sector accounting for about 65 per cent of the demand.[77] Earlier projections had shown steeply rising demand for natural gas, and the state-owned natural gas and pipeline company BOTAŞ signed an agreement with Gazprom (December 1997) to construct a gas pipeline that would bypass third countries. The new line would cross the Black Sea from Russia directly onto the Turkish mainland, near Samsun. The agreement was for 365 billion cubic metres of natural gas over a period of 25 years.

From the start, 'Blue-Stream' was greeted with scepticism as a technically difficult project. It involved laying lines at the hitherto untried depths of 2,150 m. Furthermore, due to the peculiar geochemistry of the Black Sea, high concentrations of dissolved hydrogen sulphide below 200 m make for a highly corrosive environment. The opposition faced by the Turks from their principal NATO ally was almost equally corrosive. Washington issued dire warnings against increased dependence on Russian natural gas.

During the Cold War, the USA went to great lengths, apparently including discreet sabotage ' ... In order to disrupt the Soviet gas supply, its hard currency earnings from the West, and the internal Russian economy ... '.[78] The first Russian gas crossed the Czech–German border in 1973. In the early 1980s, the USA vehemently opposed increased Soviet gas exports; the new gas was to come from the super-giant Urengoi field through the Yamal–Europe pipeline. It appears, however, that the Reagan administration had no alternative to propose and did not threaten sanctions, while the Europeans were getting ready to sign $15 billion worth of contracts for pipeline equipment.[79] L. L. Martin describes how Reagan spoke to the then Japanese Prime Minister Suzuki to ask Komatsu (a Japanese company) not to complete its contract to sell pipelayers to the Soviets, while, only ten days later, the US Department of Commerce issued an export licence to a direct competitor, the giant engineering company Caterpillar, for selling pipelayers to the Soviet Union: '… It fed the notion that US concerns were more commercial than security-oriented.'[80]

But that was during the Cold War. US opposition to 'Blue-Stream', nearly a decade after the end of the Cold War, seemed a little peculiar. Or did it? In the context of NATO's eastward advancement and Russia's growing suspicions regarding Western intentions throughout the 1990s, it seems reasonable to assume that, after some initial vacillation, long-term US policy reverted to identifying the Russian Federation as a strategic competitor. In the light of postures adopted in Moscow and Washington during the past several years, the phrases 'Cold War' and 'cold peace' roll off the tongue rather more easily than they would have, say, in the mid-to-late 1990s.

Blue-Stream nevertheless went ahead and turned out to be an engineering marvel. Gazprom co-opted Italy's ENI as equal partner, forming a company that owns and operates the marine section of the pipeline. ENI's technical know-how in deep-sea pipe-laying was crucial to the technical success of the project. In the summer of 2001, amid adverse comment from Washington and much fanfare in the Turkish press, ENI's 'Saipem 7000' giant crane and pipe-laying vessel slowly sailed up the Bosporus, and in the autumn of the same year began laying the deepest section of the line. Costing $3.5 billion,[81] Blue-Stream first pumped natural gas in February 2003.[82] According to the agreement, the flow of gas was expected to rise gradually to 16 billion cubic metres in 2007. That, however, was where problems began to emerge.

In Turkey, the 1990s saw a succession of unstable governments, where competing coalition partners anxiously outbid each other to initiate large, costly projects. Among others, a modern and entirely unused – probably unusable – second Istanbul airport behind Pendik bears testimony to this bout of joyful profligacy. Several natural gas projects and allied gas purchasing agreements appear to have been signed in similar vein. Although the Turks were not involved in paying for the construction of much of the Blue-Stream system, they did actually sign a 'take-or-pay' agreement that leaves them vulnerable in case of non-purchase. Whilst this type of contract is not unusual, the total amount of gas signed for by successive governments, and the prices they committed to, later became the focus of attention.

During the same period, a similar 'take-or-pay' contract was signed to import about 6 billion cubic metres of gas from Iran by pipeline. A 3-billion-cubic metres LNG import contract was also signed with Algeria and Nigeria, to supply the combined cycle power plant constructed adjacent to an LNG degasification facility at Marmara Ereğlisi, near Istanbul. Readers may be left wondering how LNG shipped over such great distances could appear economically sound, when the country had already committed to buying more piped gas than could be absorbed by current *and planned* infrastructure. More worrying, the economic crash of 2001 in Turkey cascaded to slow down the expansion of internal gas distribution networks. BOTAŞ then revised Turkey's natural gas demand projections for 2005–6, sharply down from about 45 to 25 billion cubic metres.[83]

Many of the contracts signed in the 1990s have been severely criticized by the AKP (Justice and Development Party) Government, which swept to power in late 2002. Quite apart from being baffled by the amounts of gas they were contracted to take, the incoming government also questioned the high contract prices charged by Blue-Stream. The country has since been rocked with allegations of corruption by past governments. In November 2004, two former Turkish energy ministers went on trial for corruption related to these projects.[84] The probes have proved popular, although, to date, none of the allegations have been proved in a court of law.

In negotiations with Gazprom during late 2002 to early 2003, the Turks demanded a 40 per cent reduction from $114.2 per 1,000 cubic metres to 74.25.[85] To reinforce their point, in March 2003, Turkey stopped taking gas through Blue-Stream for six months, apparently in accordance with a clause in the contract. Gazprom, who also do not come out of this story smelling of roses, has since announced that a 'competitive' price had been agreed upon and that the agreement was back on track.[86] The affair triggered rumours that Gazprom chief Alexey Miller might lose his job for 'building such an expensive pipeline for only one customer'.[87] However, several years down the line, Mr Miller appeared well settled in his post.

Meanwhile, Gazprom representatives have pointed out that, whilst demurring to buy more gas through Blue-Stream, Turkey is pressing on with the construction of *two* pipeline links with Azerbaijan. Successive Turkish governments have contracted to take a further 22 billion cubic metres from Azerbaijan, 16 billion cubic metres from the Baku–Ceyhan–Erzurum line, and 6.6 billion cubic metres from the Shah Deniz project. Moreover, the AKP Government had set itself a target to reduce Turkey's natural gas dependence on Russia to 30 per cent of total imports – an apparently political rather than economic objective and a difficult target to attain. By the year 2010, the Turks are contracted to take-or-pay for 50 billion cubic metres of natural gas, about 55 per cent of it from Russia, through the 'Progress Line' (through Bulgaria) and Blue-Stream. It is not, therefore, clear how the country can reduce its acceptance of Russian gas without tearing up commercial agreements.

Furthermore, BOTAŞ has revised its demand estimate for the year 2010 downward, from 55 to 40 billion cubic metres.[88] The US Energy Information Agency projects Turkish demand at even lower levels.[89] Meanwhile, the Turks have been looking for ways of avoiding the 'take-or-pay' penalties, estimated to run to $1 billion by 2010. Storage facilities are being planned and underground cavities surveyed on the Thracian peninsula, the Sea of Marmara and the Salt Lake region in Central Anatolia.

The price issue between Turkey and Gazprom has since gone into the melting pot of rising and wildly fluctuating gas prices everywhere.[90] We have seen above that Gazprom is charging $255 per 1,000 cubic metres to grateful buyers in Western Europe, while even Ukraine agreed to pay $95 in 2006 and $135 in 2007. Meanwhile, prices charged by Gazprom to BOTAŞ of Turkey appear to have been promoted to the rank of a state secret. As late as 20 February 2006, Mr Medvedev of Gazprom '... noted [that] ... the natural gas price for Turkey has never been announced and will be kept "undisclosed" ... '.[91] Whatever its rewards, energy forecasting in Turkey is clearly not a profession for analysts with a weak constitution.

Turkey as an energy export corridor

There have been suggestions that Turkey was well placed to serve as a westward energy export corridor for gas from the Caucasus,[92] Iran or indeed Russia. On the face of it, this seems a valid strategic objective. Indeed, an agreement to construct a small pipeline for gas exports to Greece and a second agreement for a line extending to Italy have already been signed.

The purchasing agreements signed by BOTAŞ during the past decade were for fairly expensive gas, compared to the going prices at the time. In a higher price environment, Turkey may find some breathing space from these contracts and perhaps realistically consider positioning herself as a regional energy hub. However, with Blue-Stream II shelved, at least for a time, and large amounts of gas from Iran vetoed by the USA, Azerbaijan and Kazakhstan appear as the only likely gas providers. We will see in Chapter VI that these two countries do not have much gas to spare, above and beyond the gas-supply contracts they have signed already. Furthermore, in the absence of any serious planning, let alone actual construction of necessary infrastructure, these suggestions do not seem to be for the short to medium term.

7 Russian Perspectives: Who is Friend and Who is Foe?

If Russian media dispatches on the subject are to be believed, one of Mikhail Khodorkovsky's principal trespasses was an attempt to internationalize Yukos: 'But think for a moment what might have happened if the Yukos owners had managed to sell control of their company last July to Chevron-Texaco or Mobil, as Khodorkovsky intended ...'.[93]

True or false, the nature of the allegation is interesting. We merely need to consider that any attempt to register or sell a flagship British corporation in a foreign country (choose any country!) would be unlikely to end in police raids and handcuffs. Clearly, in Russia, Yukos and its assets are regarded as national patrimony, and an allegation of its attempted sale – an ordinary commercial transaction – constitutes an accusation. The author of the article answered his own question as follows: 'Russia as an independent oil exporter would have been on its way to a level of independence that is less than Aramco, the Saudi oil company.' Part of the title of this probably officially inspired article was 'Putin to the oil pump!'

According to another (possibly officially inspired) dispatch by Novosti, ' ... [during 2004] Russia's main economic partner, the EU ... turned out to be its main foreign policy headache'.[94] The criticism appears to have been triggered by perceived EU support for ' ... illegal actions of those on the losing side at the presidential election in Ukraine ... and demanding new rounds of the election until the candidate that suits Europe wins ...'. Reading on, we find that ' ... Russia tolerate[d] similar situations in Georgia and Yugoslavia but its patience has run out ...'. It is difficult to interpret the inculpation of the EU here in preference to the USA, which seemed '... still a rung or two above Europe'. In an extraordinary follow-on, it is explained that 2004 had been

> a time of unrestrained growth in Russia, which created ...
> confidence ... Besides, Russia put on combat duty new strategic and other types of weapons ... which also bolstered national confidence. In a word, the weakness of the 1990s is gone and forgotten, even though Russia has not regained the status of great power. [The article goes on to explain] Humiliated by the economic troubles of the past, the Russian nation was prepared to tolerate any injustice and blows. But it has regained its normal state now.

Whatever one may surmise about the Russian political psyche (and grammar!) in 2004, these larger-than-life articles probably reflected images deliberately projected by the Putin presidency. The contempt for the drift, the drunkenness and the plunder of the Yeltsin era is palpable. After several years of unprecedented high oil prices, Russia's coffers are filling up and the country is on its way back, even if ' ... Russia has not *regained* [my italics] the status of great power ... '. For our purposes, it is intriguing to find such explicit political pronouncements in articles ostensibly devoted to problems of oil and gas transmission. According to the same article quoted above, ' ... Washington has been backing the Turkish and Azerbaijan governments to steer the export of Caspian region crude oil *away from Russia* [my italics] ... as it tries to redraw the geography of the Caucasus on an *anti-Russian map* ... [my italics]'. A little further on: 'The Russian government has always understood this pipeline was part of a broader US strategy to cut all links with Moscow of the former Soviet states in the Caucasus ....'

Elsewhere in the former Soviet sphere, the changes that followed popular demonstrations in Georgia, in Ukraine and (how could we forget?) in Serbia have had unexpected consequences. From Belarus to Uzbekistan, the ex-Communist oligarchies that had inherited state power during the post-Soviet transition are now regrouping under banners that reject 'foreign' notions of democracy. Several post-Soviet states openly entered into political and military collaboration with the USA, particularly after the attacks of 11 September 2001. These oligarchies have now had sufficient time to observe that moving closer to the West might actually have contributed to the fall of the regimes in Georgia and in Ukraine. The Andijan massacre by Uzbek security forces has shut the gate on the face of peaceful transition in Uzbekistan and probably also further afield within the CIS. It is difficult to visualize a new Iron Curtain descending around this smaller and poorer rump of the Soviet Union, at a time when Moscow's vulnerabilities as an economic power are evident and doing business with the West is so lucrative. However, a new period of retrenchment by the ruling oligarchies to prolong their time in power is clearly on the cards. High energy prices since mid-2004 have helped Russia to consolidate and gather in some of her prodigal sons.

Meanwhile, looking back over the past decade and a half, Russian confusion at postures adopted by the West is understandable. Early expectations by sections of the Russian foreign policy establishment to be gradually integrated into the European framework have not been realized. During the 1990s, the Europeans have not had the confidence to engage Russia politically, on trans-European terms. Instead, during this period, the EU and NATO advanced eastward in tandem. Both organizations have absorbed the three ex-Soviet Baltic republics and a raft of Warsaw Pact countries with very different levels of socio-economic development than the rest, to the point of putting intended further EU integration at risk. It is possible that the three-cornered relationship sought by some of Europe's visionaries may someday take root, but discussions of a new architecture between Russia, Europe and the USA do not seem likely in the short term. More probably, the continent is reverting to the architecture of the 1970s and 1980s, with the Russian line in the sand drawn back by about 1,200 km.

Seen from Moscow, it is now clear that the West was not, and is not, about to offer very much in the way of 'the progressive inclusion of Russia in the expanding transatlantic community'.[95] The shadows of Cold War attitudes had never completely disappeared; they now begin to re-emerge under a new guise. Who better to lead Russia in these dangerous times but a born-and-bred cold warrior? 'Putin's policies assume that such integration is no longer a western concern, if it ever had been.'[96]

As we shall see in Chapter VI, the tensions of this cold peace have spread not just over Eastern Europe and the Balkans, but over the Caucasus and the trans-Caspian basin as well. The prize appears to be power and influence in the newly independent former Soviet republics, including the jewel in the historical Russian crown, Ukraine; and the new cold peace is being played out over oil and gas, and the pipelines and tanker ports that are used for their transmission.

With oil and gas prices at levels inconceivable only a few years ago, exporters of these commodities will be surveying the field with increasing confidence.

Chapter VI

Russia, the trans-Caucasus and the trans-Caspian Republics

Russia has been fighting multiple rearguard actions in Eastern and Central Europe since the dissolution of the Soviet Union, hoping to salvage some of the power and influence the Soviet Union once commanded in this region. The Russians also need to ensure free movement along their energy export corridors towards the West. Before the increases in energy prices (mid-2004), this was largely a defensive posture. However, in the Caucasus and the trans-Caspian basin, Moscow quickly adopted pro-active policies after 1991. The Russians consider these regions as part of their 'near abroad', their sphere of influence and more simply their patrimony.

Historically, Russian presence south of the Caucasus goes back to the reign of Catherine the Great in the late eighteenth century. The Army crossed the mountains in October 1783 at the invitation of Georgian King Irakli II, who sought protection from the newly emerging regional superpower against the arrogant ways of the Shah of Iran, his traditional suzerain. Georgia's saviour on the day was Lieutenant General Count Paul Potemkin (a cousin of the Empress's then 'favourite'), who entered Tblisi in an eight-horse carriage. Few people watching the military parade on that autumn day could have imagined that in just 16 years, Georgian sovereignty would be transferred to the Russian crown (1799).

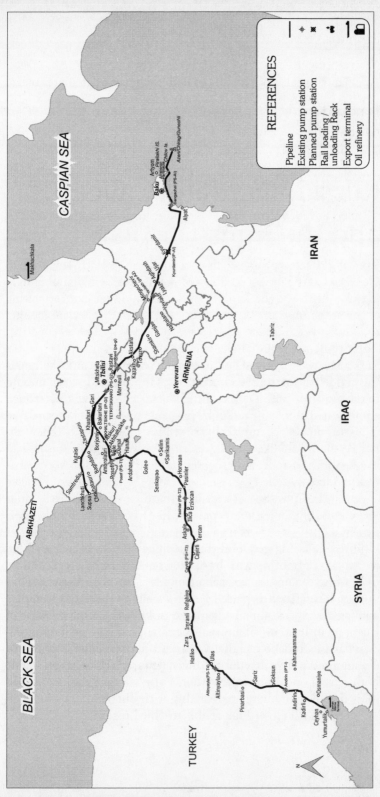

Figure 6.1 The Baku–Tblisi–Ceyhan oil pipeline. Adapted from 'Crude Oil Pipelines of the Former Soviet Union', Centre for Global Energy Studies, UK London, 2005; http://www.cges.co.uk

A few more years saw Daghestan and Baku, vassal khanates of the Persian Empire, become 'permanent possessions of Russia'.[1]

In his 1908 classic, *Russian Conquest of the Caucasus*, Baddeley reflected that

> doubtless ambition and political expediency played their part; but the succour of the Christian States ... from the total ruin threatened by the unspeakable Turk, and still more unspeakable Persian, was as righteous a cause as ever inspired a military or political undertaking.[2]

The world has become a more complicated place since then. Georgia and the former Khanate of Baku, the Azerbaijan Republic of today, have both broken free of Russian domination. Despairing of the arrogant ways of their traditional overlord, they are looking to draw in yet another superpower, the USA, as a counterweight. Their principal regional ally is none other than the 'unspeakable Turk'. Meanwhile, Russia is pursuing its 'righteous cause' by insisting on collecting tolls and taxes from the region's so far meagre harvest of oil. She is also selling nuclear hardware to her new strategic partner, 'still more unspeakable' Iran. The latter, above all, is mindful of the implacable hostility of the USA. Neither Iran nor Russia would like to see American power consolidate itself in the region, nor indeed for Azerbaijan and Georgia to succeed as independent states.

The other post-Soviet republic south of the Caucasus, land-locked and impoverished Armenia, has waged war and occupied nearly a fifth of Azerbaijan during the break-up of the Soviet Union. She is engaged in a strategic alliance with Russia and in a widening relationship with Iran, whilst maintaining strong lobbies in Washington and in European capitals. The other regional state, Turkey, has fashioned herself a role within western initiatives for commercial and political advantage in Eurasia, at the expense of Russian influence. She has been anchoring Georgia's and Azerbaijan's links with the West and acting as an alternative energy conduit towards the Mediterranean, which aims to exclude both Russia and Iran. In response, Putin's Russia has decided to 'slow down' their energy partnership with Turkey.

Let us take a closer look at this troubled region.

1 South of the Caucasus: Red is the Colour of Rust

As late as the 1930s, Baku and Grozny provided about 65 per cent of all crude oil extracted in the Soviet Union. The region's production peaked in 1940 at about 31 million tons.[3] After the War, new oilfields were developed in the Volga-Ural basin, peaking in the 1970s at over 215 million tons. The Western Siberian fields discovered in the 1960s gave even greater volumes of oil, peaking at a spectacular 410 million tons in 1986. During this period, Baku provided much of the technology and manufacturing base required for these developments. Baku's oilfields, however, were starved of men and of investment. It remained a backwater, with a countryside darkened with oil spills and hundreds of abandoned, rusting derricks, the ghosts of a century or more of hasty and wasteful exploitation.[4] At independence, Azerbaijan was struggling to produce 12 million tons a year. That amount of oil could not even keep their two ageing refineries working at full capacity.[5] When war broke out with Armenia, Azeri crude oil production dipped further to around 9 million tons.

Looking back, it now seems clear how the People's Commissar for Nationalities, Josip Stalin, played havoc with the borders of many of the Soviet republics. He left behind a checkerboard of nationalities in each of the republics, making it difficult for potential monolithic national units to emerge and to extricate themselves from the Union. Bukhara and Samarkand, historically great centres of Persian learning, were awarded to Uzbekistan, whilst the Uzbek-speaking Ferghana Valley was partitioned between Uzbekistan, Kyrgyzstan and Tajikistan. Crucially for the Caucasus, Stalin placed Armenian majority upper-Karabagh under Azeri jurisdiction as an 'autonomous' province.

Far older than the Russian presence in the region, the nationalist passions and rivalries of trans-Caucasia were more or less kept dormant during Soviet times. However, 'union' under the Soviets neither resolved endemic historical resentments nor the irreconcilable territorial claims of these peoples against each other. With Soviet power visibly weakening in the late 1980s, these ancient nationalist demons returned to occupy centre stage.

From about 1987 onwards, the Armenian population of Karabagh ('autonomous' in Azerbaijan) demanded union with

Armenia. Violence was visited upon ethnic Armenians living in Azerbaijan in 1989 and the Armenians responded in kind. The disaster was exacerbated by the Soviet army troops opening fire on Azeris in Baku (1990), ostensibly to stop violence against Armenians. In August 1991, Azerbaijan declared independence, closely followed by the Karabagh Armenians in early 1992, who declared *their* independence *from* Azerbaijan. In the war that followed, Russia and Iran alongside the USA supported Armenia, where, in 1992, Congress passed 'Section 907 of the Freedom Support Act, banning direct aid to Azerbaijan'.[6] After securing Karabagh, Armenians overran and continue to occupy five other Azeri provinces located outside Karabagh.[7] By the time a ceasefire was declared in May 1994, about 25,000 people had been killed, nearly a million Azeris and somewhere between 250,000 and 400,000 Armenians had been displaced. Some 300,000 of these Azeri refugees have spilled over into Georgia. The ceasefire in 1994 has brought an uneasy calm to the region, which still appears intact – just.

These developments have had profound effects on Azeri politics. At independence (August 1991), Ayaz Mutalibov, then the First Secretary of the Communist Party, became the country's first president, as had happened in most other post-Soviet republics. Only a year later, however, Mutalibov was forced to resign, blamed for being unable to prevent the massacres of unarmed Azeri peasants by Armenian militias in Karabagh. Presidential elections were called. Amazingly, Mutalibov then attempted a comeback by cancelling the elections and declaring a state of emergency. The move was opposed by the Popular Front Party (PFP), which swept him from power, and their leader Ebulfez Elchibey was elected as president.

The new Azeri administration failed to get a grip on the economic collapse brought on by the war and the break-up of the Soviet Union. War losses mounted. There were accusations of corruption. Newly elected Elchibey was swept from power by a military *coup d'état* and fled. Ominously, the coup came only 12 days after Elchibey had signed a 'Declaration' with a consortium of 'foreign' oil companies. The coup of 18 June 1993 brought Speaker of Parliament Heydar Aliev to power. A former KGB general, a First Secretary of the Communist Party of Azerbaijan and a former member of the Politburo in Moscow, Aliev was a well-known and authoritative figure. His elevation to the Presidency was welcomed and possibly helped along by the Yeltsin adminis-tration. One of his first moves was to tear up Elchibey's 'Declaration', which Moscow had deeply resented.[8]

Post-Soviet developments in Georgia

Across the border in Georgia, Zviad Gamsakhurdia had spent a lifetime in and out of prison, opposing Soviet rule in the name of human rights and national independence. The leader of the Georgian Helsinki Group, he was also instrumental in organizing 'anti-imperialist' actions of various kinds when, in April 1989, the sparks ignited a major conflagration. Soviet troops under Generals Rodionov and Lebed fired on peaceful demonstrators, killing 47, many of them women and children. The ensuing ferment brought Gamsakhurdia to the forefront of the independence movement, which swept to power (October 1990) in the first national elec-tions since the beginning of Soviet rule. Some months ahead of the formal break-up of the Soviet Union, Gamsakhurdia led the Georgians to declare independence (April 1991).

During these turbulent months and years, three ethnically dis-tinct provinces of Georgia erupted in rebellion against Tblisi, more or less openly helped by Moscow. In August 1990, the first of these regions, South Ossetia, with scarcely a population of 100,000, declared independence. Gamsakhurdia promptly invaded the province. With substantial Russian backing, the Ossetians fought the Georgians to a stand-off in a conflict that lasted until 1992. The incident cost over a 1,000 lives and dis-placed nearly 40,000 people.

However, Gamsakhurdia's presidency did not survive this largely artificial crisis. He was overthrown by a Russian-inspired military coup some six months prior to the Ossetian ceasefire and replaced by Eduard Shevardnadze, former First Secretary of the Georgian Communist Party and a former Foreign Minister of the Soviet Union. Gamsakhurdia and his entourage withdrew to Armenia and later to Grozny, at that time controlled by separatist leader General Dudayev. He eventually returned to continue the fight from a base near Zugdidi, in North-western Georgia. With

Russian help, the Georgian military eventually prevailed against Gamsakhurdia's rebels. He was found dead on the last day of 1993 in unexplained circumstances. Meanwhile, Shevardnadze was forced to accept Russian mediation. A ceasefire patrolled by Russian 'peacekeepers' still underpins the 'independence' of South Ossetia.

During the same terrible year of 1992, separatists in the autonomous republic of Abkhazia declared independence from Georgia. The province was depopulated in the nineteenth century, when its Muslim majority was removed by Russian ethnic cleansing. It was instead resettled with peoples of various ethnicities, including Georgians and Mingrelians, Armenians and Russians. Prior to 1992–3, less than a fifth of the population were estimated to be ethnic Abkhazians.[9] During the ensuing civil war that cost over 10,000 lives, ethnic Georgians were expelled from the country. Many Armenians and Russians fled the war zone, leaving the breakaway province with less than half a million inhabitants. In the event, the Georgian military were found wanting and Russian military support, in the form of Chechen mercenaries, won the Abkhaz an uneasy ceasefire during 1993 that survives to this day. Shevardnadze was yet again forced to accept the military stand-off, whilst Abkhazians in large numbers were admitted to Russian citizenship, as indeed were most South Ossetians.

The third rebellious province of the Republic of Georgia was the Ajaria Autonomous Republic, with the port city of Batumi as its capital. In many ways, this province is a throwback to Ottoman times, when mass conversions to Islam not only absolved the local population from paying the poll tax, but opened the road to service in the Ottoman Empire, with hopes of power and influence. During the crisis days of Gamsakhurdia's presidency, Aslan Abashidze succeeded in snatching power in Ajaria, apparently with support from the large Russian military base near Batumi.

Before 1991, 'President' Abashidze's career in the Georgian Soviet Socialist Republic had never gone much beyond the ministry of public utilities. He was said to be a descendant of the hereditary princes of the region under Turkish suzerainty. He claimed to have brought prosperity to Ajaria during his decade in power, explained by his apologists as fruits of the leader's training in economics. Others have described this surge of well-being in terms of some very lively contraband trade through the port of Batumi. In any case, Abashidze seems to have quickly turned the predominantly Muslim province into a sort of personal fiefdom. In the face of Russian support, the Georgian army were incapable of intervening to reimpose the authority of the state. Shevardnadze was thus forced to live with yet another secessionist movement at his doorstep.

Following the overthrow of Shevardnadze in Autumn 2003 and the rise of M. Saakashvili to power, Ajaria came under renewed pressure from Tblisi. For reasons yet to be explained, Putin's Kremlin appears to have decided to let go of Abashidze. On 5 May 2004, Igor Ivanov, Secretary of the National Security Council, flew to Batumi and returned to Moscow with Abashidze in the same plane. From the margins, it looks as if the Russian Government did not think Abashidze's position in Batumi could be easily defended.

While the Ajaria rebellion may thus have been resolved with Russian acquiescence, the two other breakaway regions, which have adjoining borders with Russia, are currently resisting re-integration into the Republic of Georgia. In the present climate, Moscow would see no advantage in allowing the two breakaway regions to acquiesce to Tblisi's control. We will also see below that the – as yet incomplete – Russian withdrawal from two Soviet era bases in Georgia is being carried out with extreme reluctance.

Armed militias in the Caucasus

Remarkable during these bitter struggles were the activities of various private armies, which uncannily appear to have second-guessed the intensions of Yeltsin's Kremlin every time. Tengiz Kitovani's 'National Guard' took an active part in the coup against Georgian President Zviad Gamsakhurdia in late 1991. Before that, together with Djaba Ioseliani's Mkhedrioni, Kitovani's group had touched off the fighting in Abkhazia and South Ossetia. In Azerbaijan, another private army led by Colonel Suret Huseinov was armed with equipment generously left behind by Russian troops, when the newly elected president Ebulfez Elchibey asked Russian forces to leave the country. They led the

161

coup that toppled Elchibey in June 1993 and prepared the return to power in Baku of former Soviet stalwart, Heydar Aliev, mirroring Shevardnadze's ascent to power in neighbouring Georgia.

As it transpired, local conditions allowed neither elder Soviet statesmen to adopt the policy agendas expected of them by kingmakers in Moscow. Aliev eventually signed 'the contract of the century' with Western oil companies, whilst both Shevardnadze and Aliev committed their countries to the strategic Baku–Tblisi–Ceyhan pipeline. Private armies were also active in Armenia, where the 'Yerkrapah' detachments formed by Vazgen Sargsian to fight in the Karabagh war helped him rise to the post of defence minister and eventually to the office of Prime Minister of the Republic of Armenia.[10] Their tasks accomplished, many of these people were 'effectively neutralized'.[11] Sargsian was assassinated in parliament in October 1999, together with seven other officials. The killings were condemned by the US Senate ' ... the House of Representatives concurring ... ', in a resolution which 'continues to cherish the strong friendship between Armenia and the United States'.[12]

Among its many momentous consequences, the Moscow putsch of August 1991 against Gorbachev also triggered a separatist referendum in Armenia, leading to independence in September of that year. In the elections that followed, the Armenian National Movement defeated the Communists and Levon Ter-Petrossian became the country's first president. He led the country during their successful war against Azerbaijan and won a second term in 1996. However, he was forced to resign when his faction in Parliament abandoned him, nullifying his efforts to patch up some kind of peace over Karabagh. He was replaced by his Prime Minister Robert Kocharian, former resistance leader in Karabagh, whose tenure has seen peace efforts frozen and internal opposition stifled. Not unlike his counterpart Ilkham Aliev's election in Azerbaijan, Kocharian's re-election in 2003 has been greeted with less than admiration by international election monitors.[13] Meanwhile, all across the resource-rich Caucasus, a series of precarious ceasefires continue to dominate daily life, alongside astonishing levels of corruption, internal violence and economic insecurity.

2 Arrival of the Oil Majors and the Debate on Caspian Reserves

Of the three former Soviet republics south of the Caucasus range, only Azerbaijan owns economically significant reserves of crude oil and natural gas. After nearly 140 years of exploitation, the countryside near the old oil-producing regions, notably the Apsheron peninsula, were left irredeemably polluted. Many onshore fields have been exhausted and functioning wells produce relatively little oil. Moreover, the refineries and other installations left over from Soviet times were 'primitive by Western standards'.[14] It appears, furthermore, that available Soviet technology did not allow drilling at anything beyond the nearby shallows, where the rusting frames of disused oil derricks still stick out of the water. In the late 1980s, Azerbaijan, together with Kazakhstan across the Caspian, began negotiations with western companies, with the aim of getting their oil and gas industries moving again. These negotiations continued, in fits and starts, during the troubles of the early 1990s.

As already signalled, President Elchibey of Azerbaijan was ousted immediately after signing a preliminary agreement with a consortium led by BP and Atlantic Richfield (ARCO). The Russian Government viewed the process with open suspicion, while Lukoil and Transneft sought to be party to the agreements on offer. Like the coup in Georgia that brought Shevardnadze to power in Tblisi, Aliev's accession to power in 1992–3 in Baku was probably assisted by, and certainly received favourably in, Moscow. As a prominent figure in Soviet intelligence and political circles, Aliev would have been expected to show sensitivity to Moscow's views about its 'near abroad'. Indeed, one of the first acts of his presidency was to cancel the agreement on oil exploration. This is a region '... where Russians want to be the sole guarantor of security and a key arbiter of major geopolitical shifts'.[15]

In retrospect, the prospect of closer collaboration with Moscow could not have appeared particularly alluring to the hard-pressed leaders in Baku and Tblisi. With its largely low-grade technology base, little investment capital on offer and much-depleted industrial muscle since the days of the Soviet Union, the regional superpower had little to offer in return for geopolitical conformity.

163

Before the rapid rise of oil and gas prices in mid-2004, Moscow did not possess the resources to tempt the trans-Caucasian republics into its economic sphere of activity. It still does not have the technical know-how to drill and explore at the depths that oil and gas are now being extracted in the Azeri sectors of the Caspian.

'Contract of the century'

Squeezed between Armenian military and Russian political pressure, Aliev managed the situation as best he could. He signed a Russian-sponsored ceasefire with the Armenians, whilst taking an active hand in the negotiations begun in the days of Elchibey that eventually led to the 'contract of the century'.[16] The formation of the Azerbaijan International Operating Company (AIOC) committed the participating companies to invest some $7.4 billion towards the development of three of the more promising offshore blocks in the Caspian, the Azeri, Chirag and Güneshli sectors. Having previously acquired ARCO, BP took up 34 per cent of the shares and the role of main contractor, whilst the State Oil Company of Azerbaijan Republic (SOCAR) took a meagre 10 per cent in addition to agreed higher levels of tax revenue.[17] That agreement opened the floodgates. Some 20 production-sharing agreements relating to the development of Caspian oilfields have since been signed and ratified by the Azeri Parliament.[18] Much new investment has been pledged by companies from France, Italy, Germany, the USA and even Iran.[19]

At present, much of Azerbaijan's exploration and production work takes place offshore, carried out at depths of 1,000–1,100 m of water. This is not far short of the state of the art. 'Thunder Horse', the largest-ever oil platform, constructed for service in the Gulf of Mexico, is designed to drill at record depths of 1,600 m of water.[20] In post-Soviet Azerbaijan, new technology brought from the west by companies such as BP, with operating experience in the North Sea, has been helpful. The first oil to flow from the offshore Chirag-1 block came from a platform abandoned in half-finished state during Soviet times and rebuilt by the AIOC in about three years.

Meanwhile, Washington's initial enthusiasm for the Armenian cause appeared to have been somewhat tempered by the attractions of Azerbaijan's hydrocarbon reserves. The Russian

Government's initial refusal to recognize the contract was countered by pressure from the Clinton administration, whilst US oil majors took up increasingly strategic positions in the region. In 1995, under pressure from Washington, Iran was pushed out of the 'contract of the century', and the 5 per cent initially allocated to the National Iranian Oil Company was given to Exxon.[21] The distant echoes of the Iraq Petroleum Company agreement were unmistakable; once again, Exxon was the beneficiary.

Not surprisingly, the transmission route for Azeri oil became the next tug of war, with Transneft insisting on pipelines crossing into Russian territory and discharging at the port of Novorossiysk. US policy-makers only accepted the transmission of Azeri 'early oil' through the 'Northern Route Export Pipeline' to Novorossiysk. The line was quickly completed, in part using segments of the former Soviet pipeline network.

There were additional difficulties. The original Baku–Novorossiysk pipeline passed near Grozny, the capital of Chechnya. The opening of the line was delayed in late 1997, whilst the Russians and Chechens discussed terms regarding Chechen participation in the decision-making process and transit fees. When Russia invaded Chechnya again in 1999, the line stopped pumping and Azeri oil was diverted by rail through Daghestan, whilst Transneft constructed a new 'Chechnya-bypass' to circumvent the war zone.

In April 1999, Aliev and Shevardnadze ceremonially opened a second 830-km-long 'Western Route,' carrying oil to the new Georgian tanker terminal at Supsa on the Black Sea. Taken together, the 'Northern' and 'Western' pipelines annually carry a relatively unremarkable 10 million tons. For the longer term, however, US policy-makers were determined to avoid the high transit fees charged by Russia and the various other difficulties Transneft seemed capable of coming up with. During the mid-1990s, similar Russian rearguard action had prompted Chevron to scale back its investments in Kazakhstan.[22] US policy-makers were also 'determined not to place the Caspian reserves at the mercy of Iran, nor to increase the West's dependence on the stability of the Persian Gulf and the compliance of the Arabian states'.[23]

Construction of the 1770-km Baku–Tbilisi–Ceyhan (BTC) pipeline began in September 2002. The line cost $4 billion and has an eventual capacity of 50 million tons. It runs from the Sangachal Terminal near Baku, across Georgian territory, through Eastern Turkey to the Mediterranean port of Ceyhan (Figure 6.1). Oil from the Azeri–Chirag–Güneshli fields, in the Azerbaijani sector of the Caspian, started filling the line in May 2005 and the terminal at Ceyhan began loading tankers in June 2006.

The trajectory of this new line goes counter to all Russian strategic aims in this region. It excludes Russian political influence, as well as countering her ambitions to control oil and gas exports out of the region. It also denies Russia any share of the profits in the form of transit fees: 'The former Soviet state oil sector invested heavily in existing Caspian oil facilities and Moscow's oil men believe this entitles Russia to control and compensation.'[24] The Iranians have similarly been excluded, despite having proposed a number of competing and economically attractive alternatives. We will review some of these options later in this chapter.

Caspian oil reserves

Before becoming immersed in problems of transmission, it is interesting to revisit the motivations behind the rush to the Caucasus and the trans-Caspian. Some of the companies that have entered the fray are amongst the world's largest (Exxon-Mobil, BP-Amoco), and some, such as Unocal, erstwhile interlocutors of the Taliban in Afghanistan are among the world's most aggressive. Would such companies scour this difficult region for small pickings! Or would they?

In the near frenzied rhetoric of the early 1990s, the region was portrayed as a 'second Gulf', a new Texas! Former Secretary of State James Baker famously talked up the region's potential as being in the range of 200 billion barrels of oil. So did Clinton's Deputy Secretary of State, Strobe Talbot, in 1997.[25] A total of 200 billion barrels of reserves would have ranked the region well above Iraq and Iran, in the same league as Saudi Arabia (est. ~270 billion barrels). Others who would minimize the region's potential – perhaps to shoo away greedy interlopers – have talked down the Caspian's hydrocarbon potential, to as low as *four* billion barrels in all.[26]

Like nearly everything else in this fractious corner of the world, the truth about oil and gas reserves seems to be protected (loosely borrowing from Winston Churchill) by a strong bodyguard of lies. The discrepancies grew quite alarmingly in the run-up to the construction of the Baku–Tblisi–Ceyhan pipeline. Are we to believe that 'Azerbaijan, Kazakhstan and Turkmenistan could, in different ways, become new Kuwaits'?[27] Is the Caspian basin a new Gulf? Or is it a pitiful little corner of the world, best left to the tender mercies of Russia and Iran?

Comparing current levels of Caspian oil production with those of Kuwait provides a sobering assessment. In 1971, Kuwait produced 153 million tons of crude oil and condensate. Total production has since been drifting downwards. It touched 98 million tons in 2002 and has somewhat recovered since then. By contrast, annual rates of crude oil production in Turkmenistan and Azerbaijan hovered between 10 and 15 million tons each, whilst Kazakhstan has climbed rapidly, from about 30 million tons in 1999 to nearly 51 million in 2003, about 61 million tons in 2004 and 63 million tons in 2005.[28] We must conclude that, to date, Caspian oil has not flowed in quantities that would fundamentally affect world markets, although marginal amounts can strongly influence spot prices. The sums of money that these levels of production correspond to, however, would profoundly affect the economic lives of the countries concerned. Furthermore, current levels do not necessarily reflect the *potential* for future production. So, what do we know of the oil and gas *reserves* in the Caucasus and the trans-Caspian basin?

In 1998, Ruseckas[29] suggested 3.6 billion barrels as the 'proven' oil reserves of Azerbaijan and 10 billion barrels for Kazakhstan. He explained that these numbers were rather conservative; it *might* be legitimate to think in terms of perhaps doubling these estimates. The US Energy Information Agency (EIA) quotes Azerbaijan's recoverable oil reserves as between 7 and 13 billion barrels, which is above the range quoted by Ruseckas, whilst the Azeri Government prefers to think in terms of 17.5 billion barrels.[30] In early 2005, the corresponding US EIA figures for Kazakhstan ranged between 9 and 17.6 billion barrels of oil, in line with official Kazakh estimates of approximately 16 billion barrels. One year later, the EIA upgraded Kazakh reserves to between 9 and

29 billion barrels, comparable to OPEC members Algeria at the low end and Qatar at the high end.[31] The BP Statistical Review of World Energy of June 2006 puts Kazakh reserves as nearly 40 billion barrels.[32] Kazakhstan's own recently completed assessment gives the sum of proven and probable oil reserves at approximately 30 billion barrels of crude oil.[33] In the same dispatch, however, the Kazakh Information Agency added a joker-in-the-pack: '*Probable* reserves of oilfields situated in the [Kazakh] sector of the Caspian Sea account for more than 124.3 billion barrels.' More to the point, officially Kazakhstan anticipates production rates of 120 million tons by 2010 and 180 million tons by 2015. *That* amount of oil would, indeed, start sounding like Kuwait … and a little more. It would make a difference.

We must nevertheless keep matters in perspective. Doubled or halved, these figures are not (yet?) of game-changing proportions. The proven oil reserve estimates for Iran, Iraq and Saudi Arabia combined exceed 450 billion barrels. Furthermore, Middle Eastern oil is cheaper to extract, costing less than $3 in Saudi Arabia, compared to an average of perhaps $15 per barrel in the Caspian. There is still much exploration taking place in the Caspian basin; more oil and gas may be discovered. But at present, in the Caspian as a whole, ' … Production levels are expected to exceed 4 million barrels per day in 2015 compared to a projected 45 million barrels per day for the OPEC countries in that year'.[34] *On present evidence*, which new exploration may change at any time, we do not seem to be looking at a new 'Gulf'. There nevertheless appears to be sufficient oil to turn a decent profit for the companies involved and to provide a steady and sizeable income for the countries of the region.

3 Baku–Tblisi–Ceyhan: The Pipeline and its Opponents

It is difficult to piece together how and when US policy for the region changed from one of non-interference in the 'internal' affairs of the former Soviet Union to the more ambiguous posture of the late 1990s. Was the evolution in US policy related to developing negotiations over the 'contract of the century'? Did the

USA consider and then abandon ideas of giving Russia the breathing space Moscow thinks it needs? Whatever the course of internal debates, probably by the middle of the 1990s, and certainly no later than 1998, US strategy had been shaped to exclude Russia, as well as Iran, from playing an important part in the transmission of oil extracted in Azerbaijan.

Even so, when 'new oil' began to flow from the offshore Chirag-1 block, the only available export route was the refurbished Transneft line to Novorossiysk, running through Russian territory. The 'Western Route' to the new *Georgian* tanker terminal at Supsa followed in April 1999. However, these two pipelines were never meant to service the greater flows from Azeri offshore fields expected after 2005–6. *That* particular task was assigned to the Baku–Tblisi–Ceyhan line, intended to bypass Russian and Iranian territory. It is possible that the peculiarly acid relationship that developed between Russia and Azerbaijan over the war with Armenia loomed large in Azeri minds during the inception of this project. Certainly, Kazakhstan would not have allowed herself such cheerful declarations of independence from the former imperial power. Neither the timing and volume of Kazakh oil production, nor the nature of the relationship between Russia and Kazakhstan, would have allowed that. In the event, the Baku–Tblisi–Ceyhan crude oil pipeline and the accompanying Baku–Tblisi–Erzurum gas pipeline projects have proved hugely controversial.

Azeri oil; should Russia care?

Ordinarily, the Russian giant should not have taken any notice of relatively marginal amounts of oil produced in Azerbaijan. The Russians are hovering around production levels of 500 million tons or more. Current Azeri production does not even come up to 5 per cent of this total. So why the fuss?

Another intriguing aspect of the Baku–Tblisi–Ceyhan pipeline is its very capacity. The line has a diameter of 46 in and will eventually be capable of carrying 1 million barrels per day, approximately 50 million tons per year. This is the throughput many authors agree is necessary to operate the line profitably.[35] Back in Azerbaijan, however, oil production had almost recovered to about 14 million tons in 1999. In 2003, the total reached 15.5 million tons, two-thirds of which was available for export. The offshore 'Azeri block' of the Azeri–Chirag–Günesli complex coming on stream in 2005 has raised this total to 22.4 million tons and to nearly 30 million tons in 2006. Again, some of this oil will go for domestic consumption. Does Azerbaijan alone have the potential to fill the BTC line? More to the point, should Russia worry about the amounts of oil produced in Azerbaijan?

We have already seen in Chapter V that these matters are far from being politically neutral. According to one Russian report, the BTC pipeline was meant to 'steer the export of Caspian region crude oil *away from Russia* [my italics] ... [as]... part of a broader US strategy to cut all links with Moscow of the former Soviet states in the Caucasus ...'.[36] The expected switch of Azeri oil transmission from Novorossiysk to the BTC line invited reaction from the semi-official Novosti Russian News Agency:[37]

> Azerbaijan is beginning to methodically oust Russia from its oil market ... State Oil Company of Azerbaijan will stop exporting oil along the Baku–Novorossiysk pipeline less than a month from now ... Baku may only be putting up a trial balloon to test Moscow's reaction, but Russia might be ousted from the regional oil market by late 2005 if it reacts too weakly ... The Baku–Tbilisi–Ceyhan pipeline will start exporting oil in fall ... [2006] which means Novorossiysk will stop receiving Azerbaijani oil.... The Russian route will gradually be frozen out ... The expert believes Russia must, first of all, try to enhance its influence in other CIS countries, the former Communist bloc and Turkey if it wants to prevent this.

Meanwhile, the Russian Interfax agency reported without comment that ' ... Antitank mines have been discovered near the village of Klde in Georgia's Akhaltsikhe district about 100 meters from the oil pipeline Baku-Tbilisi-Ceyhan, which is under construction'.[38]

The Russians are also wary of a future east–west trans-Caspian line from the Kazakh port at Aqtau to Baku, linking the Kazakh pipeline system with the BTC line. Pumping Kazakh oil would be one obvious way of filling the BTC line without waiting for Azeri production to pick up to 50 million tons a year. This has already been discussed in evaluating the possible role of the BTC line, but the Kazakhs have not yet committed to a *pipeline* across the Caspian. The financial cost would probably be rather high, of the order of $2.5 billion, and the political cost in respect of Moscow's adverse reaction might well be higher still. Instead, during 2005–6, about 3 million tons of Kazakh oil was carried by barge across the Caspian for transmission through the two smaller pipelines to the Black Sea ports. Bending a little with US pressure, the Kazakhs have also signed an agreement for shipments through the BTC pipeline, about 7.5 million tons 'over the medium term' and rising to 25 million tons when the pipeline reaches full capacity.[39]

We will review below the competing 'Caspian Pipeline Consortium' line, which at present pumps Kazakh oil mainly from the Tengiz field on the north-eastern rim of the Caspian to Novorossiysk. For the last two years the Russians have been delaying granting the Consortium permission to expand the capacity of the line from its present 28 million to (the pre-planned) 67 million tons per year. The expansion effectively pre-empts future increases in production from the Tengiz field for the foreseeable future and probably the output from Karachaganak (further to the north) as well.

Depending on how Kazakh oil exports develop, fierce competition between the CPC and the BTC consortia seems possible, with Russia fully expecting the Kazakhs to remain true to their earlier commitment to the CPC line. However, the Russians have one more string to their bow. The agreement for the Bourgas–Alexandroupolis line was signed by Russia–Bulgaria–Greece in March 2007. The expansion of the CPC pipeline has now been tied to the producers in Kazakhstan committing to send their oil out of the Black Sea through the Russian-controlled Bourgas–Alexandroupolis line, when the line is completed (2010–11).

However, there is another unknown, in the shape of the giant Kashagan field discovered in 2000 in the Kazakh sector of the Caspian shallows, a 'super-giant' field with estimated reserves between 7 and 13 billion barrels. That development seems to be BTC's hope for staying in business without upsetting the political equilibrium around the CPC line. Tanker traffic between Aqtau and Baku is thus expected gradually to increase once the BTC is fully operational and the Kashagan field is progressively developed. The Kazakhs were planning to construct five 12,000-ton tankers for this purpose. The first of these tankers, the 'Astana', was launched in the autumn of 2005.

Georgia, cockpit of the Caucasus

The BTC pipeline invokes a catalogue of geopolitical consequences, not just for Azerbaijan, Georgia and Turkey on its trajectory, but also for several other regional states. As explained by the Russian Information Agency Novosti: 'The Baku–Tbilisi–Ceyhan pipeline is not acceptable for Russia owing to both economic [it is too expensive] and political considerations.'[40] The very existence of the project hinges on Georgia's adherence to its pro-western alliance, since her territory provides the land bridge between the shores of the Caspian and the Turkish mainland. The Russians are displeased and western policy-makers must be hoping that the Georgians will not blink. The present Saakashvili regime in Tblisi is openly aiming to place the country outside the Russian geopolitical orbit, but that is not going to be easy.

In addition to the two secessionist provinces under the protection of Russian 'peace-keepers', there are two large Soviet-era Russian military bases on Georgian territory, which the Russians have agreed to vacate by 2008 – after much pushing from Tblisi and pressure from Washington. During his visit to Tblisi in February 2005, the Russian Foreign Minister, Sergei Lavrov, creatively proposed to convert the two bases into 'anti-terrorist' centres, with unchanged structure and armaments. In response, the Georgians hinted that they might declare Russian bases on Georgian territory as illegal. As a signatory to the *Conventional Forces in Europe Treaty*, the unhurried Russians might have relished some legal skirmishing, prolonged at the leisure of her diplomats.[41] A little brazenly, they proposed a period of 13 years for the withdrawal. An altogether more lively response appears to have been elicited by the Georgians, however, by suggesting that water, gas and electricity to the 'illegal' bases might be cut off.[42]

'Our gas! Our electricity!' pointed out outraged Russian officials, scathing about Georgian 'ingratitude'.

Meanwhile, Gazprom has made several of its usual attempts to purchase the main Georgian trunk gas pipeline, in return for settling unpaid gas bills. Much as in Ukraine, these approaches have been met with a vociferous nationalist response, although Georgia has never definitively ruled out the possibility. The adverse reaction to this particular 'privatization' move has come with a difference. According to the Georgians,[43] US Presidential Adviser on Caspian Energy Issues, Steven Mann, suggested that the sale of the trunk pipeline would interfere with Georgia's future 'energy independence', presumably meaning future independence from Russia. The Georgians have also been warned that the sale of the line to Russia would impede the progress of the Shah Deniz project, which is intended to pipe natural gas from Azerbaijan to Georgia and Turkey. Meanwhile, BP denied that it was in the market for the Georgian main gasline, in a bid competing with that of Gazprom. Others have speculated that the Georgians might have proposed an exchange, involving Russian support for Georgian reunification with S. Ossetia and Abkhazia. The downward progression from the sublime to the less than serious is unmistakeable. Once again, it seems wise to wait for the dust to settle.

In April–May 2005, rather reluctantly and probably under pressure from the USA, the Russians agreed to evacuate the bases in Batumi and Akhalkalaki by 2008. To the intense annoyance of the Azeri government, most of the hardware from the two bases is being transported to Armenia, which hosts the last Russian military base south of the Caucasus mountain range. Nervous observers are well aware that the BTC pipeline also passes well within striking distance of Armenian forces, who might just take it into their heads to attempt to deny Azerbaijan 'significant oil revenues that could be channelled into arms acquisition programs'.[44]

Armenia's transport problems

Nearly 20 per cent of the land mass of Azerbaijan has been under Armenian occupation since the war of the early 1990s, including five Azeri provinces over which Armenia officially claims to have no territorial ambitions. From the sidelines, Turkey has eyed Armenian activism with less than favour and, since the invasion of Azerbaijan, the border with Armenia has remained closed. During the thaw of 1995–6, the Kars border crossing was about to be opened and Turkey came close to signing a deal with the then president TerPetrosyan. However, the (then) relatively newly re-elected (1996) Armenian president was promptly disowned by his parliamentary allies and forced to resign. He was replaced by Robert Kocharian, a former nationalist commander in Nagorno-Karabakh, whose administration rejects the Treaty of Kars (1920) between Armenia and Turkey. The Turkish Government considers this as 'code' for Armenian territorial claims on Eastern Anatolia. The accusation has not been denied in Yerevan.

Meanwhile, tensions between Russia and Georgia over Abkhazia have led to the interruption of Russia's rail communications with Armenia. This is the rail-line running along the coast from Tuapse in Russia into Sokhumi (Abkhazia) and Tblisi, terminating at Yerevan, the Armenian capital. The Georgians are refusing to allow the railway to function between Abkhazia and Georgia before the Abkhaz Government in Sokhumi aligns itself politically with Tblisi. Added to the closure of the Turkish and Azeri land borders since the war in 1991–3, the Georgian ban severely limits Armenia's trade and transport options. More recently, it was announced that the much-heralded India–Finland transport corridor, sponsored by Iran and Russia, would have to pass from Iran into Azeri territory to continue northward. Due to the Georgian ban, the project has been constrained to avoid Armenian territory.

Armenia has expressed strong opposition to the India–Finland project in its present form. They have also objected to the new railway line that would improve communications between Turkey, Georgia and Azerbaijan. This latter project involves completing the gap between the Turkish rail system ending in Kars (Eastern Turkey) and the Georgian railway terminal at Akhalkalaki. The discontinuity is a vestige of the Cold War, when Georgia was a part of the Soviet Union and insulated from NATO member Turkey. The project also covers the revamping of the line from Akhalkalaki to Tbilisi (both in Georgia). Some $350 million will be spent in the initial stages of the project, which is worth a total of $600 million.[45] Armenian reaction to the developments has been expressed by Foreign Minister Oskanian:

> We have the Kars–Gyumri railway which does not function because of Turkey's wrong policy. We think that every investment in the construction of the railway that is bypassing the already existing railway is pointless. We will struggle against it.[46]

The Banking Committee of the US Senate has accepted a proposal blocking prospective Washington credit for the project.[47] Meanwhile, there has been speculation that Kazakhstan and China are interested in this project, to join ' ...Kars ... with Shanghai'.[48]

In late 2005, reports emerged of an agreement whereby Armenia would return the occupied Azeri provinces in return for Azerbaijan agreeing to self-determination in Nagorno-Karabagh. Whether Russia will see any advantage in allowing this particular conflict to be brought to an end remains to be seen. Meanwhile, Armenian officials have denied a Russian role in the 1999 assassination of Prime Minister Vazgen Sargsian and seven other political figures inside the Armenian Parliament. The issue resurfaced when a former FSB Colonel, Aleksandr Litvinenko, (then) living in Britain, alleged that the October 1999 attack on Armenia's parliament had been organized by Russian Military Intelligence (GRU). According to Litvinenko, the GRU

> 'hatched the plot to prevent a resolution of the Nagorno–Karabakh conflict.' Some relatives and friends of the assassinated officials, among them two of Armenia's most popular opposition leaders, suspect Kocharian of having a hand in the killings ... The gunmen led by Nairi Hunanian, a former journalist, were sentenced to life imprisonment in December 2003 following a lengthy trial.[49]

In the conspiracy laden atmosphere of the Caucasus, it seems difficult to discern the truth behind these allegations. Colonel Litvinenko was subsequently murdered in London in November 2006.

Motivations of the BTC-pipeline host countries

Judging by their results, Russian interventions in the wars between Azerbaijan and Armenia, and in South Ossetia and Abkhazia, have not served them well. Their territorial integrities under attack, Georgia and Azerbaijan have been led out of the Russian security orbit by former Soviet statesmen, Shevardnadze and Aliev, respectively. The Russian drive to extract profit from Azeri resource exploitation has similarly been unsuccessful. There are clear indications that in Tblisi and in Baku, the BTC pipeline system is seen as a vehicle for distancing themselves from Russia, in terms of their energy linkages, their economic ties and, more generally, their geopolitical allegiances. Only Armenia has remained within a strategic alliance with Russia.

A different set of driving forces have determined the nature of Turkey's involvement in the project. The country paid a high price for the role it assumed during the Cold War, and for the internal repression it inflicted on its own people. Between 1975 and 1990, Turkey was among few countries that recorded falling annual per capita GDP rates 'while [the] world, OECD, and Asia all saw increases'.[50] Following the dissolution of the Soviet Union, the Turkish regime felt the cold winds of its diminished geopolitical significance within the NATO structure. The country has welcomed its new role within the cold peace developing in the Caucasus, to anchor Georgia and Azerbaijan's links with the West and to serve as a conduit for the flow of hydrocarbons towards the open seas.

4 Iran: The Idle Hinge?

Iran occupies a central position on the regional map, wedged between the Middle East, the Caucasus, Central Asia, Afghanistan, South Asia and the Indian Ocean (Figure 6.1). She is potentially an ideal conduit for oil and gas transmission, as well as being a large producer of these vital commodities.

In the 1970s, Iran produced nearly 300 million tons of oil annually and exported all but 25 million tons of it. During the 1973–4 oil shock, prices were buoyant and the Shah of Iran seemed both rich and powerful. His large purchases of expensive armaments from the USA only partly offset the then growing imbalance in cash flows between oil producers and consumers. The Shah will also be remembered for his magnificent uniforms and his newly found look of self-confidence. At home, he had always been repressive and unpopular, but few observers expected him to leave his capital as quickly as he did in the face of street protests in 1979.

The Islamic *cordon sanitaire*, so assiduously cultivated during the closing stages of the Cold War, was ostensibly meant as a line of defence against the spread of Communism in Western and South Asia. That strategy has never received the criticism it deserved, either after the rogue behaviour of Saudi and Pakistani-sponsored mujahedeen groups in Afghanistan, or after the outrages of 11 September 2001, organized by named CIA-trained operatives. Similarly, Washington has only itself to blame for the regime that emerged in Iran in the aftermath of the Shah's departure. At that time, Iran's traditional religious hierarchy based on Qom was considered as 'a second line of defence', should the Shah go under. After the revolution, such claims could not be verified, as the groups that occupied the US Embassy publicly *burned* the files they came across, rather than publicize their contents. Far from accepting being fielded as the B-team, Iran's mullahs reached out and claimed state power for themselves. They have not been forgiven.

Iran has since lived in a world of unrelenting American hostility. Among others, this enmity has produced open US (and European) support for Saddam Hussein's war against Iran during the 1980s. Western powers watched in deafening silence as Saddam's forces undertook missile attacks on Iranian civilian centres and used poison gas against Iranian infantry – as well as on dissident Kurdish population centres in Northern Iraq. The nerve-gas-production equipment was bought in the West. No one has owned up to selling these plants to Saddam, although it is rumoured that some of the equipment carried the emblem of a prominent German chemicals firm and that visiting Russian officials admired the quality of the machinery.

At present, Iran still labours under a 'sanctions' regime put in place by the USA. According to the US Energy Information Agency:[51]

the 1995 executive orders prohibit US companies and their
foreign subsidiaries from conducting business with Iran ...
virtually all trade and investment activities by US citizens in
Iran are prohibited and finally, US Iran–Libya Sanctions Act
(ILSA) of 1996 (renewed for five more years in July 2001)
imposes mandatory and discretionary sanctions on non-US
companies *investing* [my italics] more than $20 million annu-
ally in the Iranian oil and natural gas sectors.

Soon after the overthrow of the Shah, Iran had summarily
expelled foreign oil companies from her soil. Shortly afterwards,
the country was invaded by Iraq across Khuzestan, the oil-rich
province. Production quickly fell to a quarter of its peak of nearly
6 million barrels per day.

The slow but reasonably steady recovery after the war brought
Iranian production back up to nearly 4 million barrels per day
(~200 million tons per year). During these difficult decades, Iran's
oil and gas infrastructure has been starved of investment and new
technology. This is partly due to the war and its aftermath and in
part to US sanctions, but probably also to the indifferent quality
of their management and planning. Characteristic of an age with
fewer cars and more basic needs, Iran's largely unreconstructed oil
refineries still produce a heavier mix of products than most modern refineries and only 16 per cent automobile gasoline. The
country annually *imports* some 8–10 million tons of refined products, notably gasoline. More recently, Iran has been trying to
regain some lost ground in oil extraction, refinery capacity and
petrochemicals production. Before the election of President
Ahmadinejad, new legal frameworks had partially eased the entry
of foreign companies, and higher oil prices since mid-2004
brought in much-needed extra cash.

Despite being forced out of doing business in Azerbaijan under
American pressure, Iran has also attempted to take advantage of
its geographical position. Undeterred by efforts to isolate the
country economically, Iranian commentators have been producing a steady stream of suggestions for Iran's participation in
potential regional schemes for processing and transmitting the
Caspian Basin's hydrocarbon wealth: 'In the longer term, Iran
would like to become the hub for Central Asian pipelines.'[52]

Some of these proposals have been on the drawing-board for well over a decade.

Swapping oil with Iran?

Best known among these schemes are 'swap' agreements suggested to the oil producers of the Caspian.[53] Briefly, Iran's oil wells are mostly in the south, whilst in the north its has large urban centres, Tehran and Tabriz, as well as significant power generation and industrial capacity. The Iranian proposal involves oil deliveries by tanker to Iran's Caspian ports of Anzali and Neka. From there, the oil would be pumped to one of three refineries in the north. Together, the Tehran, Tabriz and Arak refineries can at present process somewhere between 500,000 and 650,000 barrels of oil per day, and there are plans to expand this to about 800,000 barrels per day (about 40 million tons annually).

In return for receiving Caspian crude in the North, Iran would sell Iranian crude on behalf of her Caspian suppliers, from oil terminals in the Persian Gulf. Due to lower export rates than in the past, the country has excess handling capacity in her Gulf ports. This way, Iran would save the expense of the northbound transit of her own oil and would charge a swap fee of between $1.5 and $2 *per barrel* of Caspian-owned oil put to sea. Some of these mechanisms have already been activated at low tonnage levels, with about 130,000 barrels per day of Russian, Turkmen and Kazakh oil being taken by tanker to Neka and piped to the Tehran refinery.[54]

Expanding this route would make economic sense. At present, the Kazakhs are paying transit fees that have gone up (in 2005) from $27 to $29.50 *per ton* for the privilege of pumping oil through the Caspian Pipeline Consortium line to Novorossiysk. With somewhere between seven and eight barrels in a ton, the CPC transit fee paid to reach the Black Sea comes to more than double the Iranian swap fee; and instead of Novorossiysk, the oil would be loaded in the Gulf, for a far shorter haul to East Asia. The Kazakhs must be wistfully looking over their shoulders. However, most of their oil production is tied up with US oil majors, who have already been in difficulty with the US Government and the American media over 'suspected' swap deals.

In a lengthy article seductively entitled 'What was Mobil up to in Kazakhstan and Russia?',[55] Simon Hersh takes the oil giant Mobil to task for participating in oil swap deals between the Kazakh and Iranian governments. The story, mainly told by two middlemen who complained they were frozen out of the proceeds, is laced with enticing hints of bribery in high places. Chevron's people are mentioned as telling US National Security Council officials that *Chevron's* 'hands were clean'. The article suggests that perhaps some of Mobil's employees might have been less than entirely vigilant in this respect. For our purposes, it suffices to know that it might have been legal for the Kazakhs to arrange oil swap deals with Iran, but that *any involvement* by US companies or personnel would have contravened US Federal Law. However, even in the less ideological days of the Clinton Administration, it appears that US government officials were not shy of leaning on *anyone* doing business with Iran. According to Hersh's article, an intermediary

> who was on a routine visit to Washington on behalf of the Kazakh government, was told by [Sheila] Heslin [then an official of the National Security Council-RK] that the Nazarbayev government would face huge political problems with Congress and the Administration if it did a swap with Iran. Giffen [the intermediary] quickly emphasized that it was Mobil, and not just Kazakhstan setting up the swap. When he was reminded that Mobil could not legally participate, he tried to reassure her, according to the official, that Mobil was '... smart. They'll do it through a European trader'. [Giffen denies making the statements.][56]

Iran is having similar problems with US policy in South Asia. We have seen in Chapter IV how the delicate balancing act between India and Pakistan may yet earn Iran a lucrative contract for exporting gas to the subcontinent. However, in the spring of 2005, the US Secretary of State entered the fray (not for the first time), openly advising India to 'refrain from signing a pipeline deal with Iran'. Whilst publicly maintaining that India has ' ... no problems of any kind with Iran ... ',[57] Indian diplomats are rumoured to be advising Iran to comply with Western demands relating to her nuclear programme. It would be interesting to know whether a little reticence over the nuclear issue might gain the Indians some advantage during negotiations over the gas price. Meanwhile the 'New Kerala' website has reported that ' ... on her maiden visit to the Indian capital, [US Secretary of State] Rice held talks with [prime minister] Singh and discussed several issues, including regional security issues and the possible sale of F-16 fighter jets to neighbouring Pakistan'.[58]

Iranian gas to Armenia?

Yet another regional gas pipeline project is creating far greater echoes than its size would ordinarily have warranted. As part of improving their strategic cooperation with Armenia, the Iranians have signed an agreement to build a pipeline by 2007 to export 1.1 (eventually rising to 2.3) billion cubic metres of gas for power production. According to the contract, the gas would be paid for by electricity sold back to Iran.[59] The gas volumes involved are modest and the Iranians appear happy to finance the construction of the pipeline, expected to cost a total of $225 million. Work on the 42-km Armenian sector started in November 2004, financed by a $34 million loan provided by the Iranian Government. It all seems straightforward, with Iran extending a helping hand to an impoverished neighbour.

However, nothing concerning oil or gas is simple in the Caucasus. Until the inception of this contract, Gazprom had supplied all natural gas consumed in Georgia and Armenia. Furthermore, Russian companies nearly wholly own the electricity distribution network in Armenia, including the operating contract for the Metsamor nuclear power plant. A lease of the latter facility had been granted to Russia's Unified Energy Systems, in return for writing off the plant's US $40 million debt to Russian nuclear fuel suppliers.[60] To complicate matters, part of the gas Iran is proposing to sell to the Armenians may originate in Turkmenistan.

In a roundabout way, all this worries the Russians. Iran already imports some natural gas from Turkmenistan to supply the energy hungry north, since most of its (Iran's) gas reserves are in the south. The $190 million Korpedzhe–Kurt Kui system is the first

181

gas pipeline from central Asia that bypasses Russian territory, bringing 5–6 billion cubic metres p.a. from Turkmen fields into Iran.[61] With Turkmenistan's gas production potential in part held back due to low prices paid by the Russians, the threat to Russian gas purchases from Turkmenistan, as well as the threat to their gas sales to Armenia and Georgia, is far from imaginary.

The pipeline presently supplying Russian gas to Armenia through Georgia is the Georgian-*owned* trunk pipeline that the Russians have been trying to acquire in return for unpaid gas bills. The Georgians occasionally appear interested in reversing the flow and importing Iranian gas through the new Armenian connection with Iran. If – as planned – the Georgian network is connected to the Baku–Tblisi–Erzurum gas pipeline, which is scheduled to begin operating in the last quarter of 2006, the new Iran–Armenia line would effectively be connecting gas wells in Turkmenistan and Iran with the Turkish network, and the Turks have already signed a contract to connect their network with Greece and Italy.

Although the initial capacity of the Iran–Armenia line is small, the implications for potential Iranian competition for gas sales to Turkey in the first instance and to Western Europe in the longer term worries Gazprom. With disarming candour, Gazprom's Alexander Ryazanov was reported to say: 'If we [Gazprom] do not take part in the construction…no one knows where the gas will go … '. According to the same Armenian website, Gazprom ' … is extremely worried about … Iranian gas pipeline extension to Ukraine through Georgia and Black Sea. The emergence of a competitor in the European gas market may have extremely undesirable consequences for Gazprom …'.[62]

Iran and Russia may have a strategic understanding in efforts to moderate the power and influence of the USA in the region. However, Gazprom is alive to the possibility that Iran and Turkmenistan could provide a source of competition to Russian gas sales at levels far beyond Armenia's meagre needs. True to form, Gazprom is on the market to buy the Iran–Armenia gas pipeline:

> Armenian authorities avoid evaluations and clear answers … insisting … that they are not going to sell the pipeline to the

Russians. Still Vice Chairman of the Gazprom board Alexander Ryazanov once again stated on June 30th [2006] they plan to purchase the pipeline and complete its construction ... Iran is said to be reluctant to have the pipeline owned by the Russians.[63]

The betting seems to be that ' ... [Armenian President] Kocharian agreed with Russian President Vladimir Putin last year to hand the new pipeline's section on Armenian territory over to Gazprom via the ArmRosGaz Company, in which Gazprom and its offshoot Itera hold a combined 68 per cent interest'.[64] With the Iran–Armenia link officially opened and conducting tests, and weeks away from Armenian parliamentary elections, no one appears prepared to say who will operate the new pipeline.[65]

Whilst the Armenian and Iranian governments have discussed extensions of a possible gas line to third countries, 'the diameter of the pipeline currently under construction is smaller than was originally planned, making re-exports of Iranian gas highly problematic. The decision to limit its capacity is believed to have been taken under Russian pressure'.[66] Meanwhile, Iranians have glibly proposed to construct a second larger diameter line in a bid to explore further export prospects.[67] It must be said that the region's geopolitical alignments do not immediately suggest where a projected second line would go next, once it reaches Armenia.

Meanwhile, in early 2006, Armenia has been forced to sign for higher prices (from $54 to $110 per 1,000 cubic metres) for gas from Gazprom, who agreed to postpone the increase for three months until 1 April 2006. Armenian Prime Minister Andranik Markarian has ruled out fresh asset handovers, suggesting Armenia would not take any loans from Russia: '... we could borrow from the West and international organizations on much more favorable terms ... . Nor can we compensate for anything with assets. We would thereby sort things out only for one year.'[68] According to the same source, the Russian side was interested in an incomplete but modern thermal power plant ' ... as well as Armenia's entire gas pipeline network. The Hrazdan plant is currently being completed by a state-owned Iranian company that signed a $150 million investment agreement with the Armenian government last fall'.

It is not clear how Armenia's developing relationship with Iran is being viewed by the US Government. The USA is home to some 1.5 million ethnic Armenians and the relationship with Armenia is an intricate one. Armenia also provides Russia with her last military base south of the Caucasus and periodically engages in joint military exercises.[69] There have been gentle reminders from Washington that Armenia would have some room for manoeuvre, should she choose to edge a little closer towards the West. The tone compares favourably with US State Department pronouncements regarding other countries (e.g. Pakistan, India) considering business deals with Iran. Perhaps these contradictions need not be resolved, so long as the US–Russian relationship does not take on a yet more competitive edge in the Caucasus and the trans-Caspian basin, or on the larger world stage.

Within this complicated matrix, it does not seem geographically fanciful to design a conduit for pumping large quantities of gas from Turkmenistan and Iran, through Turkey into Southern and Central Europe, with a possible spur to Italy. The long heralded 'Nabucco' pipeline was meant to reduce European reliance on Russian gas – and was duly opposed by the Russians. Nabucco might also have carried some Caspian gas, but could not proceed without plentiful Iranian supplies. It has stalled in the face of resistance by the USA. An 'alternative' Nabucco project would have pumped Kazakh and Azeri natural gas to the West across Asia Minor, but would have required an expensive and politically troublesome trans-Caspian connection to Kazakhstan. However, the Azeris and Kazakhs, together, will *not* have an extra 30 billion cubic metres to export in the near future,[70] and anything less would not be worth building such a long pipeline for.

Not surprisingly, the plan is languishing. In March 2007, Hungarian gas trader Emfesz announced plans for the construction of a small pipeline from Ukraine, carrying an eventual 3.5 billion cubic metres of Russian gas to a new power station in the northeast of Hungary.[71] This was promptly followed by an announcement in the Bulgarian media that 'The execution of Nabucco gas pipeline project is halted because one of the participants, Hungary, decided to take part in an alternative energy project …'.[72] We were told, meanwhile that ' … Emfesz was established in

2003 by the Ukrainian Dmitry Firtash, who is the co-founder of RosUkrEnergo AG (Switzerland), Ukraine's sole natural gas provider since 2006'.[73] We have already come across RosUkrEnergo in Chapter V. It seems Gazprom has found yet another way of undermining the Nabucco project.

5 Across The Caspian: Finding a Way for Kazakh Oil

Simplifying a little, Kazakhstan principally exports oil and Turkmenistan primarily natural gas, although both countries would like to export more gas *and* more oil. The case of Uzbekistan is a little more complicated. The country consumes about 45 billion cubic metres of domestically produced gas. Their *declared* reserves are not far short of those in neighbouring Turkmenistan, although it is rumoured that the regime has been exaggerating the level of gas reserves. The country's main export commodity is cotton – not gas! The limited level of Uzbek gas exports may be due to the lack of outlets other than the Russian grid, coupled to the far lower price paid by Gazprom for Central Asian gas, always assuming the gas exists.

Taken as a whole, Central Asian resources are even more land-locked and farther from market than those of Azerbaijan. Both Turkmenistan and Kazakhstan export small amounts of oil to Iran, and Turkmenistan a small amount of gas. However, until the opening of the Atasu–Alashankou pipeline to China (Chapter VII), nearly all Kazakh oil exports were pumped through Russian territory, whilst nearly all Turkmen gas is similarly exported to Russia – to be resold by the Russians.

Exporting Kazakh oil

Of all the Central Asian republics, Kazakhstan has the closest ties with Russia. Six million of her 17 million people are ethnic Russians, mostly concentrated in the north, while less than 40 per cent of the population are ethnic Kazakhs. The country is mostly desert, sparsely populated and spread over 2.7 million km^2. Much of the present day oil and gas production is in three large onshore fields: Tengiz, Uzen and Karachaganak. The more recently discovered 'super-giant' offshore Kashagan field is still in the development phase, expected to come on stream initially with 75,000 barrels per day sometime in 2010, then quickly expected to increase to about half-a-million barrels. With further development, Kashagan may eventually pump over 1 million barrels per day – over three-quarters of present-day production.

The oilfields are mostly in the west of the country, on or near the Caspian rim, while most of the population and industrial centres are in the east and south-east. The two Soviet era refineries, Pavlodar in the north-east and Chimkent in the south-east, draw their crude oil from Western Siberia through Surgut and Omsk. According to a swap agreement with Russia, part of Kazakh oil goes to the refinery in Samara (Russia) in exchange. The rest of Kazak oil extracted in the west is pumped, either through the Atyrau (former Guriev)–Samara oil pipeline into the Russian system or through the Caspian Pipeline Consortium (CPC) line directly to Novorossiysk. Similarly, gas-producing areas in the west are not connected to consuming areas in the populous south-east. The former capital Almaty receives its gas supplies through a pipeline from Turkmenistan that comes across Uzbek territory. These arrangements date from Soviet times, when present-day international frontiers were simple administrative demarcation lines within the Union and all energy distribution plans had been optimized to serve the Union as a single unit.

It is not surprising, therefore, that after the break-up of the Soviet Union, Kazakhstan found herself hopelessly enmeshed in an energy infrastructure controlled by the Russian Federation. Similar difficulties have arisen with her electricity distribution grids. Worse, her main export commodities are the same as those of Russia, and the Russians control the transmission lines. In the mid-to-late 1990s, when oil prices and sales were slack, Transneft gave only limited and erratic access to Kazakh oil shipments from the Tengiz fields through the Atyrau (Guriev)–Samara line.[74] For access to Novorossiysk, the Kazakh quota was restricted to a mere 76,000 barrels per day.[75] Exasperated Chevron officials were forced to scale back their Kazakh investment programme.

We have shipped oil by train, barge, and pipeline … we have considered shipping it out by camel … Recently we completed a shipment from Tengiz to the Black Sea. First, we filled rail cars with oil at Tengiz and moved them to Aqtau on the Caspian. From there, the oil moved by barge across the Caspian to Baku, where a pipeline moved the oil to Ali Bayramli in Azerbaijan for reloading into rail cars, and then on to the port of Batumi on the Georgian Black Sea Coast. From there it moved by tanker out to the Mediterranean.[76]

During those difficult years, despite pressure from the US State Department, the Kazakhs entered into swap agreements with Iran that still continue at relatively low levels, perhaps 6 or 7 million tons per year. Kazakhstan also opened a small oil route to China, moving 1 million tons of oil by rail from Atasu to the Chinese border at Alashankou. The railway carriages have now been replaced by a 10-million-ton per year crude oil pipeline that could be upgraded to 20 million tons providing a sizeable new outlet for future Kazakh oil production (see Chapter VII). The project that really unlocked Kazakh exports, however, was the CPC line to Novorossiysk.

The CPC oil pipeline to Novorossiysk

The CPC was formed by 11 partners,[77] aiming to carry crude oil mainly from the Tengiz field (and some from Karachaganak) to the new tanker terminal of Yuzhnaya Ozerevka, near Novorossiysk. The Karachaganak and Kenkiyak spurs join the main CPC pipeline at Atyrau.[78] Completed in 2001, it cost $2.6 billion and was based on a refurbished Soviet era pipeline with a length of 1,575 km and an initial annual capacity of 28 million tons. From its inception, the system was designed with a potential (eventual) annual capacity of 67 million tons.

The transit fees for the CPC have risen from a rather expensive $27 to $29.50 per ton. Added to a projected capacity increase from 28 to 67 million tons announced in early March 2005,[79] the income Russia hopes to receive from the line appears substantial. Even so, the Russians slowed down the original project during the planning phase, among others, by delaying the granting of rights of way and other 'legal documents allowing pipeline construction through Russian territory'.[80] That, of course, was during a period of surplus oil on the markets.

Unlike the BTC project, the CPC line allows for the realization of all Russian policy aims in the region. With Transneft in charge as project operator and the pipeline passing into Russian territory, Russia retains overall control of the operation as well as taking a share of the surprisingly high transit and port fees. The announcement that the CPC line capacity will more than double comes just in time to thwart any ambitions to fill the Baku–Tblisi–Ceyhan line, with increasing production from Tengiz and Karachaganak. However, initial Russian calculations did not include the subsequent discovery of Kashagan, from which oil may be shipped using the BTC line. As we will see below, the Russians have also delayed the *approval* of the CPC enlargement project, partly blocking plans to expand production in Kazakhstan.

As an aside, it may be recalled that the Ukrainians were charging $5.20 per ton of Russian oil conveyed in the direction of Eastern Europe and $4.40 per ton for oil shipped to Odessa. Both Transneft and the Russian Government have insisted that the Ukrainian rates were punitively high. By way of comparison, the marginally longer CPC pipeline charges $29.50 per ton for conveying Kazakh oil to Novorossiysk. Even so, Transneft has complained of losses by the CPC and suggested that the only way to turn a profit for Russia would be to raise the transit fees to still higher levels.[81] It is likely that further rises would begin to price Kazakh oil out of world markets.

Meanwhile, decoding US policy for the region has not been difficult. As enunciated in 1998 by Bill Richardson (US Department of State), it reads as ' … freeing Central Asian and Caucasus states from overdependence on Russia, continuing to isolate Iran, and weaving Central Asia and the Caucasus into the fabric of the international economic and political system … '.[82] It seems clear that, in this region at least, a low-level locking of horns between the USA and Russia has been quite deliberately put in place and that the BTC line is part of that project.

The Kazakhs are thus a little uncomfortably wedged between the two giants. They have trod gingerly and so far avoided coming to permanent harm, as happened in Georgia and Azerbaijan. Nevertheless, the large Russian minority in the country is dissatisfied with the Government's low-key, undeclared de-Russification policy. They make their voices heard through several nationalist groups of variable virulence: ' ... they desire dual citizenship with Russia, a privatisation policy that does not favour Kazakhs, and that the official state language be Russian . . .'.[83] So far, the Kazakhs have avoided both the loss of the north through civil war and the mass departure of the Russians, the relatively skilled element of the population.

Unlike the trans-Caucasian republics, Turkmenistan, Kazakhstan and Uzbekistan have entered the post-Soviet era with their Communist Party First Secretaries firmly in charge. While the loss of Soviet subsidies affected their economies adversely almost overnight, no great shocks were visited on the political structures of the three countries during the transition. Indeed, over 15 years later, the same cast of characters are nearly all in place. The death of Niyazov in December 2006 has not led to visible political changes. It must be assumed that the three groups in power knew how to talk to Moscow and had a well-developed sense of just how far they could diverge from the centre's will, without provoking cataclysmic interventions: 'Nazarbayev insisted in Moscow ... that Kazakhstan and Russia were energy partners, not competitors. Kazakhstan remained committed ... to exporting a major share of its energy resources via Russian pipelines . . . .'[84] In the Caucasus, the hapless Gamsakhurdia would not have known where to begin and by the time Aliev and Shevardnadze had been installed in Baku and Tblisi, respectively, the damage had already been done.

The CPC agreement may thus be viewed as a Kazakh concession to Russian ambitions in the region. They accepted that they would need to place at least one major export pipeline through Russia, whilst looking for additional export routes. The Chinese option is being developed slowly but steadily. The other major Kazak options involve hooking up to the BTC line through tankers or a trans-Caspian pipeline connection, or, indeed, reaching the open seas through Iran.

Interestingly, US-based observers are not unaware of the *economic* wisdom of establishing energy transport corridors through Iran:

The United States has a major long term interest in securing energy routes from the Caspian Basin through Iran, and indeed all adjacent states, and ultimately seeing Iraq and Iran fully develop their oil and gas resources for one basic reason – maximum access and production in the region will help to ensure that future energy demand can be met at moderate prices. Furthermore, if the benefits from increased energy production are shared in a relatively equitable manner, political accommodation and hence stability could be attainable.[85]

In this region, politics tends to trump economic and technical considerations every time. It seems safe, furthermore, *not* to expect a rapid Iran–US political accommodation. If Georgia is able to maintain its present posture, a looped (i.e. parallel *second*) BTC line would not be inconceivable within the coming decade. In the short term, however, the amount of Kazakh oil available for tankering across the Caspian Sea does not appear to be much greater than some 7–10 million tons p.a.[86]

6 Gas From Turkmenistan: Russian Friends and Russian Foes

Turkmenistan covers nearly half a million square kilometres, inhabited by less than 5 million people. It has a relatively homogeneous population, over 70 per cent of who are Sunni Turkmens. Nearly 80 per cent of the country is covered by the Kara Kum desert: 'Agriculture, especially cotton cultivation, remains the country's major source of employment, and most agricultural workers continue to live on Soviet-era collective farms.'[87]

Apart from pipeline connections, which we shall discuss, Turkmenistan is less intimately entangled in Russian infrastructure, compared to Kazakhstan or Uzbekistan. It has no common border and only a small Russian minority to worry about. The Turkmens share common ethic origins with the Turks of Turkey and Azeris, from whom they are separated by divergent historical evolutions and political traditions. Historically an impoverished Russian (and later Soviet) backwater, Turkmenistan is culturally closer to Iran, where, as late as the nineteenth century, Turkmen tribesmen carried out most of their plundering and slaving raids. An element of competition is unavoidable, as Iran itself is potentially a natural-gas-exporting country. However, Turkmenistan has been largely inhibited by US diplomatic pressure from engaging in what would otherwise have constituted a natural progression of relationships with Iran.

Like Uzbekistan, Turkmenistan is not quite a natural gas giant,[88] but it has sizeable reserves, developed during Soviet times and directly connected to the Soviet-era Central Asia-Centre (CAC) gas pipeline system, constructed in stages between 1960 and 1974. Since 1992, the Russian sector of the network is owned and operated by the reorganized state monopoly Gazprom. The combined capacity of the CAC system is currently estimated at 90 billion cubic metres per year.[89] At independence, this configuration left no alternative for Turkmenistan but to continue selling gas to Russia.

Ideally, the Turkmens would have preferred to pay Gazprom a transit fee and sell gas to European customers, who are known to *pay*, and to pay far higher prices than Gazprom. However, Gazprom would not expect to carry competing gas through its pipelines to 'her' lucrative European gas markets. Furthermore, Gazprom was (and is) in need of gas from Turkmenistan's Daulatabad and Yashlar gas fields, which have lower well-head costs, to meet Russia's domestic needs.[90] Cheap Turkmen gas serves to make up for low-priced, state-regulated Russian domestic gas sales. More expensive 'Russian' natural gas from the Tazovskiy and Yamal peninsulas, near the Arctic Circle, can then be pumped to the higher-priced European market (currently 140 billion cubic metres). What is not often mentioned is the possibility that some of the Siberian fields might begin to run out of gas. Simmons has suggested that the Russians need Turkmen gas to replace falling production in the now mature Urengoi field, which peaked at 304 billion cubic metres in the 1980s and is now nearer the 140 billion cubic metres mark.[91] However, the Russians are building more pipelines connecting the region with Europe, which suggests that they, at least, think there is more gas in this region.

In the years after independence, President Niyazov could have been excused for feeling squeezed on all sides, as Turkmen delegations negotiating with Gazprom were 'made up of former senior members of the Soviet gas industry':

> By 1993, President Niyazov was becoming highly suspicious of the motivation of those in Turkmenistan's gas industry. One of the first to go was former Deputy Prime Minister and Minister of Oil and Gas Nazar Soiunov who in the early days of independence traveled abroad seeking potential investors in Turkmenistan's gas industry. Soiunov now lives in exile in Moscow.[92]

As if to say 'things could get worse', in the early 1990s, Gazprom claimed to have sold Turkmen gas to Armenia and Ukraine, who had consistently been in arrears with their gas bills since independence. The Russians cheerfully transferred some of the unpaid Armenian and Ukrainian gas bills to Turkmenistan at a time when the country was borrowing on international markets to finance its current account deficit. At that stage, the Turkmens found no reason to export gas that no one would pay them for. By 1994, production dropped to nearly half the peak production rate in 1993. It dipped further in 1997–8, when Turkmenistan cut off gas supplies to Ukraine and produced only what they needed for domestic consumption, some 10–15 billion cubic metres. It does seem that during these difficult years, Gazprom treated Turkmenistan rather roughly:

> By the spring of 1997, Ukraine owed Turkmenistan 450 million dollars for its gas shipments ... when Russia decided not to sell Turkmen gas on European markets, the Gazprom chief said he would promise to do what he could to keep the Turkmenistan population from 'starving to death'... in dealings with Gazprom, Niyazov commented that he 'smelled old Soviet ambitions'.[93]

Turkmenistan's links with Iran[94]

The world into which Turkmenistan was released at independence was still dominated by Russia, with Yeltsin at the helm and apparently unwilling to give up the desire for dominance over Russia's 'near abroad'. Niyazov looked for alternative alliances to help his country drift away from Russia's outer orbit. Kazakhstan in the north and Uzbekistan in the east were struggling with the effects of sudden cuts in subsidies from Moscow. In the south-east, the Red Army had withdrawn from Afghanistan, where *mujahedeen* factions sponsored by a constellation of foreign intelligence services continued to fight each other with undiminished dedication. Finally, the Turkmens could have hooked up to the Baku–Tblisi–Erzurum gas pipeline, then only in its early stages of inception. The latter alternative would have required constructing a trans-Caspian gas pipeline, from Turkmenbaşi on the Eastern Caspian shore to Baku. Niyazov had consistently rejected this alternative, because it contradicted his own vision of how sovereign rights should be apportioned and regulated in the Caspian. The only other neighbour with whom the Turkmens could have done business was Iran.

For Iran, a closer relationship with Turkmenistan promised useful swap agreements and access to the potentially lucrative Turkish market. The more remote prospect of reaching Europe through Turkey would have put both Iran and Turkmenistan on the map as competitors to Gazprom. Iran therefore would have considered the 6 billion cubic metres Korpedzhe (on the Caspian shore of Turkmenistan)–Kurt-Kui line as a useful first step. Much of the line was funded directly by Iran, with the Turkmen debt to be repaid by gas deliveries. For Iran, a new line linking gas fields in the south (of Iran) to the populous and industrial north-west would have cost far more than the Korpedzhe–Kurt-Kui pipeline.[95]

A rail link was also established at about the same time between Meshed (in Iran) and Tedzhen (in Turkmenistan). A little optimistically, it was estimated that in the first year the line would carry 2 million tons of freight and half-a-million passengers. Meanwhile, in 1996, the Turks and Iranians signed an agreement to proceed, in principle, with the planning of a 56-in gas pipeline, annually carrying 28 billion cubic metres, 65 per cent of which was intended for Turkish consumption and the rest for export to the European mainland. The project was then estimated to cost between $1.6–2.5 billion.

According to O. Roy,[96] ' ... during his trip to Washington in May 1998, Niyazov unsuccessfully battled to have the Turkmenistan–

Iran–Turkey pipeline excluded from the ILSA [Iran–Libya Sanctions Act]'. A subsequent attempt by Shell to put together a project that would extend over 3,000 km from the Turkmen fields to Eastern Europe, the Nabucco project, has similarly withered on the branch, in the face of opposition from Washington. It appears that former US Secretary of State Alexander Haig had organized the first discussions about this project, back in 1993. Niyazov finally withdrew from the Turkmen–Iran–Turkey gas pipeline 'when it became clear that continued US opposition to projects involving Iran would not get international funding'.[97]

One final vestige of the larger project remains alive. The Turkey–Iran pipeline connection has been completed and Turkey has started taking small amounts of gas. However, the Turkish Government has been in negotiations to reduce the gas price and has been intermittently halting purchases to reinforce the point. Iran returned the courtesy by cutting off supplies during the desperately cold winter of 2005–6. According to the contract, by 2010, Turkey is expected to take-or-pay for 10 billion cubic metres of natural gas, part of which is understood to originate in Turkmenistan.

The trans-Afghan pipeline

From the start, President Niyazov of Turkmenistan appears to have favoured an alternative pipeline, proposed first by Bridas of Argentina back in 1991 and then by Unocal. Its history has been described in patient detail by Ahmed Rashid in his book *Taliban*[98] and by Olcott.[99]

Briefly, the project was originally promoted by Carlos Bulgheroni of Bridas. It involved a 1,400-km-line from the Dauletabad fields in South-east Turkmenistan, crossing about 450 km of Afghan territory and ending at the pipeline hub near Multan in Pakistan. Extending the line to India would make economic sense. The cost of the line, initially estimated at $1.9 billion, was later revised to about $2.5 billion. In 1996, Bridas's plans had reached an advanced state when Niyazov decided to undertake the same project with Unocal and Delta Oil of Saudi Arabia. The Argentineans were bundled out of Turkmenistan, leaving behind a pile of contracts torn up by the Turkmen Government, for which

Bridas has been suing both them and Unocal in Texas courtrooms ever since. Notwithstanding the pending law suits, in 1997, Turkmenistan and Pakistan signed with Unocal and Delta Oil for a line carrying 20 billion cubic metres to Multan in Pakistan, with a possible extension to the Indian distribution system.

Strangely missing at these gatherings were representatives of the Government of Afghanistan. The Taliban in Kabul appear to have taken umbrage at being offered a transit fee of $0.15 per million BTU (about $5.4 per 1,000 cubic metres), without prior consultation. More to the point, they could hardly have offered security guarantees for the enterprise in the middle of a civil war with the Northern Alliance and General Dostum's Uzbeks, even if they controlled – at that point in time – the particular tract of land through which the pipeline was expected to pass. It seems difficult to comprehend how anyone could seriously have planned the construction of a natural gas pipeline through the chaos of Afghanistan. Speculating for a moment, the discernible attraction of the project for Niyazov could have been the participation of a large American company (Unocal), with the concomitant benefit of a little backing from Washington.

Amazingly, Unocal appears to have negotiated with Taliban officials as the legitimate government of Afghanistan, with visits back and forth between half-destroyed Kabul and Unocal offices in Texas and California. As Ahmed Rashid's book suggests, officials in the Clinton's administration tacitly approved these negotiations until the Al Qaeda attacks on two US Embassies in East Africa. After 1998, Unocal had to pull back, leaving the Gazprom network as the only outlet for the bulk of Turkmen gas.

Back to work with Russia

The late Nihat Erim, a politician of modest talent in mid-twentieth-century Turkey, was once heard to reflect that 'This country [meaning Turkey] cannot function, without leaning on either America *or* on Russia'. Niyazov appears to have had some such predilection for great power patronage. Soon after Clinton's cruise missiles exploded in Sudan and Afghanistan in retaliation for the attacks on the two US embassies, Niyazov went back to work with

Russia. He had found no backing for a gas line through Iran to Turkey and there was no trans-Afghan pipeline in prospect. In 1999, he signed with the Russians to deliver gas to Ukraine and to Russia. No new gas-well developments were required to raise production to pre-1997 levels and the decrepit CAC-pipeline system was still in place ... just. By the year 2000, Turkmenistan was exporting nearly 35 billion cubic metres of natural gas. These agreements were made on the basis of Gazprom receiving a transit fee, for a gas sale between the Turkmen and Ukrainian gas companies. By 2003, the volume of Turkmen exports had risen to 42 billion, when Turkmenistan and Gazprom signed a new, comprehensive contract.

What Gazprom did in 2003 was to draw in Kazakhstan, Turkmenistan *and* Uzbekistan into one massive contract. By the year 2010, Gazprom needs 100 billion cubic metres of Central Asian gas, bought on favourable terms, to maximize profits from their European gas export trade. The contract committed the Turkmens to ramp production to 60 billion cubic metres by 2007, 70 billion by 2009, eventually reaching a ceiling of 80 billion cubic metres per year. Kazakhstan and Uzbekistan have committed to selling about 10 billion cubic metres each. The *Asia Times Online* headline on 12 April 2003 said it all: 'Russia Gains Big in Central Asian Gas Game'. Taken together, the agreements represented a giant step toward developing a unified gas system across Central Asia, with a price structure that suited Gazprom.[100] In 2005, Gazprom paid $42 for 1,000 cubic metres of Uzbek gas. For 2006, they agreed to pay Uzbekistan $60,[101] while exporting to Europe at $255 per 1,000 cubic metres.

The conditions to which President Niyazov put his signature in 2003 could not have been to his liking. The gas was priced at $44 per 1,000 cubic metres,[102] with *only half* the price paid in cash and the rest in kind, as pipes, compressors and other supplies for the gas sector. All concerned appear to think they lose out in these barter deals. Ashgabat estimated they were receiving, in effect, about $36–7 for their gas, after 'factoring-in market prices of Russian barter supplies to Turkmenistan'.[103] The contract was meant to run until 2028, although the price was to be renegotiated in 2006–7. In January–February 2005, the Turkmens again complained about the low price. At that stage, the Russians were refusing to talk about a new pricing structure '... before 2006'. When President Niyazov reduced gas supplies, however, Alexey Miller turned up in Ashgabat in person and agreed to pay $58 per 1,000 cubic metres on a straight cash basis (April 2005).

Elsewhere, this move was widely seen as Russia pre-empting Ukraine by signing up (yet again) *all* possible Turkmen gas production. For a while, Turkmenistan had not been particularly interested in selling to Ukraine, with President Niyazov accusing '... Ukraine of not fulfilling the barter part of an accord on payment ... failed to supply 60 million dollars worth of goods in 2004 ... '.[104] Later, however, Niyazov tried to improve on the price paid to Turkmenistan by Gazprom ($44 per 1,000 cubic metres) by negotiating directly with Ukraine. Even after Gazprom had agreed to pay $58, it appeared, Gazprom or their Swiss subsidiaries would be making a substantial profit by selling Turkmen gas to Ukraine at $95 per 1,000 cubic metres. The only loser from the deal would have been the Turkmenistan treasury. However, there was scant evidence that the proceeds ever reached the state treasury anyway. *Global Witness* has suggested that large portions of the gas revenue 'resides' in offshore bank accounts and that nearly 75 per cent of state spending in Turkmenistan takes place off budget.[105]

At $58, Niyazov was still clearly dissatisfied with the Russian gas price. Attempts to restart negotiations on the trans-Afghan pipeline in 2004–5 were led by the ubiquitous Unocal (by then acquired by Chevron-Texaco) and encouraged by the US State Department, anxious to draw Indian and Pakistani attention away from the Iran–Pakistan–India pipeline project. Gazprom reacted sharply, suggesting Turkmen reserves were insufficient to service both their contract as well as a future trans-Afghan pipeline. At the other end of the ill-fated trans-Afghan pipeline, India raised similar objections, as did the Asian Development Bank, that there was simply not enough Turkmen gas.[106]

With negotiations over the Myanmar–Bangladesh–India pipeline in abeyance due to Bangladeshi indecision, and talks on the Iran–Pakistan–India pipeline stalled (during 2005–6), officials in Pakistan and India could have been forgiven for thinking they needed another option. *Talks* about the trans-Afghan pipeline were therefore kept alive for a while longer and India was reported to be preparing to participate.[107] At that stage, some observers interpreted the new approach by Delhi as code by Murli Deora, the new Indian Petroleum Minister, for drawing away from the Iran–Pakistan–India pipeline. As the war in Uruzgan, Helmand and Kandahar provinces increased in ferocity, however, the project gradu-ally fell away from the agenda – no doubt to surface another day.

The only chink in Gazprom's armour in securing *all* of Central Asia's gas production for its own purposes has appeared fairly late in the perennial contract-signing game between President Niyazov and Alexey Miller. In January 2006, several news agencies reported that Turkmenistan had entered into negotiations with a 'powerful Chinese delegation' for constructing a 30 billion cubic metres gas pipeline to China. The Chinese delegation was visiting Ashgabat in the run-up to Niyazov's landmark visit to China in Spring 2006:

> The package ... could include establishment and modernization of oil and gas exploration and extraction facilities and supply of related technology and equipment. In addition ... China has offered to set up a silk fabric production facility and a velvet weaving plant in Turkmenistan.[108]

It is, of course, early days yet, but the Russians might well need to point out, *again*, that their contracted purchases for the next 25 years cover all known recoverable Turkmen gas reserves. Although the Chinese deal was meant to be some years away, however, the Chinese negotiations appear to have worked a treat! Gazprom CEO Miller's visit to Ashgabat in September 2006 ended with a victory of sorts for the Turkmens. Gazprom agreed to pay $100 per 1,000 cubic metres for three years, starting with 2007. 'First of all, we will be supplying gas to Russia', Niyazov was quoted as saying with commendable loyalty: 'Do not think that Turkmenistan wants to go elsewhere with its gas.'[109]

At the other end of the pipeline, incoming Ukrainian Prime Minister Yanukovych was forced to accept paying Gazprom $130, amid doubts about RosUkrEnergo, rampant corruption in high places and pointed questions from Yushchenko's former Prime Minister Yulia Tymoshenko.

7 Who Wins and Who Loses in Eurasia?

The BTC and its implications

As elsewhere, politics in Eurasia deals as much with perceptions as it does with realities. Looking at the overall picture, the much-heralded BTC pipeline, in itself, deserves relatively little attention, on a par with low-level western military assistance to the countries of the region. The moves that have really mattered for Georgia and Azerbaijan have been the Russian thrusts aimed at breaking up the two countries. These moves have left both Georgia and Azerbaijan struggling and with little incentive to stay within the Russian security orbit. As a consequence, the Kremlin's interventions in both countries in the 1990s now appear inept and damaging to long-term Russian interests. If attention spans in Washington turn out to be as short as they have been in Afghanistan, Georgia and Azerbaijan could still be dragged back into the fold through military intimidation and energy arm-wrestling. In this sense, western investment in the BTC pipeline is viewed by Georgia and Azerbaijan as a sign of more permanent commitment to the region.

Within this context, it is as well to dispel one misunderstanding that seems to have preoccupied some observers, including several UK-based 'experts'. Opponents of the BTC line, including pro-Russian and pro-Iranian commentators, have frequently argued that the BTC line was aiming in the 'wrong' direction. Much simplified, the argument runs as follows. Mostly, the expansion in crude oil consumption is taking place in east Asia. Increased flows of oil must, therefore, aim towards the East. The BTC line does not do that (so the argument goes). To go east from Ceyhan, tankers would need to pass though the Suez Canal, the straits of Bab-al-Mandab and then head east. It would be quite impractical. Far better, runs the argument, to send the oil through Iran and out through the Gulf and the Straits of Hormuz.

As a criticism of the trajectory of a single pipeline, the argument is specious. The BTC line is intended to carry a maximum of 1 million barrels a day. By comparison, Saudi Arabia alone produces somewhere between 8 and 9 million barrels a day, a large proportion of which is shipped daily to the east via the Straits of Hormuz. Iran herself ships out over 2 million barrels a day through the same channel, and we have not yet counted in the UAE and Kuwait and, of course, Iraq. Within this framework, switching an extra million barrels a day eastward from Hormuz and picking up oil from Ceyhan for Western Mediterranean refineries is a sizeable but routine operation. Depending on the level of pipeline charges, it might also cut transport costs. There is therefore little need for comparing 'eastward flows' versus 'westward flows' with respect to piping 50 million tons a year. In the greater scheme, it is a minor amount of oil. The real point at issue is that the Iranian route is based probably on sounder economic judgement, whilst US policy has aimed to ignore the economic argument and isolate Iran. In this sense, the BTC line is deliberately designed to bypass Iran, as well as Russia, a point keenly felt by Moscow's and Tehran's analysts.

Going East or going West?

In Central Asia, the oil rich Kazakhs have made their choice. After much wiggling in the little extra space they had gained for themselves as a post-Soviet republic, they seem to have found they had no real alternative but to stay with the Russians. The Turkmens, who could not be faulted for effort, have similarly failed to find alternative outlets. After the Andijan massacre and the accompanying opprobrium in the West, Uzbekistan has similarly committed to aligning herself with Russia and, incidentally, also with China, through the Shanghai Cooperation Organization. Significantly, America's definitive failure in Central Asia was announced not in Moscow but during a meeting in Astana, the capital of Kazakhstan: 'An alliance of Russia, China and Central Asian nations called for the US and coalition members in Afghanistan to set a date for withdrawing from member states, reflecting growing unease over America's regional military presence.'[110]

Washington's political thrust has thus matched neither the economic muscle provided by western oil companies, nor the substance and persistence of the Russian effort to maintain their grip on the region. America's much vaunted strategic penetration into the region has turned out to be half-hearted. In fairness, the USA could not have gate-crashed the Caucasus and Central Asia without a concentration of diplomatic, financial and possibly military resources that it was never prepared to mobilize. In any case, neither the political geography of the region nor the nature of local political reflexes would have allowed an easy fit. The disastrous dialogue of the deaf with Uzbekistan is a case in point.

It is also doubtful whether the USA had any intention to confront the Russians in such a provocative way and on such a wide front. Judging by the consequences of their actions, it seems that all they ever intended was to gather a little of the low-hanging fruit in this vast and not very fertile Russian garden. In the end, their efforts have amounted to befriending Georgia and Azerbaijan, and to drawing Azeri and some Kazakh crude through the BTC pipeline. The promise of rewards in Iraq and her spectacularly rich oil and gas reserves appears to have been far more alluring.

The Russian monolith

In Chapter V, we discussed alternative trans-Balkan oil-pipeline strategies. The Russian handling of the problem suggests that they are far better prepared than before for the equally competitive but far subtler post-Soviet environment. Despite the commissioning of the BTC pipeline and the presence of foreign oil companies in Azerbaijan and Kazakhstan, it is useful to note that Russia remains the dominant power in this region. Of late, it has forced the hand of US-based companies in Kazakhstan to lobby Washington in favour of a Bourgas–Alexandroupolis pipeline:

> If built, [the Bourgas–Alexandroupolis] pipeline will become, in effect, a prolongation of the Caspian Pipeline Consortium's (CPC) line ... Proceeding with Burgas-Alexandropolis and a commitment to its use by Western companies in Kazakhstan is a Russian precondition to the planned enlargement of the CPC pipeline from Kazakhstan ... The US, European, and Kazakh oil companies face production delays and financial losses because Russia has blocked that pipeline's capacity expansion in the last three years. To allow that expansion,

Moscow wants those companies to export their oil from
Kazakhstan through Russia, as opposed to exporting it across
the Caspian and the South Caucasus to the open seas.[111]

The CPC line is controlled by Transneft and the Bourgas–
Alexandroupolis line will be 51 per cent owned by Transneft,
GazpromNeft and Rosneft. With the Kremlin fully in charge and
the giant state-owned companies securely in harness, Moscow is
increasingly turning the energy tool into a powerful weapon in
Eurasia, as well as in Eastern and Central Europe.

Meanwhile, in the south of the region, US policy could have
made a profound difference on the regional chessboard by engaging with Iran, the idle hinge! Natural gas from Turkmenistan and
Iran *could* have flowed to Europe through Turkey! Azeri, Kazakh
(and a little Turkmen) oil *could* have flowed to the Gulf, providing the global market with a large consignment of cheaper oil and
Iran with a profitable trade. Through Iran, the West could have
effectively influenced the cultural and political evolution of
Eurasia. Furthermore, the Iran–Pakistan–India gas pipeline project could have gone ahead without the protagonists constantly
looking over their shoulders. With Washington having failed to
find an accommodation with Iran, the region has been deprived of
alternative outlets and the Russians have been allowed yet
another opportunity to reassert their influence in Central Asia,
along the axes of their creaking oil and gas pipelines.

Chapter VII

Oil and gas transmission in East Asia: The options

Few people who knew China in the 1930s, or even in the 1960s, would have imagined that she could ever become the second largest crude-oil consumer in the world. In the past decade, China has also joined neighbouring Japan and Korea as a major importer of oil. All three countries have potential supply problems. Nearly 50 per cent of China's oil imports (149 million tons crude plus products in 2004, 168 million in 2006)[1,2] are shipped from the Middle East, whilst for Japan and Korea,[3] the share of Middle Eastern oil is nearer 80–90 per cent. Given the state of the Middle East and the vulnerability of shipping through the Straits of Hormuz and Malacca, the three East Asian majors require alternative energy sources and supply routes.

The picture for natural gas is more complex. Japan, South Korea[4] and China (Taiwan) already account for nearly 80 per cent of all traded LNG. Much of it comes from Australia, Indonesia, Malaysia and Brunei, with a smaller share from Oman and Qatar. Mainland China, on the other hand, has been constrained by the high cost of LNG, which Taiwan, Korea and Japan have been willing to pay. We will see below that China has been looking for more cost-effective ways of boosting gas utilization, without altogether discarding the LNG option. Clearly, the economic well-being of all three countries depends crucially on the cost and security of future energy imports. In fact, they might have a possible solution to their problems tantalizingly close to home. Nearby East-central Siberia and Sakhalin Island are home to oil and gas reserves that could potentially provide an excellent fit.

For the Russians, the formidable dynamism of East Asia conjures up a worrying contrast to the vast, untouched and economically stagnant but resource-rich emptiness of Eastern Siberia. It is at once a position of strength and one of weakness. How will they move? This chapter completes our survey of energy transmission along the Russian periphery and outlines some East Asian perspectives regarding access to energy supplies, describing the region's existing and possible future links with Central Asia, Siberia, the Pacific Ocean and the Barents Sea.

1 Russia's Uncut Diamonds: Irkutsk, Yakutsk and Sakhalin

The Irkutsk basin, in the East-central Siberian plateau, is the first of the potentially hydrocarbon rich areas to consider. Hydrocarbon extraction in the Yakutsk basin, further to the north-east, requires transmission through permafrost. On Sakhalin Island, most onshore hydrocarbon reserves have already been depleted, and current exploration and production is mostly taking place in the cold, deep waters offshore.

Irkutsk and Yakutsk

The hydrocarbon resources of the Irkutsk basin have not yet been fully explored and resource estimates vary widely. One estimate puts 'confirmed' reserves at between 8 and 11 billion barrels of oil and about 2 trillion cubic metres of natural gas. Intriguingly, *confirmed* reserves are thought to represent perhaps less than 5 per cent of existing resources.[5] A more generous estimate was provided by the *New York Times*:[6] 'Russia has as much as 67 billion barrels of untapped oil reserves along the [East Siberian] pipeline route.' While future exploration is thus expected to increase proven reserves, there is relatively little regional *production* taking place. Even the refinery near Angarsk, the capital of Irkutskaya

Oblast, receives *Western* Siberian crude oil, supplied by pipeline from the hub at Taishet, 570 km to the northwest.

Expectations are also high regarding the hydrocarbon reserves of the Yakutsk basin. Once again, exploration is far from complete. Operation and hydrocarbon transmission in the region requires working and constructing in permafrost, which is technically feasibly, but expensive. The 1,300 km trans-Alaskan oil pipeline, crossing similar terrain, cost a stupendous $8 billion in the mid-1970s. Taken together with estimated reserves in the Krasnoyarsk basin to the north-west, the oil and gas potential of this region is probably of staggering proportions. However, much work remains to be done to mobilize these hard-to-get resources, although the need to fill the East Siberia–Pacific Ocean pipeline (see below) has accelerated the exploration process along the pipeline route. In this respect, progress on Sakhalin Island is more advanced.

Sakhalin Island[7]

There are several oil and gas projects making progress offshore, primarily on the north-eastern shelf of the island. Of these, Sakhalin-I and Sakhalin-II have reached the field development (production) stage. The Sakhalin-I consortium includes Exxon Neftegas as the operating company, several Japanese companies,[8] Rosneft and India's ONGC Videsh,[9] with investment plans exceeding $12.8 billion.[10] Gas production began in September–October 2005 at a rate of 0.6 billion cubic metres and is expected to rise to over 2.5 billion cubic metres per annum. First, gas will go to regional utilities serving Komsomolsk-na-Amur and Khabarovsk City, through pipelines constructed by Rosneft across the island to the mainland. Eventual gas exports to China are being contemplated.

Oil production at Sakhalin-I is expected to rise from an initial 50,000 to about 250,000 barrels per day (~12 million tons per year). The construction of an oil pipeline bound for De Kastri on the Siberian mainland (near Khabarovsk) has been completed and exports by tanker have begun, using the 100,000-ton berths at De Kastri. The port is able to operate all year round, including during months when the Sea of Okhotsk surrounding Sakhalin Island is icebound.[11] In addition to the Chaivo field currently in production, the group's licences cover the offshore Odoptu and Arkutun Dagi blocks, awaiting development.

A consortium led by Shell, including several major Japanese companies, initiated the Sakhalin-II project.[12] This group developed an oilfield with associated gas, and a predominantly gas field with associated condensate and an oil rim.[13] First, oil was produced in 1999 and production to date has averaged at about 12–13 million barrels per *year*. It is estimated that there are 150 million tons of recoverable oil and 500 billion cubic metres of gas. Gas and oil from Sakhalin-II are being conveyed to shore and then pumped 800 km to Prigorodnoye at the southern tip of Sakhalin Island. Both the oil and LNG terminals have been completed.

Initial investment estimates for this project were about $10 billion. However, the novel technologies required by extreme climatic conditions and the doubling of steel prices since the launch of the project have led to cost overruns. To reduce its exposure, Shell signed a memorandum of understanding with Gazprom in July 2005, to exchange a 25 per cent share in the Sakhalin-II project for a 50 per cent share in the Zapolyarnoye–Neocomian oil and gas fields in the north of Western Siberia. The difference in the value of assets being exchanged requires Shell to come up with an extra $1 billion. What made the project particularly attractive for Gazprom was the fact that contracts for nearly the entire volume of natural gas to be produced had already been signed (see below).

By common agreement, Production Sharing Agreements (PSAs) signed by Russia during the early 1990s were advantageous to foreign investors. In addition to the major tax benefits built in to the contracts, Russia was to begin receiving its share of the profits only after the investors had recovered their costs. By their own admission, the Russians were infuriated when the Sakhalin Energy consortium declared that their costs had doubled – nearer the time when the swap deal with Gazprom was due to take place.[15]

These projects were, in any case, being realized against intense pressure from environmentalist groups, criticizing potential damage to grey whale and other wildlife habitats.

No one wants to take issue with the environmental community ... Royal Dutch Shell ... was forced to stop construction and then alter the main pipeline route for Sakhalin-II. It emerged the line was to pass through the 'feeding grounds' of grey whales, an endangered species.[16]

Nevertheless, in mid-2006, the Russian Federal Service for the Oversight of Natural Resources found numerous environmental violations by the Sakhalin-II project. The alleged infractions included illegal routing of an oil pipeline, mass fish and crab deaths in Aniva Bay, where LNG facilities were being constructed, and that toxic chemicals were being illegally released to the environment.

To the outsider, Russian officialdom would easily count among the worst environmental offenders on the planet. In late 2006, *both* Sakhalin-I and II projects have been threatened with the withdrawal of their operating licences. Similar warnings by the Prosecutor general's office to TNK-BP, over alleged environmental violations in the exploitation of the Kovykta natural gas field, have surfaced very soon after Gazprom expressed an interest in acquiring shares in the Kovykta project. Gazprom and TNK-BP had also competed for rights to build gas distribution networks in the Irkutsk region.[17]

It had also been reported in mid-summer 2006 that the Federal Tax Service had blocked the accounts of the Caspian Pipeline Consortium and proceeded to collect 4.7 billion roubles (about $175 million) in back taxes. The spin put on the news by *Kommersant* (Moscow) was intriguing: 'The tax difficulties of CPC signal that, in Russia, the sole route of shipping crude via pipelines that are not controlled by the state-run Transneft is in danger now.' The emerging pattern has sufficiently worried the US State Department to call on Russia to 'uphold [her] commitments on energy'.[18] Foreign Minister Lavrov was quoted on the Russian Foreign Ministry website as saying that his country is a 'long way from backing out of agreements we have reached, no matter how difficult the conditions were when they were agreed to'.

In a dispatch of 21 December 2006, Novosti reported that Gazprom had acquired '50 per cent plus one share' in the Sakhalin-II project for $7.45 billion. The price paid suggests that the Russians agreed to cost increases of nearly 50 per cent, but have *not* accepted that they had doubled. Neutral observers, *not* necessarily sympathetic to Russia, have independently suggested that the form of these PSAs left Russia vulnerable to inflated cost claims by the international oil companies. With the many tentacles of the Russian octopus acting in unison, however, foreign investors in Russia suddenly appear rather more exposed than they had expected to be.

2 Chinese Puzzle: From Where to Get Oil?

Media attempts to explain step increases in global oil prices since mid-2004 have saturated the public consciousness with stories of increased imports by 'countries such as India and China'. The figures tell a different story. An *exporter* of oil until 1993, China's imports have reached the 140–50-million-ton level over a period of 13–14 years. It is difficult to see how year-on-year increases in imports of 10–14 million tons by any single country would have had a dramatic impact on the markets. The case about Indian imports is even weaker; during 2000–4, Indian imports grew from about 70 to about 90 million tons (p.a.), a mere trickle by global standards.[19]

What we really need to keep an eye on is *global* demand, which has been rising steadily by about 1–2 per cent year-on-year. In retrospect, the fall in demand during the late 1990s now looks like a transient ripple due to the financial crisis in South-east Asia. Meanwhile, during the past decade or more, the oil industry has not been investing in new exploration and refining capacity at rates necessary to keep pace with increasing demand. Previous excess crude-oil production and refinery capacity has thus been swamped by slowly, steadily increasing world demand. We will discuss these factors in greater detail in Chapter VIII.

In the first decade of the new century, China's economy is being stimulated by some $40–60 billion p.a. in direct foreign investment. It is difficult to tell how long this flurry will last. Observers looking for spectacular jumps in Chinese fossil-fuel demand would best keep an eye on Chinese *coal* consumption projections, where truly large increases are expected, primarily for electricity generation. China's crude oil needs should probably increase at the present rates during the next five years, provided the present rate of external investment continues. Clearly, there must be an element of uncertainty. Meanwhile, the Chinese, like everyone else, need to guarantee their future energy supplies, and for *that*, like everyone else, they are investing abroad. It is a new development, but it is far from being an unusual move.

In recent years, China's state-owned China National Petroleum Company (CNPC) has acquired oil concessions in numerous countries,[20] including a few where political correctness would not have allowed some other investors to operate with an easy conscience. In Sudan, both the UN and the USA have been making ineffectual gestures in protest against pro-government forces openly massacring the civilian population of Darfour. The CNPC owns 40 per cent of the Greater Nile Petroleum Operating Company (GNPOC), the Sudanese oil consortium that produces about 15 million tons annually in the south of the country. Meanwhile, China has positioned herself as a major arms supplier to the government in Khartoum.[21] She is also working with Iran, with which the USA has been in open confrontation since 1979.

> In March 2004, China signed … to import 10 million tons of liquefied natural gas over a 25-year period in exchange for Chinese investment in Iran's oil and gas exploration, petrochemical and pipeline infrastructure … The US Central Intelligence Agency has submitted a report to US Congress stating that Chinese companies have 'helped Iran move toward its goal of becoming self-sufficient in the production of ballistic missiles'.[22]

Another state-owned Chinese company, ' … Sinopec [has also won a] contract for the development of Iran's Yadavaran oil field … November 2004 … may eventually produce 300,000 barrels per day'.[23] Despite the Iran–Libya act, Japan is also involved in a $2 billion development of Iran's Azadegan oilfield, which requires Japanese government funding.[24] After the election of the new Iranian president in 2005, however, there are media reports suggesting that Iran has torn up many of these contracts. Chinese acquiescence in reporting Iran to the Security Council in respect of nuclear weapons-related irregularities followed soon after these press reports.

The new Chinese thirst for oil has also found them in conversation about participating in Canadian tar sands conversion to synthetic oil, economically feasible at petroleum prices above about $20–5 per barrel: 'Sinopec also acquired a 40 per cent stake in Canada's Northern Lights oil sands project in May 2005, which is expected to produce around 100,000 barrels per day by 2010.'[25] These seem like small beginnings. The announcement by Enbridge Inc. of a memorandum of understanding with PetroChina, 'to cooperate on the development of the Gateway Pipeline ... project to transport 400,000 barrels per day of Alberta oil sands production from Edmonton, Alberta to a port on the west coast ...',[26] takes these projects one step further.

Meanwhile, there has also been talk of constructing a pipeline from Venezuelan oilfields, across Colombia, to a tanker port to be constructed on the Pacific coast. This would give easy access to carriers bound for China. The present security situation in Colombia makes this an unlikely proposition in the short term. The Chinese have also been signing agreements with Venezuela regarding ordinary oil sales. As Canada and Venezuela provide nearly a quarter of US oil imports, oil importers into the USA are nervous.[27] Meanwhile, the Venezuelan president Chavez, who is not happy with American policies, has visited Beijing with a view to selling oil:

> After all, how would Washington policymakers feel if [the] French Foreign Minister ... spent millions of euros in support of a domestic opposition in the US, whose stated goal was the removal of President Bush from office? ... just as many US public figures are demanding that their government reduce its imports of Middle East oil, so too are Venezuelans urging Chavez to reduce his country's traditional reliance on the US's oil consumption. Now that China is offering Chavez just that opportunity, the question is, will Washington tolerate a Sino-Venezuelan petro-pact or begin dusting off the Monroe Doctrine?[28]

For the time being, there are no cataclysmic changes in prospect. Venezuela has sold about 7 million tons of crude oil to China in 2005 and has signed an 11-million-ton contract in mid-2006. The

Venezuelans are also looking to expand their tanker fleet, using Chinese shipyards.[29]

Chinese expansion in the USA?

In 2005, the China National Offshore Oil Corporation (CNOOP) put forward an $18.5 billion bid to buy Unocal. It was a surprising move, blocked by the US Congress on grounds of national security. Unocal was instead sold for $16 billion to Chevron-Texaco. If nothing else, the episode provided China with a cogent response to US complaints that China only floats small percentages of the shares of their major corporations on the open market.

The Chinese have also been investing in oil and gas fields in Kazakhstan, where CNPC runs three exploration projects, four oilfields and two pipeline projects.[30] PetroChina and its parent company CNPC (China National Petroleum Corporation) have competed for the purchase of Calgary-based PetroKazakhstan against Lukoil of Russia and ONGC-Mittal Energy of India.[31] The CNPC bid was eventually successful; the Indians complained that they were not allowed to match CNPC's last-minute improved bid.[32]

The Siberian pipeline story

When a pipeline-based alternative is available, truck and rail transport are rarely used, because their costs are higher than pipelines. The difference in transport costs may at times be greater by as much as a factor of five.[33] In the absence of existing pipeline facilities, in 2004 the Russian Government confirmed its commitment to increasing Western Siberian oil exports to China by rail. The oil was to be shipped from the pipeline terminal at Angarsk to Daqing, the pipeline hub in North-east China. The Russian railways transported about 6 million tons of crude to China in 2004, nearly 8.5 million tons in 2005 and about 11 million tons in 2006. The figure quoted for 2007 was 11 million tons. This seems a relatively expensive way to buy oil, even if Russian railways apply a preferential tariff. For several years, China also imported about 1 million tons of crude oil annually from Kazakhstan by rail, over the Alashankou Pass (Dzungarian Gate), to the north of the Tien Shan range. In addition to limitations imposed by carrying capacity, Chinese crude oil imports from Russia and Kazakhstan by rail thus incur a cost penalty. The construction of the pipeline link parallel to the Atasu–Alashankou railway line, was completed in late 2005. It has an initial capacity of 10 million tons p.a.

Oil pipeline from Russia

Some time before Yukos was taken in hand by the Russian government, China had signed an agreement with them, approved by the Kremlin, to construct a 2,400-km-long oil pipeline from Angarsk to Daqing. In the absence of actual East-central Siberian production, the oil conveyed through this line was to be pumped from Western Siberian fields. The construction of the line was expected to commence in early-mid 2004, costing (estimates varied) between $2 and $3 billion. It was to have a capacity of between 20 and 30 million tons annually. Before the start of the project, however, the Russian Government moved in on Yukos, at once to eliminate a centre of alternative political power and, not least, to regain control of a major former state asset, 'privatized' during the colossal plunder of the Yeltsin years. The move was also in line with President Putin's aim of realigning the objectives of Russia's large private corporations more closely with those of the state. Meanwhile, despite prior Russian government approval, the Angarsk–Daqing pipeline deal was shelved.

As the Putin administration settled in, it became clearer that private energy companies in Russia would come under closer official control. However, the apparent demise of the Angarsk–Daqing project was partly connected with a competing Japanese proposal, for the construction of an oil pipeline to the Pacific Ocean.

3 A Pipeline for Japan: All Her Own?

The Japanese proposal was for a longer, larger (4,200-km, 122-cm diameter) and more expensive pipeline of 80 million tons capacity, running from Taishet north of Lake Baikal, circumventing Chinese territory and reaching Nakhodka, near Vladivostok. To make the offer more attractive, the Japanese initially offered about $5 billion of the (then) estimated $8–10 billion that the line was expected to cost. The Nakhodka outlet would have allowed all comers to bid for Siberian oil, including buyers from Japan, Korea and, indeed, the USA. It is likely, however, that the Japanese would have claimed some sort of primacy among equal bidders, for having contributed to financing some significant part of the project.

At the beginning of April 2003, the Russian Government was expected 'shortly' to decide which of the East Siberian pipeline options to adopt. By mid-2004, this decision had been postponed for another six months, awaiting 'the completion of ongoing studies'. Clearly, there were difficult choices to be made, not least regarding what to do with the standing commitment to the Chinese Government, to build the line to Daqing. *That* line would have been less costly and probably easier to complete than the line to Nakhodka. However, Putin's people were clearly reluctant to tie up a large pipeline investment for a single customer. From March to April 2004, periodic unofficial dispatches coming out of Moscow were affirming Russia's preference for a Taishet–Nakhodka line.

After prevaricating for nearly two years, it was announced on 28 December 2004 that the Russian Energy Ministry had submitted a draft resolution to the Government for constructing an 80-million-ton-capacity pipeline from Taishet, running through Kazachinskoye, Skovorodino and Khabarovsk to Perevoznaya (*not* Nakhodka), near Vladivostok. Two days later, the Prime Minister signed an ordinance to build the line to the Pacific. That should have been the end of the matter. But was it?

Tugging at pipelines

Japanese sources remained cautious. Partly, the reason had to do with the ambiguity of the Russian proposal. For one thing, the Kremlin had not provided a timetable. Secondly, it was announced that the pipeline would be filled only partly from Western Siberia (Tomsk region, the Khanty-Mansi autonomous district), and partly from yet-to-be-developed fields in the Irkutsk region and the Talakan field in Yakutia. Disagreements surfaced early on. Speaking

213

as Japan's visiting Foreign Minister, Nobutaka Machimura, listened, Industry and Energy Minister Victor Khristenko told his audience: 'Russia counts on getting loans that won't be linked to the purchase of Japanese equipment or technology.'[34]

Russo-Japanese negotiations progressed slowly over the capacity of the line, the amounts to be borrowed and conditions tied to the loans. All the while, Russian coffers were filling with the proceeds of rising oil prices, which had reached unprecedented heights in the middle of 2004. Meanwhile, Chinese disappointment and several high-level official visits in either direction during early 2005 appeared to have somewhat softened the impact of Russian decisions on Chinese ambitions. Moscow then began leaking news about the possibility of constructing a spur from the main line at Skovorodino to supply Daqing (see Figure 7.1). In April 2005, 'Moscow issued an order for the pipeline to be built from Taishet to the halfway point at Skovorodino near the Sino-Russian frontier, triggering worries in Tokyo that oil supplies might go to China first'.[35]

Under the headline, 'China to get oil before Japan: Russian envoy', the same *Japan Times* dispatch suggested that Japan's fears were compounded by the departing Russian ambassador to Beijing, Igor Rogachev. His speech, carried by the Interfax news agency, was worrying for the Japanese:

> China is our next-door neighbour, so the distance is very short [Rogachev said] From an economic point of view [supplying oil to China] is very effective … I think we do have much more (reserves), so in passing time, of course we can supply other countries,

including Japan and South Korea. For good measure, the ambassador found it opportune to criticize visits by the Japanese Prime Minister Koizumi to the Yasukuni shrine: '*Japan has told Russia it may not offer financing for the pipeline project, expected to cost $12 billion, if the prospect of Russian oil reaching the Sea of Japan coast diminishes*' [my italics].[36]

A 30 May 2005 Novosti dispatch, citing Industry and Energy Minister Victor Khristenko, revealed the Russian thinking behind the delays: 'The first section of the oil pipeline will link Taishet in

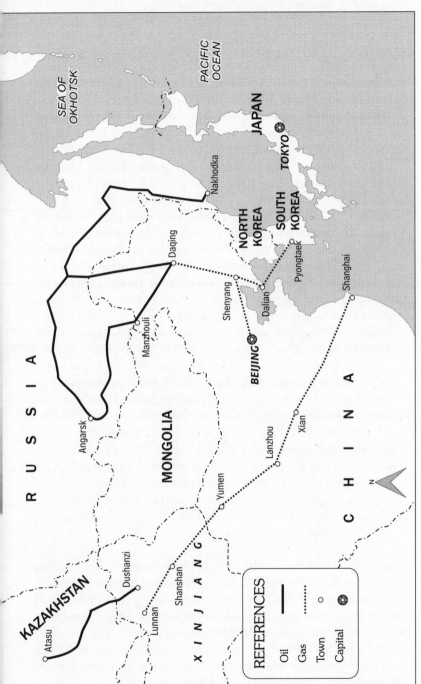

Figure 7.1   Pipeline prospects in Central and North-East Asia. Courtesy of http://www.eia.doe.gov/

the west with Skovorodino ... The capacity of the first section is 30 million tons. It will be loaded with West Siberian oil.'[37] This was the closest the Russians came to admitting publicly that they did not have the extra 50–80 million tons p.a. to export to Japan. The dispatch continued in inimitable Kremlinese, effectively stating that filling the second section from Skovorodino to the Pacific will need the development of *new* Eastern Siberian oilfields.

That could take anything up to ten years and the Japanese would know that. Later in the same year (14 October 2005), a Prime-Tass dispatch attributed similar remarks to Trade Minister German Gref. Upon receiving the news that part of the oil brought to Skovorodino could be shipped by train, or a short pipeline, to nearby Daqing in China, Japan finally blinked: 'Japanese Minister of Economy, Trade and Industry Shoichi Nakagawa said: "If the pipeline is stopped halfway it may never reach Japan. I told Russia that we would not be able to spend money of our taxpayers on such a risky project".'[38]

In late 2005, a Novosti political commentator summarized the position as:[39]

> What is now called the Eastern Pipeline is a compromise. The first phase is to transport [30 million tons] over 1,200 miles to a point within 42 miles of the Chinese border ... 400,000 barrels of oil a day will then be diverted into a direct Chinese link pipe and the remaining 200,000 barrels a day will be transported by rail to the Pacific Coast for shipment to Japan. The second phase of the proposed pipeline ... in 2010, will see capacity increase to 1.6 million barrels of oil a day and the pipeline extended the remaining 1,200 miles to the Pacific Coast – seemingly to favour Japan over China.

There were clear signals that the Japanese were far from feeling favoured by the arrangements, although reading between the lines, the Russians would probably have elected to construct the line to the Pacific, if only they had had the oil to fill it with. There have been straws in the wind: 'Oil production has recently been launched at the Verkhnechonsk deposit, one of the biggest in Eastern Siberia ... This deposit will play a major role in the projected Eastern Siberia-Pacific (Taishet-Nakhodka) main pipeline ... .'[40]

216

What price Amur leopards?

The trajectory of the pipeline and the choice of the virgin bay of Perevoznaya for constructing the new tanker terminal attracted furious opposition from environmentalists. The line was originally designed to follow the existing railway, passing just 800 m away from Lake Baikal, with all the attendant dangers of polluting the largest freshwater reservoir on earth. Furthermore, at the tail end, approaching Vladivostok, the trajectory of the line was to cross the habitat of the last extant 50, maybe a hundred, Amur leopards, beautiful animals judging by their photographs. In Perevoznaya, the 200 marine species that spawn in the bay and young fish swimming out to the ocean annually were said to be at risk if the bay – currently a popular summertime beach for the residents of Vladivostok – was turned into a tanker terminal. The reasons for overlooking the existing and perfectly serviceable deep-water port of Nakhodka-Vostochny were unclear.

Transneft responded in their usual wooden tones that 'state experts' had concluded that Perevoznaya was the 'most preferable place', despite objections that the intended area is really an open bay and shallow for tankers. The argument rapidly descended into farce, when critics alleged the governor of the Primorye region had the route changed because he had financial interests in Perevoznaya. Meanwhile, the 'feasibility study' submitted by Transneft to the Natural Resources Ministry was rejected within days.[41]

No one really expected the habitat of the Amur leopards to impede pipeline progress. London's *Independent* may have got a few details wrong, but was appropriately full of moral indignation: 'Kremlin fast-tracks lake pipeline despite protests of greens.'[42] All was not as it seemed, however. During a meeting with local authorities shortly afterwards, President Putin stunned his audience by declaring that the line should be constructed at least 40 *km* north of Lake Baikal. Transneft President Semyon Vainshtok, who had just finished defending the company's decisions, is said to have remained speechless. Transneft has since got down to planning a route passing further away from the Lake and nearer some of the possible *oil production sites* in the zone some 400 km north and east of Irkutsk.[43] Environmentalists claimed a second victory before the end of summer, when Vainshtok himself announced that the tanker port was to be constructed in the far more suitable Kozmino Bay.[44]

4 Old Disputes: Revival or Resolution?

At a meeting with western analysts at the beginning of September 2005, President Putin reiterated the latest Russian position that oil would go first to China and 'only later to the Pacific coast ... But we will also build to Nakhodka'.[45] The remarks, later confirmed by a spokesman, suggested that the economics of selling oil by pipeline to China first were more favourable. Almost in the same breath, he mentioned expanding Chinese military orders, as ' ... keeping Russia's arms industry alive ... ', and praised the agreement with China resolving all border issues between the two countries.

In fact, the Chinese have taken steps to liquidate *all* their border disputes with Russia in the north and India in the south. With the Russians, China has agreed a straightforward 50–50 split of all disputed territory along the 4,300-km border. The object of the exercise appears to have been simply to end the long-standing dispute itself.[46] Following this historic step in October 2004, the two countries went on to cement their strategic understanding with joint military exercises on the Shandong coast in the summer of 2005. In April 2005, the Chinese also signed an agreement with India at prime ministerial level, setting out 'guiding principles' to resolve their decades-old border dispute.[47] China has officially recognized Indian sovereignty over the border province of Sikkim and agreed to open the Nathula and Jelepla border crossings to stimulate trade. The same dispatch quoted intentions to increase levels of bilateral trade from some $13 billion in 2005 to $20 billion by 2008.

The contrast between these developments and Japan's relations with Russia and China is significant. In the interview cited above, President Putin '... had harsh words for Japan, accusing it of intransigence over the Kuril Islands territorial dispute which has held up the signing of a peace treaty between the two countries since World War II . . .'. We will have more on the Kurils a little later. Coincidentally, the Chinese have not been getting on very well with the Japanese either. Sparks have flown with overtones of resurfacing historic antagonisms, in surprising contrast with the vertiginous expansion of trade between the giants of East Asia.

The dance of the dragons

Officials in Beijing remain guarded about the latest announcements from Moscow about the East Siberian pipeline. In late 2005, there were signs that the Russians may shift their positions yet again, depending on how their negotiations develop with the Japanese. One thing, at least, has been clarified. The Russian Government has decided that state funds will not be used to look for oil for the pipeline project. Instead, they will strive to attract private venture capital for exploration and reserve development in East-central Siberia. We have nevertheless reached an interesting point. Without new oil, the large pipeline to the Pacific cannot be filled. Both China and Japan appear to have the funds to invest for reserve development, but neither has been asked to come in on the act. It must be concluded that medium-to-long-term Russian aims regarding the region remain to be defined.

One obvious question is why Japan did not enter into a dialogue with China over the issue of East Siberian pipelines? Instead, we have been comparing the merits of competing bids. Visits by the Prime Minister of Japan to the Yasukuni shrine have been discussed, where 'class A war criminals' are buried. No doubt, Koizumi was pandering to his right-wing following, as part of his vision of statecraft, without necessarily wishing to irritate anyone on the international stage. In truth, a minimal interest in Chinese sensitivities would have alerted him to the dangers of his actions. Belittling atrocities, committed by the Japanese army during their destruction of large swathes of Shanghai in 1937 as a minor 'incident' (as new Japanese school textbooks have done since 2005), could not have been expected to improve matters. Meanwhile, it is possible to identify a deeper rift behind diplomatic exchanges, provoked by apparently superficial irritations.

There is a hardening dispute over natural gas fields in the East China Sea: 'Japan now claims that nine of China's concessions encroach upon Japanese territory, including the Chunxiao gas field.'[48] In April 2005, Japan had granted exploration licences to some of its oil and gas companies to work in the vicinity of the Diaoyu (Senkaku) Islands:[49]

> a territorial dispute between China and Japan in the East China Sea ... is being further fuelled by reports of vast supplies of oil and gas in the region. The disputed territory includes the Diaoyu (or Senkaku) islands and the Chunxiao gas field northeast of Taiwan, which ... holds 200 billion cubic metres of gas. Japan regards the median line as its border while China claims jurisdiction over the entire continental shelf. In 2003, China began drilling in the area after the Japanese rejected a Chinese proposal to develop the field jointly. Although the Chunxiao gas field is on the Chinese side of the median line, Japan claims that China may be siphoning energy resources on the Japanese side.[50]

The Chinese have also been concerned by the more assertive strategic posture adopted by Japan. For the first time, the Japanese 'National Defence Program Outline', released in December 2004, identified China as a potential security threat, in respect of natural resources in the South China Sea, the Diaoyu (Senkaku) Islands and over Taiwan.[51] The latter item lends credence to Chinese concerns that the USA would like Japan to take a greater role in the defence of Taiwan.

It thus seems increasingly difficult to distinguish old animosities from present-day rivalries. One would have thought that these are matters which peacetime diplomats are paid to handle in search of reasonable levels of cooperation. None of the above goes far to answer questions regarding why, if India and Pakistan can begin to talk about cooperation, are China and Japan unable to do so. Observers[52] have suggested that Japan is adopting deliberately provocative postures, in order to force the Chinese into comprehensive discussions. There appear to be no indications that the Chinese position will do anything but harden in the face of such a policy. Meanwhile, Japanese ambitions to become a permanent member of the UN Security Council, which would have required Chinese assent, have been quietly shelved.

The tensions in East Asia are deep-seated. It seems unlikely that Koizumi's successor as Prime Minister (September 2006), Shinzo Abe, has a mandate to alter the existing matrix of relationships, or absence of them, in any fundamental sense. The new Prime Minister belongs to the same conservative, nationalist political grouping, although he has hinted that he might select policies *more* acceptable to China and South Korea. On the surface, however, postures have visibly relaxed since Koizumi's departure.

5 Russian Options: Pump East or Pump West?

At present, Russia is dependent on the European market for about 80 per cent of present oil exports. This is not a concern in times of tight supplies. In the longer term, however, the limited nature of their export outlets is a strategic worry for Russian planners. They would naturally aim to diversify.

Back to the Barents Sea?

Alongside the much-heralded East Siberian pipeline projects, there are on Russian drawing boards two alternative pipeline trajectories, linking the Western Siberian pipeline system with the Barents Sea. The first is through the port of Murmansk, which can accommodate tankers up to 240,000 tons. It sounds a little surprising at first, but the Murmansk–Houston route is nearly half the distance between the Gulf and Houston. However, Murmansk is nearly 600 km away (even) from the port of Arkhangelsk. A pipeline to Murmansk would have to go around the shores of the White Sea (Beloye More) or cross the strait from Zimiy Bereg to Terskiy Bereg. A far shorter pipeline is required for a terminal further east along the shores of the Barents Sea, possibly at Indiga or at Kolguyev Island. The project was first proposed in 2000–1 by a private consortium, led by the now jailed Mikhail Khodorkovsky of Yukos. A pipeline of 80 million tons' capacity had been mooted,[53] of similar size to the line contemplated from Taishet to Nakhodka.

A Novosti dispatch of 12 November 2004 tended to confirm that Moscow was running several projects in parallel:

Transneft company to start construction of an oil pipeline between Western Siberia and the Barents Sea coast ... 1,788-km long will begin in the area of Surgut ... to ... the Barents Sea ... The overall throughput capacity of the oil pipeline will be 50 million tons of oil a year, of which two-thirds will be provided by Western Siberia.[54]

The numbers quoted in the dispatch are interesting. Two-thirds of 50 million tons is a little over 30 million tons, a number we had seen before. We were told that the Western Siberian network has no more than 30 million tons (annual) to spare for the *northern* route. With Russian oil production totals drifting upwards by only 2–3 per cent annually since 2004, it is possible that this was the same 30 million tons mentioned in relation to the Taishet to Skovorodino line. Secondly, the northern line is considerably shorter and appeared within the means of Transneft to complete quickly with her own resources – even before the oil price rises of 2004. In terms of reaching open seas, the Barents Sea option appears attractive. On the other hand, exports through the East Siberian line would do much for regional development and enhance Russian influence in East Asia – when the necessary production levels are reached.

The Barents Sea project would have fitted in well with the Russia–US energy dialogue that was much-discussed before Bush and Putin came to power. In October 2005, the Russians said they might cancel the two pipelines to the Arctic Ocean, 'to focus on expanding sales to China and the rest of Asia'.[55]

Russia, Japan and the Kuril Islands

In the dying days of the Second World War, Stalin declared war on Japan and occupied the four southernmost of the Kuril Islands (Habomai, Shikotan, Kunashiri and Etorofu), lying between the tip of the Kamchatka peninsula and the north-eastern tip of Hokkaido Island. The fate of these islands has complicated Russo-Japanese relations ever since and have been the primary cause for the lack of a formal peace treaty between the two countries.

The Japanese continue to view the Soviet offensive in the northern theatre as a violation of the Soviet-Japanese Neutrality

Pact of 1941. They have maintained their claim to the four islands not just *per se*, but also as an assertion and reminder that they have suffered betrayal at the hands of the Soviets. With the 1951 peace treaty, Japan renounced all rights and claims to Southern Sakhalin and the Kuril Islands. However, in 1956, the USSR and Japan signed a joint declaration agreeing to divide the disputed group between the two nations, with Russia keeping the two northern-most islands and ceding Shikotan and Habomai to Japan, *if the two countries signed a peace treaty*. It was never signed and Japan now claims all four islands, which are referred to as the Northern Territories.[56]

Without progress on the territorial issue, it should have been unlikely for Japan to contemplate a multibillion dollar loan or investment for the Taishet–Nakhodka line. Indeed, as late as 2001, observers did not believe Japan would become involved in LNG contracts with the Sakhalin-II project, before some progress had been achieved on the Northern Territories. The Japanese have since shown varying degrees of flexibility in their negotiations with the Russians, but always with an eye to the return of the 'Northern Territories'.[57] The purchase of Sakhalin gas by the City of Tokyo may be viewed within the framework of this flexibility. This has been followed up by several other Japanese LNG purchasing agreements. It seems that the seductions of energy supplies have a power all their own.

The tone of Russo-Japanese exchanges has hardened since then. In late September 2005, German Gref, personally close to Putin, said to Novosti that 'ceding' the Kuril Islands to Japan was 'inadmissible'.[58] The contrast between this posture and the Russian '50–50' agreement with China, over *all* disputed territories, seems quite significant.

By early 2007, the Russian die was definitively cast in favour of the 30-million-ton crude-oil pipeline to Skovorodino, which initially answers Chinese needs. According to the 'prospectus' for a seven-year benchmark Eurobond in dollars, Transneft will spend at least $11 billion for the first leg of the ESPO pipeline 'up from initial estimates of $6.6 billion. Phase 2 foresees expansion of the link to 1.6 million barrels per day and construction of a second leg to the Pacific coast, where a terminal would be already built as part of Phase 1'.[59] Due to harsh terrain, the line will cost about $4 million per km, compared to $2.2 million for Baku–Tblisi–Ceyhan and $1.7 for the far easier CPC pipeline. Significantly, Transneft has initiated the actual construction of the line to Skovorodino. It is a meandering route, running close to several oilfields under development. Meanwhile, in February 2007, MOSNEWS.com ran the following news item:

> Japan has offered to share the costs with Russia for extending a Siberian oil and gas pipeline to the Pacific coast, apparently to help more output to be routed to Japan rather than China, the *Wall Street Journal* reported on Tuesday, Feb. 27, citing Japanese Finance Minister Koji Omi.[60]

6 Gas Transmission in East Asia

As a proportion of their total primary energy requirements, both South Asia and East Asia consume less natural gas than, say, North America or Europe. This is due mainly to supply problems. Nevertheless, in the first decade of the twenty-first century, nearly all great cities of Asia are queuing up to replace coal and heavy fuel oil with natural gas, in order to reduce air pollution.

In Japan, gas supplies to power generators and population centres are imported as LNG. The country has few indigenous resources and imports 99 per cent of its fossil fuel needs. Up to the 1960s and early 1970s, domestic gas supplies consisted mainly of coal-based town gas, gradually replaced by gas manufactured from oil, until the first oil shock of 1973–4. The first imports of LNG go back to the late 1960s. Curiously, the prosperous and crowded Island of Honshû does not have a thoroughgoing gas pipeline network. This is partly because high population density areas only make up 3 per cent of the land mass. Separated by mountainous terrain, these centres are widely dispersed. The configuration has resulted in LNG supplies arriving at over 20 regasification plants distributed along the shores, usually close to electricity generation plants and population centres.[61] Furthermore, safety standards on Honshû are stringent and real estate prices are high. Purchasing the 'right of way' for new pipeline construction is expensive and most trunk pipelines are constructed underneath intercity roads.

The estimate for a 100-km gas pipeline, to be completed by 2010 for supplying the Gunma prefecture north of Tokyo, was about $2.6 million per km.[62]

With international gas markets becoming progressively less predictable, Japan would have been well served by steady, piped supplies of gas from the nearby mainland or from Sakhalin Island. Historically, the Cold War and the 'northern territories' issue have stood in the way of developing pipeline links with Russia. The latter dispute has precluded the drawing up of exclusive economic zones around the islands in question, giving rise to potential legal problems for companies considering investments in the area.[63]

Assuming that these difficulties could somehow be finessed, which has not happened to date, one proposed scheme involved carrying gas from Korsakov on Sakhalin Island, by pipeline to Ishikari Bay on the northern edge of Hokkaido Island, then pumping to Tomakomai on the southern shore of Hokkaido. In the second phase of the project, the Tsugaru Strait would need to be crossed to the main island of Honshû, involving laying pipes at relatively feasible depths of 350 m. Two alternative schemes would then carry the gas along the shore to either Niigata on the Western edge of Honshû or to Sendai and Tokyo on the Eastern edge. Despite the frigid atmosphere between Koizumi's brand of Japanese nationalism and Putin's Kremlin, several key Japanese companies have nevertheless signed up to buy LNG from Sakhalin-II. The first of these contracts was signed with the City of Tokyo (May 2003), for about 1.1 million tons per year, nearly 12 per cent of the total project capacity. Since then, several others have signed contracts,[64] including Tokyo Electric Power Co. (annual 1.5 million tons LNG), Kyushu Electric and Togo Gaz, both for 0.5 million tons annually.

Korea's pipelines in the sea

In contrast to Japan, the South Koreans have a well-developed domestic gas pipeline grid. They estimate that pipeline-supplied natural gas would come to about 25 per cent cheaper than their LNG imports. It would be technically feasible to transmit Sakhalin-I gas landed at De Kastri, down the coast and through North Korea. Leaving that to one side, the short-to-medium-term gas-pipeline options, instead, involve underwater transmission from China. Plans have been made for laying a line either from Dalian or, more likely, from the Bay of Weihai on the Shandong Peninsula to Inchon (in South Korea) on the coast, 55 km southwest of Seoul. This pipeline project would be contingent on China receiving piped supplies from the Russian Federation.

China's options; domestic and Russian gas

Natural gas currently accounts for about 2–3 per cent of total energy consumption in China. From small beginnings, China's domestic gas production has developed rapidly during the past decade, reaching nearly 50 billion cubic metres in 2005. The country's known domestic gas reserves amount to about 1.5 trillion cubic metres, located mainly in Sichuan, Bohai Bay, north-central China (Northern Shaanxi, the Ordos Basin) and in the Tarim Basin (Xinjiang).[65] The International Energy Agency estimates that *demand* will rise at an average of nearly 5.5 per cent yearly, to 59 billion cubic metres by 2010 and 107 billion cubic metres by the year 2020.[66] PetroChina officials have come up with still higher demand figures.[67] Although China expects to increase domestic production and build a second west–east line from Xinjiang to Guangdong province,[68] much new gas will need to be imported, provided it can be delivered at reasonable cost.

Development in China has come at a price. During its rapid industrialization, China used large amounts of coal for power generation, as well as for industrial boilers and domestic heating. Not much attention was paid to controlling the usual emissions of soot and dust, and still less to those of sulphur dioxide and nitrogen oxides, or indeed of highly toxic arsenic, mercury and cadmium. By contrast, natural gas is a cleaner fuel. It can be rendered nearly free of sulphur and other pollutants with relative ease. For those who would link climate change to carbon dioxide releases, natural gas also produces less carbon dioxide per unit of energy released. Pollution in Beijing is now being reduced by supplanting the use of coal with natural gas from the Ordos Basin. For modern China, cleaning up the air in notoriously polluted major provincial centres such as Taiyuan and Chongqing has become a priority for improving public health. Meanwhile, with the 2008 Olympics approaching, the urgency to reduce air pollution in Beijing has become a national issue.

Like India, China would favour importing natural gas, provided it can be delivered at reasonable cost. In Chapter IV, we outlined price-related problems that several multinational groups have faced in India, where prices are kept low through central Government subsidies. Foreign investors are now trying to sell up. The lessons would not have been lost on those contemplating similar moves in China. In the second half of the decade, natural gas no longer appears as attractive a fuel as it did in 2001–2, when it sold at less than $75 per thousand cubic metres at the New York City 'gate'.

Returning to China, the country has not yet invested in many expensive LNG reception facilities. Price permitting, both the Shanghai-PuDong area and the Tianjin-Beijing complex would have been natural candidates for receiving LNG. In contrast to the Japanese and Koreans, however, the Chinese Government has proved sensitive to the long-term consequences of purchasing expensive energy. Partly their problem is that of weaning away from cheap coal a customer base with relatively low purchasing power. They also need much new investment to bring their basic infrastructure for the transmission and distribution of natural gas, in line with potential new demand.[69]

In 2004, China announced a relatively low natural gas purchase price for Shanghai from the internal West–East natural gas pipeline. This was meant to encourage market development in the Shanghai area, by making gas prices attractive for both domestic and industrial consumers. However, the move appears to have persuaded some multinational companies to withdraw from further investment in regional pipelines, and to adopt a wait-and-see attitude regarding LNG regasification projects in nearby Zhejiang province. Meanwhile, PetroChina has formally opened the 4,200-km West–East gas pipeline from the Tarim Basin to Shanghai.[70] The 1,660-km eastern sector, from Shaanxi province to Shanghai, had already begun pumping at an annual rate of 1.5 billion cubic metres since October 2003. Total capacity in 2005–6 rose to 12 billion cubic metres, although local market development is expected to take some time.

Finally, China has not entirely given up on LNG imports. Two consortia, with CNOOP as lead contractor, have committed to

LNG purchases. BP will build the country's first LNG import terminal near Guangdong. BP will take a 30 per cent equity stake in the project, CNOOC 31 per cent, with the rest held by local firms from Guangdong and Hong Kong. The gas will be supplied from Australia's North–West Shelf LNG terminal, expected to begin operation in the first half of 2007. This first plant near Hong Kong is expected to serve power plants and allied installations in the Shenzhen–Pearl River Delta area. The regasification plant is expected to enter service in 2006, with initial imports of 4 billion cubic metres, rising to 7 billion by 2008. Given the higher purchasing power of the southern industrial zones and the Hong Kong–Shenzhen area, a level of tolerance for current higher natural gas prices may be expected.

A second LNG terminal is under construction in Zhangzhou, in Fujian province farther up the coast, which is scheduled for completion in late 2007.[71,72] However, with a smaller industrial hinterland, the Fujian project does not fit the same pattern. Starting in 2007, it will be supplied with 3.6 billion cubic metres by the Tangguh partners, an Indonesia-based consortium led by BP, including among others BG (formerly British Gas). The plan is to supply two new power plants, Songyu II (1800 MW) in Xiamen and Nanpu (1800 MW) in Quanzhou, alongside five major coastal cities: Fuzhou, Xiamen, Quanzhou, Zhangzhou and Putian.[73] In an interesting – if not ground-breaking – development, the Chinese side is taking equity in the two LNG *exporting* consortia. The supply contracts had been signed before the price surges of 2004–5 and applicable gas prices for these two projects have not appeared in the public domain.

Importing piped Russian gas into China

China is also actively seeking ways to import natural gas from Russia by pipeline. For a while it seemed that the probable source of the gas would have been the Kovykta gas field north of Angarsk, with reserves of 2 trillion cubic metres. According to an interagency task force master plan,[74] however, gas from Kovykta will not be exported to Asia. Instead, pipelines have been laid from the Kovykta fields, through Sayansk, to Irkutsk, distributing gas to many communities along the way.[75] According to the gas production and distribution scenarios studied by the same 'task force', the maximum amount of natural gas that can be exported to China and Korea by 2030 is no more than 25 billion cubic metres.[76]

These decisions are not consistent with resolutions adopted at a Sino-Russian summit in Beijing in March 2006, where President Putin promised that Russia would deliver 68 billion cubic metres of natural gas, using two separate routes.[77] The first of these would carry about 30 billion cubic metres of *Western Siberian* gas through the Republic of Altai into Xinjiang, for local use and for pumping into the west–east natural gas pipeline system. Environmental activists as well as gas engineers have immediately pointed out that this route would cross into protected uplands, and be both expensive and environmentally undesirable. A shorter route through Mongolia would have eliminated both difficulties (see below). The other difficulty involves ... the price. For China, drawing gas from Western Siberia would amount to competing with Western Europe. It is doubtful that they would accede to paying European prices for the gas.

The second Russia–China route would go through the Russian 'Far East'. Figure 7.1 shows the generally familiar potential gas pipeline trajectory from Angarsk, crossing the frontier near Manzhouli into Daqing, splitting at Shenyang with spurs to Beijing and Dalian, the latter for an undersea connection to South Korea. At 4,900-km total length, this is a long line and an expensive project, with an estimated price tag of about $12 billion and an annual capacity of 30 billion cubic metres, one-third of it destined for South Korea.

An alternative route, shorter by some 1,500 km, would have run through the territory of the Republic of Mongolia. This line is technically feasible and significantly cheaper to construct. Negotiations were undertaken in 1998 involving the five possible partners: Russia, Mongolia, China, Korea and Japan. The Russians proposed to sell some of the gas to Mongolia, who are desperate to reduce air pollution in the capital, Ulaan Bataar. These negotiations have failed. China expressed concerns over political risks and possible transit fees. Clearly, the merest hint of a pipeline becoming the focus of cross-border rivalry would make it a vulnerable project. As explained delicately in an Asia Pacific Energy

Research Centre report, the regional states are not accustomed to collaborate on large projects.[78]

In any case, the readiness of the Russians to collaborate with Mongolia was always likely to attract suspicions in Beijing. During the Russian Revolution, Ulaan Bataar (translates as Red Hero) was the messenger sent to the Bolsheviks for help against the homicidal White Russian General, Baron Ungern-Sternberg. The Baron, who plundered the Mongolian capital and massacred much of its population, was eventually caught and executed by the Red Army. However, the Soviets also assisted 'Outer' Mongolia in its bid for independence from China. Behind the failed negotiations, it seems possible to detect elements of Mongolian reticence towards her southern neighbour's ample embrace, whilst the Chinese might have been loath to advantage a country, whom they occasionally tend to view as their lost northernmost province.

It is thus not entirely clear when the Russians will have how much gas they can export to East Asia and what prices they would charge for it when the time comes. The delays in decision-making appear not just related to uncertainty regarding the reserves to be mobilized, but also about the magnitude of investments required for field development and the financing of the necessary pipelines and other infrastructure.

It is a situation that finds parallels in prospects for the East Siberian *crude oil* pipeline project, where they appear to be short of the extra oil to export. The Russians have been using cheap Kazakh and Turkmen gas to supply subsidized domestic customers. They export gas, probably mostly drawn from North-western Siberia to Europe, at $255 per 1,000 cubic metres (during 2007). The question must be: do they have any extra gas to export to China, whether from the overcommitted resources of Western Siberia and Central Asia or from the as yet undeveloped resources of Central and Eastern Siberia?

7 The Joker in the Pack: China's Kazakh Options

Although still incomplete, oil pipeline connections and production agreements between Kazakhstan and China are at a more advanced stage than those between China and Russia. As early as

2002, Calgary-based Hurricane Hydrocarbons, later renamed PetroKazakhstan, had been producing about 6 million tons of crude oil annually, making it the then second largest oil producer in Kazakhstan.[79] When the China National Petroleum Corporation (CNPC) purchased PetroKazakhstan, it acquired their production-sharing agreements over the Kenkiyak and Kumkol fields in the Turgai basin.

Kazakhstan is a large country mostly covered by deserts. What makes the Chinese venture particularly convenient is that the Kumkol fields of the Turgai Basin are connected to Atasu by an 820-mm-diameter pipeline. This was originally intended to carry crude oil from Tomsk (West Siberia) to Pavlodar in Kazakhstan, through Atasu, due south to Uzbekistan (Figure 7.2), so the Kumkol–Atasu link is operational. Prior to the completion of the Atasu–Alashankou pipeline link in late 2005, 1 million tons of oil were being carried from Atasu to the Chinese frontier crossing at Alashankou by rail.[80]

In 2003–4, the Chinese decided to fast-track negotiations for the construction of the pipeline, between Atasu in East-central Kazakhstan and the Alashankou pass in the extreme west of China. Once again, the trajectory ran alongside the existing railway line. The construction of the 32-in, 988-km segment was completed in December 2005, at a reported cost of $700 million.[81] Initially intended to carry 10 million tons of crude oil per year, the line skirts Lake Balkash and runs through Balkash–Sayak–Aktogay to the frontier pass, also known as the Dzungarian Gate, into China.

On the Chinese side, crude-oil imports are viewed as crucial for the development of China's westernmost and potentially rebellious Xinjiang province. A new segment of pipeline from the frontier to the refinery at Dushanzi (in Xinjiang) has been completed. It is also planned to carry some of the oil by rail to the nearby Karamay and Urumqi refineries for processing. CNPC plans to turn Dushanzi into a large petrochemical base in Western China. The current 6 million tons' oil-refining capacity will be expanded to 10 million tons and the 220,000 tons of ethylene production to 1 million tons.[82] These are large plants!

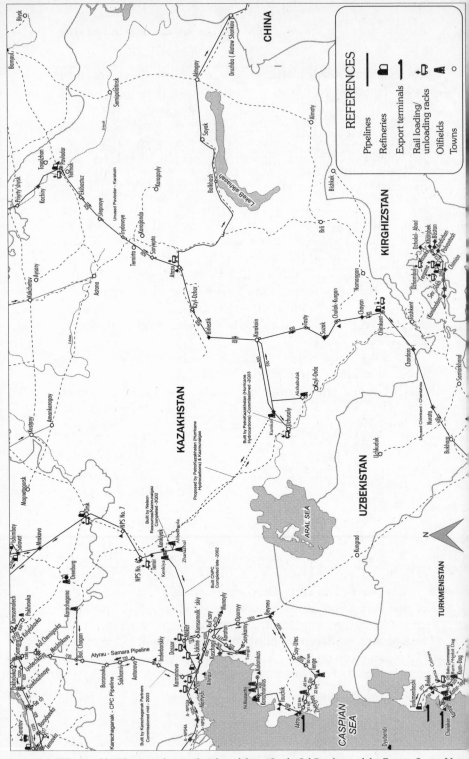

Figure 7.2   The Kazakh–China pipeline trail. Adapted from 'Crude Oil Pipelines of the Former Soviet Unio[n]
Centre for Global Energy Studies, UK London, 2005; http://www.cges.co.uk

Where to find Kazakh oil?

As usual, the devil is in the detail. The immediate need is for 10 million tons of crude oil for the pipeline to work at full capacity. However, there are discrepancies in the amounts of oil being earmarked by the various parties concerned, for delivery through the Atasu–Alashankou–Dushanzi line. According to the Kazaks and the Chinese, it is initially planned to deliver 3 million tons of oil from Kumkol to Atasu for this purpose: 'An additional 1.5 million tons should be delivered from relatively smaller deposits (Kenkiyak and Zhanazhol) currently operated by CNPC in western Kazakhstan.'[83] For the time being, the rest would have to come from Russia, and Transneft has claimed not to have the spare crude oil to pump from Tomsk through Pavlodar to Atasu. These appear to be relatively minor difficulties. However, on reaching full capacity (20 million tons) in 2010, filling the Atasu–Alashankou line will require either a part of increased Kazakh production or more Russian crude from Western Siberia, via the Omsk–Pavlodar–Shymkent pipeline.

China and Kazakhstan have also considered building a natural gas pipeline from western Kazakhstan to Xinjiang.[84] PetroChina has not secured enough domestic reserves in Xinjiang to satisfy demand for 45 years – the designated lifespan of the West–East Pipeline project. The line from Kazakhstan would connect to the West–East Pipeline and allow China to secure gas fields in western Kazakhstan as back up. Understandably, both sides are concerned about the cost of the undertaking and Putin's visit to Beijing has raised other hopes. Could it have been meant to forestall further talk of Kazakh (or Turkmen) gas for China? The Sino-Kazakh project is probably being considered in terms of a strategic reserve for the longer-term. Ultimately, however, the Chinese are conscious that the most expensive option is to run short of fuel supplies.

8 Where to in East Asia? Many Questions!

The Russians appear to have definitively set aside the crude-oil pipeline project running from Western Siberia to the Barents Sea.

Moscow has also finally admitted they only have enough oil for what has been dubbed 'Phase 1' of the East Siberian pipeline. They have begun the construction of a line running from Taishet to Skovorodino, near the Chinese frontier in Eastern Siberia, from where a spur will feed the oil towards Daqing in China. The line from Skovorodino to a tanker terminal near Vladivostok, on the Pacific Ocean, will be built 'later'.

Whether China or Japan would get the first batch of oil has wreaked diplomatic havoc in East Asia. The outcome outlined above is also in line with hardening Russo-Japanese and Sino-Japanese relations. Meanwhile, investment for developing the necessary Siberian reserves is only now being committed. With oil prices surging, cash-rich Russia is weighing her options, although we have seen that the finance for Phase 1 has been raised on the Eurobond market.

Regarding the construction of an eventual *gas* pipeline from Central Siberia to China and Korea, a trajectory through Mongolia would shorten the line by 1500 km, significantly reducing the cost. Banking and credit mechanisms for mitigating political risks associated with cross-border projects might have enhanced the viability of this route. However, China has stated its preference for a pipeline trajectory from Angarsk into northern China, which circumvents Mongolian territory.

In Central Asia, China's recent agreements with Kazakhstan point to a firm, albeit slowly expanding commitment for oil transmission into Xinjiang Province. Importing *gas* from Kazakhstan or from Western Siberia, however, looks expensive. Putin's 'commitment' may just be a way of keeping Chinese negotiators happy or may eventually serve as a strategic back-up for supplies in Xinjiang, which feed the West–East natural gas pipeline into Shanghai.

The Russian decision to send oil to China first has taken place in parallel with regional political developments. The whole of East Asia, including the Koreans, have shown adverse reactions to Tokyo's new, assertive posture. Powerful fields of force are being set up between Russia, China and Japan, with the Kurils, Taiwan and energy exploitation in the East China Sea as focal points for tension. With the USA encouraging Japan to adopt a more pro-active posture, the shape of a new 'cold peace' in East Asia is beginning to emerge.

Meanwhile, soon after the Sino-Russian border agreement in 2004, the Chinese have taken steps to liquidate border disputes with India, inherited from the days of Chairman Mao and Pandit Nehru. The Russians have offered India technical assistance and, reading the runes, diplomatic support in furthering the Iran–Pakistan–India gas pipeline project. In its outlines, closer cooperation between Russia, China and India on matters concerning energy transmission is consistent with China's and Russia's attempts to establish a less unipolar world. However, India is being tempted away from a possible Asian alignment, including the Iran–Pakistan–India pipeline, by offers of assistance from the USA, in the area (among others) of nuclear energy. As part of the process of wooing India, the US Congress has stopped impeding a possible deal on nuclear fuels with India on the grounds of nuclear proliferation.

Doubtless, this is a story that will run and run.

Chapter VIII

Where do we go from here?

In reviewing the energy transmission problems of Eastern Europe, the Middle East and most of Asia, we have traced the contours of major geopolitical faultlines in these immense regions. If nothing else, our survey suggests, it is often futile to distinguish between the role of energy transmission as 'cause' or 'effect' in regional confrontations. No two conflicts present identical configurations. Whether competition over the course of East Siberian pipelines served to trigger some of the Sino-Japanese tensions, or was simply a consequence, does not seem to be a worthy question. What we have really arrived at is perhaps the predictable recognition that, wherever relevant, energy production and transmission become significant components of regional confrontations. It seems tempting, nevertheless, to ask whether, with a little *less* oil, the Middle East would not have had an easier ride in the world after independence. We can only speculate.

In these chapters, I have tried to articulate how the 'physics of fuel transport', i.e. the technical possibilities, constraints and limitations imposed by the exigencies of matter, continuously interact with three other key factors, namely: 'demand', 'geopolitical blockages' and the 'epochal change'.[1] In closing, it would be useful briefly to examine some of the relationships between these elements. We will also have a brief look at some of the difficulties we are likely to face in powering the planet in the medium term.

236

1 Key Factors that Govern Fuel Transmission

'Demand' is not as straightforward to track down as it first sounds. We have seen that natural gas consumption in the USA and Western Europe does not change significantly over a very wide range of gas prices. However, most domestic customers in less prosperous countries, notably Eastern Europe, China and India, do not have similar flexibility. Their demand would be sensitive to the price of the gas. In these regions, the public mostly has a low purchasing-power base. Bringing the gas to Shanghai or Delhi then becomes only one part of the problem. Economists have finely honed terminology for this kind of phenomena, but all *we* need to know is that the general public in India or China have cheaper, albeit less efficient and more polluting alternatives, be it coal, charcoal or cow dung. Apart from keeping a hawkish eye on the price, marketing the gas to the mass of the population in poorer regions will require some convincing and, perhaps, even a little twisting of arms.

In relation to oil and gas consumption, the second major element to keep in mind is the contrast between the trends in oil and gas demand. There has been a rapid jump in the demand for gas over the past two decades (but not always in supply!), whilst demand for crude oil has been rising more steadily. The jump in demand for gas has occurred mostly in rapidly developing economies, where the social costs of air pollution can no longer be ignored. In these regions, constraints imposed by the 'physics of fuel transmission' are much in evidence. Intercontinental gas transport by refrigerated tankers is not as cheap or technically straightforward as the conveyance of crude oil by ordinary tanker. For conveying natural gas, overland transport by pipeline is generally more economical, at least for distances shorter than about 2,000–4,000 km, and natural gas-handling requires high-pressure equipment, which is always far more expensive – and hazardous – to handle.

When discussing 'geopolitical blockages', the examples that come to mind are the fates of major cross-border pipelines in the Middle East. Several of these were constructed in attempts to pump Iraqi oil to the Mediterranean. The IPC pipelines through

Jordan and Palestine were casualties of 1948 in Palestine, while the northern IPC pipeline was intermittently blocked by Syria, until US forces blew up a section of it in 2003. Saudi access to the Mediterranean was similarly blocked by Syria. Meanwhile, the IPSA lines connecting the Southern Iraqi fields with Red Sea ports were first blocked and then taken over by the Saudis. Only Turkey, frigid to political in-fighting in the Arab world, has chosen to view the Iraqi pipelines running through her territory to the port of Ceyhan as a simple business proposition.

We have observed erratic Russian pumping of Kazakh oil in the 1990s, when oil prices were slack. It may happen again. Furthermore, it is no use pointing a finger at the Russians; the Saudis did the same to Iraqi supplies. It could happen in the future, with Iran and Caspian (or Russian) 'swap' oil – *if* the market slackens again. The only advice available is to keep alternative routes open for oil exports – and indeed for *imports*.

In this respect, Russia's already unique hold on Central Asia has been enhanced by US pressure on Turkmenistan and Kazakhstan to limit their contacts with Iran. Turkmenistan has for decades been constrained to sell cheap gas to Gazprom, a company that behaves as an extension of the Russian state. Gazprom, in turn, exports the gas to Russia's 'near abroad' at politically modulated rates and to Western Europe at the highest prices she can muster. Until 2006, Gazprom had acted mostly with strict business discipline in respect of profitable natural gas exports to Western Europe, whilst using gas prices and indeed gas *flows* as a tool to reward or punish former Soviet republics. The latter have mostly been unable to pay their gas bills, whilst attempting, when they see fit, to steer independent political lines from that of Moscow. The evident contradictions have given rise to many of their difficulties.

The slow coming together of tectonic plates in South Asia also deserves our attention, although it is too early to label these moves as a new 'epochal change'. Major shifts in relations between India and Pakistan seem possible through slow, deliberate negotiations on possibilities offered by sharing gas pipelines from Iran, or (a less likely prospect) from Turkmenistan through Afghanistan. Meanwhile, the regime in Bangladesh has been ideologically weary of Indian influences. They have, nonetheless, been unable definitively to reject the lucrative project involving the construction of a gas pipeline from Myanmar to India, transiting through Bangladeshi territory. Internal politics permitting, it may yet happen.

Coming to the major 'epochal change' of our time, nearly 15 years after the event, we still do not see clearly why the dissolution of the Soviet Union was actually brought about. Clearly, Russia was unwilling to continue subsidizing some of the Union's more profligate republics. In 1991, cancelling the Union might have appealed to Yeltsin as a clever trick to be shot of Gorbachev, who was then President of the Soviet Union: 'No Union ... No President!' However, the dissolution was clearly unplanned and unexpected. Everything from countless commercial and industrial interconnections, to the social support system, has been shattered. Looking back, the deep economic collapse that followed in the wake of dissolution in 1991–2 does not seem entirely unavoidable. The human cost has been colossal.

A fascinating new pattern has emerged, furthermore, in post-Soviet republics, ranging from Moldova to Armenia, where the inability to pay gas bills has been compensated by Russian acquisitions of local industry and infrastructure. Inevitably, the scope for such exchanges is limited by the amount of available infrastructure that can be bartered away. There is no doubt, furthermore, that the Kremlin views this process, along with occasional cuts in gas supplies, as a legitimate lever to regain influence and control in the post-Soviet republics. The changes triggered by the Soviet collapse have yet to be played out in their entirety. Russia herself needs much primary economic development and alleviation of poverty. Meanwhile, the leadership's quest for control over the post-Soviet space has appeared single-minded, but devoid of any promise of a better life for the peoples of the former Soviet Union. Moscow's ambitions appear increasingly anachronistic, worthy of the Russian Empire of a bygone age.

Another struggle for power and influence is being played out in East Asia. The new industrial giant, China, has taken on the might of Japan. The competition is being played out over hydrocarbon prospecting rights in the East China Sea, as well as over hydrocarbon transmission from East Siberia. In the matter of the pipelines, the role of arbiter has fallen to a Russia that has her own tense relationship and territorial disagreements with Japan. One major factor drawing China and Russia together appears to be the new pro-active strategic posture adopted by Japan in taking its place alongside the USA. We do not (yet?) have a new Cold War in East Asia, but it seems reasonable to think in terms of a cold peace. Meanwhile, how to interpret the massive expansion of peaceful economic ties between the powers of the Asia-Pacific rim, from within this geopolitical confrontation? Can we expect those ties to remain untouched by the tensions and frictions of a cold peace?

2 The Changing Strategic Environment

Since 1991, NATO and the EU have expanded into large swathes of Central and Eastern Europe. The Baltic States (former Soviet republics) and Russia's former Warsaw Pact allies have all moved to what used to be called the 'Western camp'. From a Russian perspective, US aggression in Iraq and NATO enlargement in Europe possibly represent parts of the same overarching geopolitical initiative. However, it is still Russian pipelines that supply Eastern and Central Europe with natural gas and a proportion of their oil, and Moscow is mindful of her last real lever of power over the region.

It was generally thought, however, that after the debacle over Ukrainian gas, the Russians would not have used their position lightly and cut supplies, again! It was tempting to think that events of early 2006 would be regarded as a mistake by a relatively young president – by Russian standards. However, at the end of 2006, Gazprom doubled the price of gas to Belarus from $50 to $100 (per 1,000 cubic metres). 'In revenge', President Lukashenko imposed a transit fee of $45 per ton of Russian oil going west through his country. Russia refused and Belarus drew oil from the line in lieu of payment. The subsequent Russian cut in oil supplies during January 2007 to Belarus affected Germany, Poland, the Czech Republic and Slovakia, being the countries further downstream. The Russians also imposed a duty of $180.7 per metric ton of oil going to Belarus, threatening to impose duty on all imports from Belarus and to reroute all oil supplies away from Belarus. Lukashenko swiftly climbed down and, to complete Moscow's triumph, asked for a loan of $1.5 billion to pay for increased gas and oil charges. It all suggested a coercive streak in Moscow, demanding quick results and total victory.

During his meetings with European leaders, in Finland during October and November 2006, President Putin appeared ready to use a similar 'take it or leave it' approach. There was no interest in any of the EU's key demands: 'access to Russia's pipelines, greater investment security, or a level playing field for foreign investors in Russia'.[2] After the November meeting with EU leaders, Novosti reported that 'Russian Foreign Minister Sergei Lavrov said Wednesday that Moscow has no intention of ratifying the [European Energy] charter, because it is flawed'.[3]

By contrast, the European response, to increasingly well-coordinated actions of state-owned or semi-private giant Russian oil and gas companies, has been disconnected. While the companies have been taught to acquiesce to Kremlin's guidance, individual European governments are trying to make their particular accommodations with the new approach. They are beginning to look a little exposed. For all their warnings against excessive dependence on Russian fuel supplies, US policy-makers have been unable to provide viable alternatives. After all, they represent the largest importer of fossil fuels on the planet.

South of the Caucasus, Georgia and Azerbaijan have suffered from direct Russian intervention. It has led to separatism, civil conflict and war. The two republics have reacted by drifting away from the security architecture that Moscow had sought to create, in order to retain some level of control over the post-Soviet space. Armenia, the lone outpost of Russian ambitions south of the Caucasus, nurtures territorial ambitions over near neighbours and it seems to suit Russia to keep the Caucasus pot boiling.

In Central Asia, however, the Russians have managed to gather the post-Soviet republics back into the fold, including Turkmenistan whose President Niyazov had in the past eagerly looked for alternative routes to export Turkmen natural gas. This outcome was to be expected after the USA blocked the Iranian routes for oil and gas exports, without offering alternatives to Kazakhstan and Turkmenistan. The lack of imperial reach by the USA has left these governments with no choice but to export their oil and gas through Russia. It is forcing them into a docile role and costing them a great deal of money.

On the other hand, it does not seem entirely fortuitous that Russia, China and India have chosen the present time to liquidate some long-standing border disputes. These developments conform to Yevgeny Primakov's[4] vision. He had earlier proposed a Russian-Chinese-Indian triumvirate to serve as counterweight to super-power America. Within the same framework, the Indians have been handling a new relationship with the USA with consummate skill. Meanwhile, in East Asia, Japan appears ready to take a more active role in defending 'western' interests. With the exception of India's very flexible posture, the alignment of the powers is easily discernible.

It must be noted that Russia, China, India, Japan, Korea and the USA have immense volumes of trade circulating between their shores. It has led to increased levels of prosperity. No one is about to throw all this away. Nevertheless, the strengthening dipole in East Asia would be expected to influence the region's energy linkages, among which the East Siberian pipelines loom large. After blowing hot-and-cold for several years, Moscow has announced the construction of a pipeline to somewhere near the Chinese border at Skovorodino – *first*. It is eventually to be completed to the coast, where Japan too would buy oil. The Japanese are not content with this outcome, whilst the Chinese seem less dissatisfied than of late. Construction commenced during summer 2006. Meanwhile, the region's future cross-border gas pipeline trajectories have not been defined in any meaningful way. Building a gas pipeline alongside the ESPO has been mooted, without indicating where the gas would come from.

On the *western* rim of Asia, the Baku–Tblisi–Ceyhan pipeline also bears testimony to a low-level confrontation between the USA and Russia. The latter have entirely rejected the necessity for this pipeline, which they clearly perceive as 'anti-Russian'. On the whole, this is a reasonably sober assessment. Further west, the Russians have made slow, patient efforts to regain predominance in the one republic they never really saw as distinct from themselves: Ukraine. It must be galling for the Russians to observe Ukraine now preening itself for NATO and EU membership. The two countries have been enmeshed in a complicated web of relationships that will not be easy to undo. This is a crucial area, where the Russians cannot contemplate losing. Furthermore, the region is densely criss-crossed by oil and gas pipelines, in which both countries have vital interests. Winning the tug of war over Ukraine is probably more important for the Russians than all the rest of the post-Soviet space put together. How it is eventually played out remains to be seen.

3 Increasing Energy Needs: The Trends

The surge in oil and gas prices since mid-2004 has frequently been explained in terms of greater crude oil imports by 'countries such as India and China'. When matched against actual import figures, this evaluation does not stand up to scrutiny (Chapter VII). We will need to look for explanations elsewhere.

Global demand for oil has been increasing by 1–2 per cent year-on-year for quite some time. Following the large dip due to the crash of the 'Asian Tigers', demand has resumed growth after 2000–1, at the same steady pace. Careful observers have correctly anticipated this recovery, as early as 1999, during the lowest point in oil demand.[5] However, just several years down the line, the oil world appears to have been caught in short supply, as if unawares. The markets were also agitated by shortages of available refining capacity.

It is not really surprising that the early warning signals were ignored.[6] Reducing spare capacity is now established practice in the modern industrial world. Spare capacity costs money in the short term, which adversely affects quarterly company profits. Thus, the energy world has been faced with a combination of cost-cutting exercises by the oil majors and the drive for higher prices by OPEC has left world markets with short inventories, coupled with little shut-in (reserve) production *and* even less reserve refinery capacity. The recent step-up in prices has followed on the back of this close-tracking between production and refining capacities and consumption levels, where every minor disruption in supply has driven prices to panic levels. Furthermore, present price levels are obviously attractive for both producers and refiners.

The 'sudden' discovery of shortages in global refining capacity is another interesting anomaly. Partly, this was a consequence of *excess* refinery capacity over the past decade, leading to fierce competition between refiners that squeezed profit margins to near extinction. As a result, for a long spell, it did not seem worthwhile to build oil refineries. We live in a dysfunctional age where industrial managers routinely take decisions about the medium-to-long term, on the basis of short-term trends. Being mere mortals, they also often tend to move with the received wisdom of the day. The excess in refinery capacity lasted and lasted – until consumption rose to swamp excess capacity and various local events (notably hurricane Ivan and the Nigerian oil worker strikes of 2004, hurricanes Rita and Katrina in 2005 and attacks on oil installations in Nigeria during 2005–6) led to unprecedented price hikes. At present, it is difficult to see oil producers and the oil majors rushing into large-scale investment decisions that would limit their own profits. In any case, constructing new refineries and sinking new production wells are medium-term projects. At least three–four, sometimes five–six years, are needed for present investment decisions to translate into new refineries and oil wells coming on stream. The present high-price excursion is thus being driven by structural elements that are not likely to disappear quickly.

4 The Rush to Pipelines and the Global Warming Debate

The more contentious pipeline projects discussed in this book make up but a small fraction of pipeline systems that are at the planning stage, under construction or, indeed, in operation all over the world. Economic growth and improved living standards require security of energy supplies. However, we also desire a cleaner planet and fear the possible threat of climate change. Our objectives are inherently at odds with each other.

In the world of energy experts and politicians in need of exciting new visions, the present spell of high prices is a time to ponder some difficult policy options. Doubtless, some old chestnuts will reappear. Already, we are reviewing the same old glowing reports about the merits of ethanol as a motor fuel. Energy farms will be enthusiastically revisited. *Bio*-refineries, converting plant material to chemicals and transport fuels will once again be fervently discussed. We will, *again*, gloss over limitations of existing technology and the levels of subsidies required for the wider use of cultivated energy crops as sources of energy. The Brazilian Government's support for automobile-gasoline grade ethanol from maize and sugar cane was one of the more expensive examples of its kind. With recent high prices for petroleum-derived gasoline, such projects might just break even – for a while.

However, some things do not change rapidly. For example, we could not cultivate crops for large-scale power generation without competing with food production. It would take one-and-a-half-times all the arable land of a country such as South Africa to grow enough energy crops to power the UK alone[7] (about 70 gigawatts). On the other hand, there are obvious advantages in generating power from forestry residues, farming and municipal wastes, where feasible. Technically, it may not be possible entirely to replace coal-firing with wood in power stations;[8] however, marginally supplementing fossil fuels with small proportions of biomass can make several percentages difference in carbon dioxide emissions. The fact remains, however, that we still need to determine from where the bulk of our future energy supplies will come. At present, we live in a world fuelled and powered by coal, gas, oil and, alas, nuclear energy, and only a small component of renewables. While no contribution is too small in conserving resources and reducing harmful emissions, it is as well to realize that renewables cannot alter overall energy supply trends.

To make matters worse, the debate about where we go from here is laced with a number of misconceptions that seem to have taken on a life of their own. We do not really have a sound method for establishing a reliable link between the present cycle of global warming and the rise in carbon dioxide concentrations in the atmosphere. We *suspect* that such a link exists. We do not know why the planet has gone through similar cycles in the past and how the atmosphere has returned to lower carbon dioxide concentrations. The *fact* is, it would be a good idea to try to reduce carbon dioxide emissions, as much for fear of global warming as for slowing down our rate of resource utilization. Furthermore, we constantly need to remind ourselves that we should not treat the Blue Planet as an immense rubbish tip.

Secondly, received wisdom would have us believe that we must recover the carbon dioxide generated through fossil fuel utilization and store it somewhere, and that we must burn hydrogen instead of these 'dirty' fuels and make up the balance with renewables. 'Carbon-capture-and-storage' would require that we concentrate the carbon dioxide formed during fossil fuel combustion, compress the captured gases to about 200 bars, transmit them somewhere (by high-pressure gas pipelines), and pump them into underground reservoirs and hope they do not leak back up through the rock formations. Proponents of CO_2-sequestration have calculated the cost in money, energy utilization and accompanying further carbon dioxide emissions to be about two-cents per kilowatt hour.[9] This represents nearly a 40 per cent mark-up based on current US electricity prices.[10] For the UK *alone*, this would cost \$7–8 billion *every year*. Carbon dioxide capture and storage is thus both technically difficult and potentially extremely costly. It is also pointless unless every other country emitting large amounts of carbon dioxide does the same. After all, we could not ring-fence the air over any particular country.

Regarding the use of hydrogen as a common non-polluting fuel, it is useful to establish that pure hydrogen is an expensive chemical that must be produced in a chemical plant and stored under very high pressures. Both the separation plants producing hydrogen and the infrastructure for transmitting and storing hydrogen are expensive. The process would also produce amounts of carbon dioxide in proportions depending on the starting material that originally contained the hydrogen. Furthermore, every school-age child knows that hydrogen explodes when contacted with air. Our technical advice must be that compressed hydrogen is a far more dangerous substance to handle on a mass scale than natural gas. For example, we would need to accept that every traffic accident might end up with an explosion – the magnitude of which would depend on the amount of hydrogen left in the tank.

In my opinion, neither carbon-capture-and-storage nor the use of hydrogen as a fuel is likely to be applied on anything but the experimental scale. They simply cost too much. As for compressed hydrogen, it is a danger to anyone but trained technical personnel and, even then, technical personnel need to be extremely careful.[11]

We have been here for a long time

Meanwhile, it is interesting to have a look at what has happened since we first began *talking* about carbon dioxide-capture-and-storage. In the OECD countries alone, between 1990 and 2003, carbon dioxide emissions have increased by an additional 20–25 per cent.[12] Furthermore, globally, there are developments that will dwarf the economies in carbon dioxide emissions envisaged in the UK[13] or, for that matter, in Europe.

At present, the USA alone produces nearly 40 per cent of total world carbon dioxide emissions. The share of coal in total energy generation in the country has risen from about a quarter to a third since 1993 and now accounts for more than 50 per cent of all electricity production.[14] It is known that coal produces more carbon dioxide per unit of energy produced, compared to oil or natural gas. To date, the USA have not decided to curb carbon dioxide emissions; on the contrary, these are going up. Furthermore, the use of direct coal combustion is increasing worldwide, in addition to the increasing oil and gas usage that this book has been about. In China, there are plans to double coal-fired electricity generation capacity to over 650 GWe by 2020, whilst the other Asian giant, India, is also likely to vastly increase fossil fuel utilization. None of these countries are planning to capture-and-store carbon dioxide. They know and openly admit that it would stunt their economic growth.

Much of the difficulty arises from our twin, conflicting aims of wanting to run expanding economies, whilst adhering to a reasonable environmentalist agenda. In the first decade of the millennium, it is no longer a secret that major energy consuming countries, including the EU, Japan and the USA, are taking a closer look at nuclear energy again. In Europe, both coal-fired power stations and nuclear power plants are ageing. Across the continent, there has been an inability to take decisions about the next generation of power stations. In fairness, the policy drift is partly a consequence of the privatization of the energy supply industry. How the European Commission and individual member states eventually cope with potential contradictions between their perceptions of what needs to be done, and the decisions that are taken by private power companies, remains to be seen.

As the time horizon shortens, available options naturally diminish. In the medium term, available European and British alternatives appear restricted to returning to nuclear-based power generation, probably combined with increased dependence on Russian natural gas and/or increased supplies of LNG from the Middle East and West Africa. Thinking ahead for once, it might be instructive to compare the decommissioning costs of nuclear power stations with the potential costs of carbon dioxide capture and storage. In that race at least, nuclear energy appears to come out far ahead.

One clear, credible and practical route to damping down carbon dioxide and other emissions would be to economize, to use *less* energy, *less* fossil fuels for non-essential purposes. This requires a consensus based on public awareness and no one will earn brownie points for turning down the lights at Christmas. The second route would be to examine *feasible* renewables options (they exist!), while accepting up front that they will always be a relatively small component in the energy equation.

It is difficult not to observe that the energy policy community has for some years been looking for rapid solutions in places where no quick fixes are to be found. In Europe and in the UK, we are inexorably moving towards more nuclear energy and more Russian and other natural gas imports. It is, furthermore, useful to note that little else is actually being done about our future energy economy and suspected climate change problems at present.

The foregoing is submitted as a plea for doing our homework on energy and environmental matters with a little more care.

Endnotes

(All URLs were correct at the time of printing)

Introduction

1   I owe this classification to Deniz Kandiyoti. Personal communication.

Chapter I

1   http://www.eia.doe.gov/emeu/cabs/World_Oil_Transit_Choke
     points/ Background.html
2   http://en.rian.ru/world/20060119/43086818.html
3   Kumar, P., *Express India*, 'Iran gas pipeline is now dead';
     http://www.expressindia.com/fullstory.php?newsid=62218
4   Ibid.
5   According to post-Soviet authors, Russia held first place in 1901,
     when her production was nearly 11.7 million tons, out of a world
     total of 23 million tons. (Cherniaev, V. D., Vdovin, G. A., Yassin,
     E. M. and Stavrovsky, E. R., 'Oil Transportation', in N. A. Krylov,
     A. A. Bokserman and E. R. Stavrovsky (eds), *The Oil Industry of the
     Former Soviet Union* (Amsterdam: Gordon & Breach Science
     Publishers, 1998) p. 187.)
6   Churchill, W. S., *The World Crisis 1911–1918* (London: Odhams
     Press Ltd, 1938).
7   Pees, Samuel T., 'Oil History' 2004; http://www.oilhistory.com/
     pages/Pipelines/pipelines.html

8   Smaller diameter pipelines linking well-heads to storage and concentration facilities.

9   Depending on one's point of view, the great body of water surrounded by the Arabian Peninsula, Kuwait, Iraq and Iran may alternatively be called the Persian Gulf, the Arabian Gulf, or by its less well-known Turkish name of the Gulf of Basra (I think 'the Gulf' will be simpler).

10 Cherniaev *et al.*, op. cit., p. 196.

11 Tarbell, I. M., *The History of The Standard Oil Company* (New York: University of Rochester, 1996; original publication McClure, Phillips & Co., 1904). http://www.history.rochester.edu/fuels/tarbell/MAIN.HTM

12 F. Halliday mentions ' ... an American-Iranian oil entrepreneur [who] used to give out bumper-stickers saying "Happiness is Multiple Pipelines" ...' (personal communication).

13 On the need for 'overarching legal frameworks', see P. Stevens, 'Cross-Border Oil and Gas Pipelines: Problems and Prospects', Joint UNDP/World Bank Energy Sector Management Assistance Programme (ESMAP, June 2003.

14 Stevens, op. cit.

15 http://home.businesswire.com/portal/site/google/index.jsp?ndmViewId=news_view&newsId=20060913005370&newsLang=en

16 About $425 per kilowatt.

17 Efficiencies of 55–60 per cent are higher by about 15 per cent than those of modern conventional coal-fired plants.

18 Tongia, R. and Arunachalam, V. S., *Economic & Political Weekly* (1999) XXXIV (18); http://iis-db.stanford.edu/evnts/3917/Tongia_pipeline.pdf

19 Tongia and Arunachalam, op. cit.

20 1 bar is ambient pressure.

21 Robins, B., *Sydney Morning Herald* online (22/06/2004): http://www.smh.com.au/articles/2004/06/22/1087844940050.html

22 http://ktva.com/alaska/ci_4331340

23 In 1929, when the Company was reorganized, Standard Oil of New Jersey (later ESSO, then Exxon) and the SOCONY (Standard Oil Company of New York, later Mobil) took up 25 per cent ownership of the IPC (see Holden and Johns, 1982, p. 111). In the low-oil-price crisis of the late 1990s, these two giant companies split off from J. D. Rockefeller's empire and re-merged to form a new company now known simply as Exxon-Mobil.

24 See, for example, Yergin, D., *The Prize: the epic quest for oil, money and power* (New York: Free Press, 2003; original publication: New York: Simon & Schuster, 1990).

25 Yergin, op. cit.

26 McLellan, B., *Oil and Gas Finance and Accounting* 7/2 (1992) pp. 79–94.

27 Stauffer, T., 'Natural gas and Gulf oil: boon or bane', in *Gulf Energy and the World* (Abu Dhabi UAE: Emirates Centre for Strategic Studies and Research, 1997) pp. 65–83.

28 Natural gas is found in oil wells. This is termed 'associated' gas (i.e. associated with oil), in contrast to wells principally producing non-associated gas. The latter also bring up variable amounts of condensates, called natural gas liquids (NGLs).

29 Depending on the amount of natural gas liquids (NGL) recovered and the price of oil, this 'natural gasoline' may impact significantly on the profitability of operations. NGL consists of aliphatics, mostly ranging from C6 to C9 hydrocarbons.

30 Kandiyoti, R., 'Bench scale experiment design for developing co-pyrolysis and co-gasification technologies,' *Int. J. Power and Energy Systems* 24 (2004) 205–14.

31 Hatheway, A. W., website on 'Former Manufactured Gas Plants'; http://www.hatheway.net/01_history.htm

32 Hatheway, op. cit.

33 A high-grade fuel mainly composed of C3–C4 hydrocarbons. It is produced as a by-product in oil refineries and may be distributed in small steel cylinders for domestic use.

34 Aromatic chemicals were not the only danger. The plant director, a gentlemanly and competent man, died not long after our visit. I was told that his car hit a tree following a night of binge drinking, another of the occupational hazards threatening the inhabitants of this beautiful city.

35 Stauffer, op. cit.

36 The argument could be taken further, by suggesting that in the absence of North Sea gas, Gulf *oil*-derived fuels might have replaced the ageing UK coal-fired stations. Taken to extremes, this argument invites Gulf oil producers to feel suspicious about *every* other form of fuel on the planet.

37 UK Government Energy White Paper, 'Our Energy Future – creating a low carbon economy', February 2003; www.dti.gov.uk/energy/whitepaper

38 By the end of 2002, the total installed power capacity in China had reached 357 GW. The fossil-fuel-fired component of this capacity was about 75 per cent and coal-fired units accounted for more than 95 per cent of fossil-fired capacity. Total installed capacity will reach 430 GW by 2005. At the time of writing, *all* of this new capacity has come on stream.

39 http://intranet.concawe.org/1/MLLCLKNBHMMOIJGFKNG
    DGEDO5JWYP3R6Y1QEH1Q7HN9YBDA3BYT6P3BY9LTE4Q/
    CEnet/docs/DLS/CR122-OilPipelines-2003-02732-01-E.pdf
40 Lako, P. and Jansen, J. C., 'What scenario studies tell about security
    of energy supply in Europe', Dutch General Energy Council (AER)
    ECN; ECN-C—01-054, June 2001. http://www.ecn.nl/docs/library/
    report/2001/c01054.pdf
41 COMMISSION OF THE EUROPEAN COMMUNITIES;
    COM(2000) 769; Brussels, 29 November 2000; Green Paper:
    'Towards a European strategy for the security of energy supply'.
42 The Green Paper is alluding primarily to Poland, Hungary and the
    Czech Republic. At the time of writing, the accession of these
    countries has been completed.
43 As kindly pointed out by V. Vesovic, Punta Arenas is also at the end
    of a good land road from Rio Gallegos, on the Argentinian side of
    the border.
44 Total natural gas imports from Argentina in 1998 amounted to a lit-
    tle over 2 billion cubic metres p.a. By the end of 2002, this had
    increased to about 5.3 billion cubic metres p.a. The quantities
    involved are modest compared with, say, Russian gas exports of 190
    billion cubic metres p.a. in 2002. (IEA Statistics, International
    Energy Agency, Natural Gas Information 2003, Copyright
    OECD/IEA 2003, Paris, France; Part II, Table 7 and Part II, Table 9.)
45 http://www.bnamericas.com/story.jsp?sector=9&noticia=
    352478&idioma=I 'Petrobras cancels Bolivian investments, speeds
    up LNG import plans' – Bolivia, Brazil (Wednesday, 3 May, 2006
    17:22 (GMT -0400)).
46 The 'first' centre is Sasolburg, where the first South African coal-to-
    oil plant was constructed in the 1950s, with a capacity of 500,000
    tons of product liquids per year.
47 International Bank for Reconstruction and Development and
    International Finance Corporation; Report No 26757-MOZ; 22
    October 2003.
48 Ibid.
49 Variables have been devised in a Stanford University study to eval-
    uate the probable risks involved in cross-border projects. These
    depend largely on the level of political and economic integration,
    as well as the feasibility of doing straightforward business within
    each of the countries involved. The latter involves, among others,
    levels of expected corruption. The composite parameters, termed
    'proxy variables', include political risk score, total trade between the
    countries as a percentage of GDP and the strength of institutions for
    economic cooperation. http://pesd.stanford.edu/docs/2002mtg_gas/
    Briefing%20Book_3.pdf

Chapter II

1   http://www.journalnow.com/servlet/Satellite?pagename=
WSJ%2FMGArticle%2FWSJ_BasicArticle&c=MGArticle&cid
=1031777023840&path=!nationworld&s=1037645509161 [R2-001]
2   Cherniaev, V. D., Vdovin, G. A., Yassin, E. M. and Stavrovsky,
E. R., 'Oil Transportation', in N. A. Krylov, A. A. Bokserman and
E. R. Stavrovsky (eds), *The Oil Industry of the Former Soviet Union*
(Amsterdam: Gordon & Breach Science Publishers, 1998) p. 222.
3   Nigeria is Africa`s largest oil producer, with over 125 million tons
p.a. However, most Nigerians, especially those living in the oil-producing regions, live in abject poverty.
4   AllAfrica.com; Vanguard (Lagos); 30 July 2004; 'Oil Pipeline Fire
Kills Seven in Gov Nnamani's Town', Tony Edike in Enugu [R2-
002]
5   Engber, D., Slate Website; Friday, 30 December 2005; http://www.
slate.com/id/2133479/
6   *Angola Press*, 'Suspected militants blow up key Nigerian oil
pipeline,' Luanda – Saturday, 14 January 2006, 10:31:43 a.m. http://
www.angolapress-angop.ao/noticia-e.asp?ID=407513
7   Reed, T. C., *At the Abyss: An Insider's History of the Cold War* (New
York: Presidio Press, Ballantine Books, 2004) pp. 268–9.
8   http://www.kentucky.com/mld/kentucky/news/state/15129859.htm
9   http://intranet.concawe.org/1/MLLCLKNBHMMOIJGFK
NGDGEDO5JWYP3R6Y1QEH1Q7HN9YBDA3BYT6P3BY9LTE
4Q/ CEnet/docs/DLS/CR122-OilPipelines-2003-02732-01-E.pdf
10 Report No 3/06, p. IV; http://www.concawe.be/Content/Default.
asp?PageID=31
11 Cherniaev *et al.*, op. cit., p. 248.
12 Cherniaev *et al.*, op. cit., p. 237.
13 http://www.rmi.org/sitepages/pid785.php
14 http://english.eastday.com/eastday/englishedition/business/
userobject1ai2238066.html
15 http://iraqwar.mirror-world.ru/article/98020
16 http://www.baltimoresun.com/news/nationworld/bal-te.nationlede
27aug27,0,5368580.story?coll=bal-nationworld-headlines
17 http://www.stwr.net/content/view/1049/37/
18 http://www.baltimoresun.com/news/nationworld/bal-te.nationlede
27aug27,0,5368580.story?coll=bal-nationworld-headlines
19 http://marketwatch.com/News/Story/Story.aspx?guid=
%7B16CE7339-7685-4492-9814-4AB26FB6BE77%7D&siteid
=mktw&dist=
20 http://www.stwr.net/content/view/1049/37/

21 *Petroleum News*; http://www.adn.com/money/industries/oil/pipeline/ story/8192350p-8085994c.html

22 http://www.corribsos.com/index.php?id=529

23 *Human Rights on the Line: The Baku–Tblisi–Ceyhan pipeline project* (London: Amnesty International UK, May 2003).

24 'Contracting out of human rights; The Chad–Cameroon pipeline project' (London: Amnesty International UK, The Human Rights Action Centre).

25 Urhobo Historical Society (Nigeria), *Reports on Oil and Natural Gas Pipeline Problems in the Niger Delta* (2002) http://www.waado.org/ Environment/EnvironmentPage.html

26 http://www.thestandard.com.hk/news_detail.asp?pp_cat =17&art_id=23535&sid=8985810&con_type=1

27 Roland Ogbonnaya: http://www.thisdayonline.com/nview.php?id= 54528 (see also the AllAfrica.com website for 31 July 2006).

28 Africa News Dimension (15/9/2006): http://westafrica.andnetwork. com/index?service=direct/1/Home/ recent.fullStory&sp=l51878

29 The state-owned pulp and paper company, SEKA, has dumped countless tons of chemically active lignin waste into the nearby sea, since the 1940s. As a result, no live fish have been sighted in the large and beautiful Bay of Izmit for two generations. The then state-owned petrochemical installations, constructed nearby during the 1960s and later, have proceeded to dump their waste into the sea with similar impunity. Turkish state-owned industries provide many similar examples.

30 Standard Oil of California, later renamed Chevron.

31 Chris Richards, *New Internationalist* 361; October 2003: http://newint.org/issue361/; 28 September 2007

32 Ruth Morris, *Dow Jones Newswires* 'Colombia's No. 2 Oil Pipeline To Resume Pumping Monday', 25 August 2003, 14:56.

33 The 780-km, 24-in pipeline began operation in 1986, is mostly buried at depths of 6 ft. Since 1986, there have been more than 900 such incidents and a loss of some 2.5 million barrels of crude. In 2001, Colombia produced about 600,000 barrels per day and its exports accounted for less than 2 per cent of US imports. See Karl Penhaul, *San Francisco Chronicle* (Saturday, 16 February 2002).

34 See Karl Penhaul, *San Francisco Chronicle* (Saturday, 16 February 2002).

35 Like most oil pipelines, this is a multiproduct line that can carry crude oil or finished products, such as gasoline. The line has a capacity of pumping 130,000 barrels per day, a little over 6 million tons p.a.

36 Summary report of the book 'Some Common Concerns', published in September 2002 by PLATFORM, The Corner House, Friends of the Earth International, Campagna per la Riforma della Banca Mondiale, CEE Bankwatch Network and The Kurdish Human Rights Project. The full report (same title), published by Campagna per la Riforma della Banca Mondiale, CEE Bankwatch Network, The Corner House, Friends of the Earth International, The Kurdish Human Rights Project and PLATFORM, was written and researched by Greg Muttitt and James Marriott of PLATFORM, with material from several other collaborators: http://www.foe.co.uk/resource/reports/common_concerns.pdf

37 One community leader was killed in an act blamed on the paramilitaries, and a lawyer who represented the farmers fled Colombia after she discovered she was on a paramilitary hit list. She was granted political asylum in Britain in 2002.

38 http://www.thestandard.com.hk/news_detail.asp?pp_cat=17&art_id=23535&sid=8985810&con_type=1

39 In 1946, Ardahan was a sub-province of the 'vilayet' of Kars. Stalin's demand therefore covered *two* Turkish provinces. Following the break-up of the Soviet Union, Kars was subdivided into three vilayets: Ardahan, I dır and a smaller vilayet of Kars. This arrangement left Artvin and Ardahan facing the Georgian frontier, whilst Kars faces the Armenian border and I dır faces Armenia, the small Azeri enclave of Nakhchivan, as well as a small tract of the Iranian frontier.

40 The English archaeologist and diplomat Layard has left eye-witness accounts of manhunts and plundering raids by Kurdish tribes of the Mosul area (just south of the modern frontier with Iraq, agreed in 1926), targeting Nestorian villages and local Christians, whose Church organization is distinct from and predates that of the Patriarchate of Constantinople. Layard, A. H., *Nineveh and its remains* (London, Albemarle Street: John Murray, 1854), vol. I.

Chapter III

1 Anscombe, F. F., *The Ottoman Gulf* (New York: Columbia University Press, 1997) p. 29.

2 Yergin, D., *The Prize: the epic quest for oil, money and power* (New York: Free Press, 2003; original publication: New York: Simon & Schuster, 1990).

3 Longrigg, S. H., *Oil in the Middle East* (London: Oxford University Press, 1954).

4 Longrigg, op. cit., p. 76.

5 The total length of the northern leg was 856 km.

6   The southern leg was about 1,000 km long.
7   The Barcelona Transit Convention of 1921.
8   Longrigg, op. cit., p. 87.
9   He had resigned from British Government service in 1925.
10 Holden, D. and Johns, R., *The House of Saud* (London and Sydney: Pan Books, 1981) p. 81.
11 *IPC Handbook*, first edition, compiled in the Company's Head Office, London, 1948.
12 Halliday, F., *The Middle East in International Relations* (Cambridge University Press, 2005); see Chapter 3, pp. 75–96.
13 Farouk-Sluglett, M. and Sluglett, P., *Iraq Since 1958: From Revolution to Dictatorship* (London and New York: KPI, 1987).
14 Longrigg, op. cit., pp. 81, 120.
15 Longrigg, op. cit., p. 180.
16 Vuillamy, E., *The Observer* (London), Sunday, 20 April 2003.
17 'Jordanian Gov't denies plans to restart Kirkuk–Haifa oil pipeline', *Jordan Times*, 10 April 2003. Posted on 04/10/2003 3:19:34 PM PDT
18 Vuillamy, op. cit.
19 http://almashriq.hiof.no/lebanon/300/380/388/tapline/general/index.html. Excerpts from *Handbook for American Employees*, vol. 1, 1952, as issued by Arabian American Oil Company. Prepared by Roy Lebkicher, p. 45.
20 http://almashriq.hiof.no/lebanon/300/380/388/tapline/
21 Gendzier, I. L., *Notes from the Minefield: US Intervention in Lebanon and the Middle East, 1945–1958* (New York: Columbia University Press, 1997; also published by Westview Press, 1998).
22 Holden and Johns, op. cit., p. 149.
23 Longrigg, op. cit., p. 206.
24 Yergin, op. cit., p. 425.
25 Stevens, P., 'Cross-Border Oil and Gas Pipelines: Problems and Prospects', Joint UNDP/World Bank Energy Sector Management Assistance Programme (ESMAP) June 2003. http://www.dundee.ac.uk/cepmlp/journal/html/Vol14/Vol14_2.pdf
26 Stevens, op. cit.
27 Iraq Country Analysis Brief; US Energy Information Administration: http://www.eia.doe.gov/emeu/cabs/iraq.html
28 Stevens, P., 'Pipelines or Pipedreams? Lessons from the history of Arab transit pipelines', *The Middle East Journal*, 54/ 2 (Spring 2000), pp. 224–41.
29 US Energy Information Agency: http://www.eia.doe.gov/emeu/cabs/iraq.html
30 http://www.earthtimes.org/articles/show/21588.html; Thursday 18 January, 2007.
31 Yergin op. cit., pp. 490–1.

32 Yergin, op. cit., p. 492.
33 Oldest surviving son at the death of King Abdul-Aziz Ibn Saud in 1953.
34 Holden and Johns, op. cit., p. 210.
35 Holden and Johns, op. cit., pp. 220–1.
36 Alhajji, A. F., 'The Failure of the Oil Weapon'; http://www2. onu.edu/~aalhajji/ibec385/oil_weapon2.htm#_ftn3
37 Holden and Johns, op. cit., p. 283.
38 Stevens, P., 'Pipelines or Pipedreams?', op. cit.
39 Holden and Johns, op. cit., p. 298.
40 Stevens, P., 'Pipelines or Pipedreams?', op. cit.
41 Stevens, P., ibid.
42 Stevens, P., ibid.
43 http://www.eia.doe.gov/emeu/cabs/iraq.html
44 Stevens, P., ibid.
45 Stevens, P., ibid.
46 http://www.eia.doe.gov/emeu/cabs/iraq.html
47 http://www.eia.doe.gov/emeu/cabs/World_Oil_Transit_Chokepoints/ Hormuz.html
48 http://www.historyofwar.org/articles/wars_tanker.html
49 http://www.eia.doe.gov/emeu/cabs/saudi.html
50 Stevens, P., 'Cross-Border Oil and Gas Pipelines: Problems and Prospects', op. cit., p. 76.
51 http://english.aljazeera.net/NR/exeres/C42E2CC2-92AA-4D31-A338-C9B733F11649.htm
52 http://english.aljazeera.net/NR/exeres/C42E2CC2-92AA-4D31-A338-C9B733F11649.htm
53 http://www.eia.doe.gov/emeu/cabs/iraq.html
54 http://www.arabianbusiness.com/index.php?option= com_content&view=article&id=9763 (21 March 2007).
55 Ewell, M. W. Jr., Brito, D. and Noer, J., 'An Alternative Pipeline Strategy in the Persian Gulf', April 1996: http://www.rice.edu/ energy/publications/docs/TrendsinMiddleEast_AlternativePipeline Strategy.pdf
56 These reagents work by lowering friction losses between eddies, formed due to turbulence.
57 http://www.eia.doe.gov/emeu/security/choke.html#SUEZ
58 Stevens, P., 'Cross-Border Oil and Gas Pipelines: Problems and Prospects', op. cit., p. 72.
    The 320 km SuMed line runs Ain Sukhna on the Gulf of Suez to Sidi Kerir on the Mediterranean coast. The two parallel 42-in (1,067mm) lines opened in 1978 with a capacity of 1.6 million barrels per day. Completion of the Dashour pumping station capacity in 1994 increased capacity to 2.5 Mb/d.

59 http://www.mopm.gov.sa/html/en/outkingdom_e.html
60 Stevens, P., 'Cross-Border Oil and Gas Pipelines: Problems and Prospects', op. cit., p. 72.
61 Energy in Egypt (June 2005); Oil and Gas Investor (current): http://www.arabicnews.com/ansub/Daily/Day/010915/2001091542.html
62 www.oilandgasinvestor.com/pdf/Egypt.pdf
63 http://www.gasandoil.com/goc/news/ntm14192.htm
64 Second phase of Arab Gas Pipeline completed; Nicosia (14 January 2006);   http://news.webindia123.com/news/showdetails.asp?id=219913&cat=World
65 http://www.gulfoilandgas.com/webpro1/MAIN/Mainnews.asp?id=572
66 http://www.iags.org/iraqpipelinewatch.htm (23 February 2006).
67 http://www.rferl.org/featuresarticle/2006/08/7ABE73A0-0FF0-4099-B42E-93D39FE1CEC1.html
68 http://www.latimes.com/news/nationworld/world/la-fg-oil25jan25,0,7362139.story?coll=la-home-headlines
69 http://observer.guardian.co.uk/business/story/0,,2020560,00.html
70 http://www.zmag.org/content/showarticle.cfm?SectionID=15&ItemID=12342
71 http://www.platts.com/HOME/News/9324393.xml?sub=HOME&p=HOME/News
72 Stevens, P., 'Cross-Border Oil and Gas Pipelines: Problems and Prospects', op. cit., p. 78.
73 The increase between 1971 and 1973 was important, from 809 million in 1971 to 1,061 million tons in 1973. IEA Statistics, International Energy Agency, Oil Information 2005, Copyright OECD/IEA 2005, Paris, France; p. II.27.OECD/IEA 2005, Paris, France; p. II.27.

Chapter IV

1 Iqbal Siddiquee, 'Bibiyana Gas Field Production likely to start by early Dec'; The Daily Star: http://www.thedailystar.net/2006/09/20/d60920100190.htm
2 S. N. Visvanath, A Hundred Years of Oil, revised edn (New Delhi: Vikas Publishing House, 1997).
3 'Reliance Signs $4.5 Billion Contracts for Gas Fields'; Bloomberg.com; 17 March 2007: http:// www.bloomberg.com/apps/news?pid=20601080&sid=asrpDR9klWc&refer=asia

4 India was the only source of diamonds in the World until the 1760s, when diamonds were discovered in Brazil and, about a century later, in South Africa.
5 Between 2000 and 2004, Indian oil production edged up from 36.5 to 38.6 million tons p.a., whilst imports jumped from 74 to 90 million tons in 2003. During the same period, gas production has stabilized at a little under 28 billion cubic metres, where potential demand is estimated to be double these amounts.
6 http://telegraphindia.com/1040209/asp/business/story_2875474.asp
7 Visvanath, op. cit.
8 http://www.eia.doe.gov/emeu/cabs/india.html
9 IEA Statistics, International Energy Agency, Natural Gas Information 2005, Copyright OECD/IEA 2005, Paris, France; Part I, p. 21.
10 'Natural Gas in India'; http://www.infraline.com/iplus/iplus.asp?Id= 42; Monday, 13 March 2006.
11 Multiply by 36 for the price in terms of billion cubic metres, the other common unit.
12 http://www.marinelink.com/Story/ShowStory.aspx?StoryID= 201024
13 Multiply by 36 for the equivalent price 'per 1,000 cubic metres', which is the other common price unit.
14 During Hurricanes Katrina and Rita in 2005, 46 offshore platforms were destroyed, 20 were heavily damaged and more than 100 pipelines were affected. Pinon, J. R., 18 February 2006; http:// www.miami.com/mld/miamiherald/news/opinion/13902289.htm
15 http://psg.deloitte.com/spectron/L3M_UKGasIndex.asp
16 ONGC was first established as an arm of the Geological Survey of India in 1956. It was converted into a Commission – Oil and Natural Gas Commission (ONGC) by an act of Parliament in 1959. In 1994, ONGC became a public limited company: Oil and Natural Gas Corporation Limited (ONGC Ltd). Consequent upon the recent round of disinvestment, the Government equity holding in the Corporation is 74.15 per cent (Government of India, Ministry of Petroleum and Natural gas website): http://petroleum.nic.in/ vision.doc
17 http://www.lngexpress.com/shownews.asp?id=9184
18 http://in.news.yahoo.com/060308/43/62vox.html
19 http://www.consortiumnews.com/Print/123001a.html
20 http://www.rediff.com/money/2004/apr/17dpc.htm
21 India's National Thermal Power Corporation.
22 http://www.rediff.com/money/2005/oct/28dpc.htm
23 'Petronet shies off Dabhol gas contracts' (Tuesday, 6 March 2007): http://www.dnaindia.com/report.asp?NewsID=1083345

24 'Oil diplomacy pays off, India signs mega LNG import deal with Iran', *The Indian Express* (Saturday, 8 January 2005): http://www.indianexpress.com/res/web/pIe/full_story.php?content_id=62321

25 http://www.khaleejtimes.com/DisplayArticleNew.asp?xfile =data/subcontinent/2006/July/subcontinent_July845.xml&section =subcontinent

26 http://www.tribuneindia.com/2006/20060808/edit.htm

27 http://timesofindia.indiatimes.com/articleshow/1513311.cms

28 The 1,148-km pipeline from Khuzestan province runs in Azerbaijan for some 297 km. The 75-bar high-pressure line has a diameter of 42 in with nine compressor stations (three in Azerbaijan).

29 http://www.highbeam.com/doc/1G1:43019596/IGAT-1+ %7eA%7e+IGAT-2.html

30 Liquefied petroleum gas, much used for domestic cooking.

31 http://us.rediff.com/money/2005/feb/21guest.htm

32 http://www.eia.doe.gov/emeu/cabs/Pakistan/NaturalGas.html

33 http://www.eia.doe.gov/emeu/cabs/Pakistan/Coal.html

34 IEA Gas Information (2006); IEA-OECD Paris.

35 Tongia, R. and Arunachalam, V. S., *Economic & Political Weekly* XXXIV/18 (1999); http://iis-db.stanford.edu/evnts/3917/Tongia_ pipeline.pdf

36 New Delhi, IRNA report (21 February 2003); http://www.payvand. com/news/03/feb/1101.html

37 http://www.iranmania.com/News/ArticleView/Default. asp?News Code=19250&NewsKind=Business%20%26%20Economy

38 http://www.dailytimes.com.pk/default.asp?page=story_11-2- 2005_pg3_1

39 http://www.eia.doe.gov/emeu/cabs/iran.html

40 (Saturday, 26 November 2005, 01:26:26 a.m.): http://economictimes. indiatimes.com/articleshow/1308681.cms

41 (Islamabad, 6 October 2005): http://www.dawn.com/2005/10/07/ top9.htm

42 Pakistan expects delivery of two F-16s in December 2005, 20 in 2006 and the other 55 in 2007, costing about $40 million each. http://sify.com/news/international/fullstory.php?id=13954476

43 http://www.dailytimes.com.pk/default.asp?page=story_17-4- 2005_pg7_30

44 http://www.robertcutler.org/blog/archives/cat_nabuccopipeline. html

45 Ibid.

46 Ranjan, Amitav, *Indian Express* website; posted online (Friday, 2 December 2005 at 01:35 hours IST): http://www.indianexpress. com/full_story.php?content_id=83117

47 http://www.mumbai-central.com/grapevine/msg02059.html#6

48 http://www.paktribune.com/news/index.shtml?151359
49 Reuters, 'Pricing agreed, India sees gas pipeline deal by June' (Tuesday, 6 February 2007): http://in.today.reuters.com/News/ newsArticle.aspx?type=businessNews&storyID=2007-02- 06T163229Z_01_NOOTR_RTRJONC_0_India-286528-2.xml
50 http://www.hindu.com/thehindu/holnus/001200609171132.htm
51 (22 February 2007): http://www2.irna.ir/en/news/view/menu-237/ 0702221797162415.htm
52 http://newstodaynet.com/guest/2810gu1.htm
53 http://www.indianexpress.com/story/26338.html
54 http://burma.total.com/en/contexte/p_1_2.htm
55 ONGC: Oil and Natural gas Corporation. GAIL: Gas Authority of India Limited.
56 (17 March 2007): http://nation.ittefaq.com/artman/publish/article_ 34780.shtml
57 These were the same generals who later had Zulfikar Ali Bhutto executed.
58 Hali, S. M., 'Resistance movement in Bangladesh', *The Nation* (Pakistan) website (Friday, 11 March 2005): http://nation.com.pk/ daily/mar-2005/11/columns5.php
59 Ibid.
60 *The New Nation* website (22 February 2005, 21:51): http://nation. ittefaq.com/artman/publish/article_16449.shtml
61 *The Bangladesh Journal* website (2 March 2005): http://www. bangladeshjournal.com/index.php?ID=3566&tim=2-3-2005
62 Kotur Tepe, Korpedzhe, Nebit Dag, Shatlyk, Malay, Daulatabad and Yashlar
63 Rashid, A., *Taliban* (London: I. B. Tauris, republished Pan Books, 2001).
64 *Reuters India* dispatch: IST: 'Afghan gas pipeline "very real project" – Karzai' (Tuesday 4 October 2005, 6:08 p.m.).
65 British Agencies Afghanistan Group, Monthly review, November 2005.
66 http://www.adb.org/Media/Articles/2005/8418_South_Asia_gas/

Chapter V

1 Cherniaev, V. D., Vdovin, G. A., Yassin, E. M. and Stavrovsky, E. R., 'Oil Transportation', in N. A. Krylov, A. A. Bokserman and E. R. Stavrovsky (eds), *The Oil Industry of the Former Soviet Union* (Amsterdam: Gordon & Breach Science Publishers, 1998) pp. 71 and 187.

2   Mixture of light (C5 to C9) hydrocarbons that condense when natural gas is cooled down following extraction. Condensate is also called 'natural gasoline' and may be blended directly with distilled products.

3   Stevens, P., 'Cross-Border Oil and Gas Pipelines: Problems and Prospects,' Joint Report by UNDP/World Bank Energy Sector Management Assistance Programme (ESMAP), June 2003: http://www.worldbank.org/ogmc/crossborderoilandgaspipelines.pdf

4   Over 65,000 km of primary lines, 400 pump stations, and a design capacity of 600 million tons p.a. 'Pipelines to Progress: FSU Oil Exports Past, Present, Future', speech by Richard H. Matzke, President of Chevron Overseas Petroleum Inc. to the National Association of Petroleum Investment Analysts on 21 May 1997: http://www.chevrontexaco.com/news/archive/chevron_speech/199 7/97-5-21-matzke.asp

5   Cherniaev et al., op. cit., p. 196.

6   The main Druzhba line runs from the Samara hub (in Russia), through to near Saratov (Russia) and Unecha (Russia) to Mozyr in Belarus, and then splits into three lines. The first leg turns north and runs into Vilnius in Lithuania. The second leg runs west–northwest to Brest (in Poland) and eventually to Rostock in (former East) Germany. The third line runs south-west from Mozyr (Belarus) into Brody and to Uzhgorod in Ukraine, then forks into a line for Hungary and a line into Bratislava (Slovakia), which continues into the Czech Republic (passing between Plzen and Prague) northward into southern (former East) Germany, making a junction east of Berlin with the northern arm from Brest and running into Rostock. The line to Latvia (which has now stopped pumping) splits off from the main line between Samara and Mozyr. One spur adds to the line coming from Vysokoye in Russia.

7   Cherniaev et al., op. cit., p. 188.

8   Itar-Tass; 24 May 2004.

9   Bellona Foundation; http://www.bellona.no/en/energy/30532.html

10 Bellona Foundation; http://www.bellona.no/en/energy/30532.html

11 Russia Pipeline Oil Spill Study. Joint UNDP/World Bank Energy Sector Management Assistance Programme (ESMAP); desk study that was performed by Det Norske Veritas (DNV), April 2003: http://www.esmap.org/esmap/site.nsf/b5aafad54e442b5d85256cc30 06bd563/0b18576fb7bb44da85256db400600f13/$FILE/034- 03%20Russia%20Pipeline%20Oil%20Spill%20Study%20Report.p df

12 Cherniaev et al., op. cit., p. 248.

13 Ibid., p. 59.

14 IEA Statistics: Oil Information 2004; Copyright OECD/IEA, 2004, Paris, pp. II.26 and II.48.
15 http://www.interfax.com/com?item=Rus&pg=0&id=5784451 &req=
16 Up from 135 million tons in 1999.
17 In the late 1980s, the FSU produced 600 million tons and exported about 100 million tons. We assume that they consumed 500 million tons. According to IEA Oil Information (2005) in 2003, the FSU produced 555 million tons (p. 96) and exported 287 million tons (p. 119). This suggests the demand must be 268 million tons. However, the 'demand' table gives 172 million tons (p. 80) for the whole of the FSU. The drop in demand for the FSU according to the (production-minus-export) calculation is 232 million tons. According to the direct 'demand' figure, the drop in demand for the whole of the FSU is 328 million tons. Russian demand within the FSU differs by a factor of approximately (12/17). Accordingly, two calculations for the falls in calculations for Russia give 163 and 231 million tons. For want of more accurate information, we take an average of the two and arrive at about 200 million tons. The calculation is approximate but nonetheless useful.
18 Blagov, S., Article on 'KWR Advisor' website: http://www.atimes.com/atimes/Central_Asia/FF16Ag01.html
19 Ebel, R. E., 'Russian reserves and oil potential', paper presented to 'Russian Oil and OPEC's Policies' meeting, organized by Centre for Global Energy Studies, 15 March 2004. Centre for Strategic and International Studies, Washington D.C.; http://www.csis.org/energy/040315_ebel.pdf
20 Sandul, I., 'Odesa–Brody oil pipeline remains dry', The Ukrainian Weekly, 23 December 2001, 51/LXIX.
21 Matzke, op. cit.
22 http://en.rian.ru/analysis/20070222/61123316.html; 22 February 2007.
23 Peter Rutland, 'Lost Opportunities Energy and Politics in Russia', The National Bureau of Asian Research 8/5 (1997); presentation by Matt Sagers to a conference on world oil supplies at Florida International University, 16 November 2000. Cited in: Amy-Myers Jaffe and Robert A. Manning, Russia, Energy and the West, in: Survival 43/2 (Summer 2001) pp. 133–52.
24 Amy-Myers Jaffe and Robert A. Manning, 'Russia, Energy and the West', in Survival 43/2 (Summer 2001), pp. 133–52. (Data provided by PIRA Energy Group.)
25 The pipeline will cost over $500 million and the port facilities an additional $3.7 billion.
26 (March 2005): http://www.eia.doe.gov/emeu/cabs/baltics.html

27 Stevens, op. cit., p. 71.
28 *Novosti* (22 November 2005): http://en.rian.ru/business/20051122/42175298.html
29 Through the (to be enlarged) Caspian Pipeline Consortium (CPC) pipeline to the tanker terminal at Novorossiysk.
30 *Associated Press* (20 November 2005): http://www. mywest-texas.com/site/news.cfm?newsid=15610357&BRD=2288&PAG=461&dept_id=474112&rfi=6
31 Smolansky, O. M., 'Ukraine and Russia: an evolving marriage of inconvenience,' *ORBIS*, 48/1 (Winter 2004), pp. 117–34; p. 6. http://www.ingentaconnect.com/content/els/00304387/2004/00000048/00000001/art00117
32 Smolansky, op. cit.
33 Kramer, A. E., 'From Russia to Europe With a Natural Gas Pipeline,' *New York Times* (10 December 2005): http://www.nytimes.com/2005/12/10/business/worldbusiness/10pipe.html
34 'Baltic pipeline poses environmental threat – Estonian premier', *Novosti* (3 November 2005): http://en.rian.ru/world/20051103/41987041.html
35 In 2003, Russia supplied 10.2 billion cubic metres to Belarus; *Interfax* (17 March 2004).
36 Smolansky, op. cit.
37 Ibid.
38 'Barroso finally expresses support for refinery', *The Baltic Times* (14 March 2007).
39 http://www.rferl.org/featuresarticle/2005/12/21569639-8060-401A-82F1-74048E747922.html
40 Torbakov, I., *Eurasia Daily Monitor* (Friday, 6 January 2006): http://jamestown.org/edm/article.php?article_id=2370631
41 *The Associated Press* (17 January 2006): http://www. themoscowtimes.com/stories/2006/01/17/017.html
42 Comprising the 'Soyuz' and 'Friendship' pipelines and the associated 72 compressor stations.
43 Smolansky, op. cit.
44 Kupchinsky, R., 'Russia/Ukraine: Time Running Out In Gas Dispute', RFE/Radio Liberty (28 December 2005): http://www.rferl.org/featuresarticle/2005/12/21569639-8060-401A-82F1-74048E747922.html
45 Kupchinsky, op. cit.
46 The Henry Hub delivery point is a key gas pipeline hub in Erath, Louisiana.
47 Gas prices have been oscillating wildly. At the close of business on 13 January 2006, Bloomberg quoted Henry Hub spot at $307.44.
48 http://en.rian.ru/russia/20051214/42486051.html

49 http://www.kommersant.com/page.asp?id=639705
50 Ermakova, M., *Bloomberg* (2 January 2006): http://quote. bloomberg.com/apps/news?pid=10000006&sid=aPkKwoZEZhqg&r efer=home
51 Ermakova, op. cit.
52 $1.60 per thousand cubic metres for each 100 km.
53 Eckel, M., *Associated Press* (Wednesday, 4 January 2006): http:// news.yahoo.com/s/ap/20060104/ap_on_bi_ge/russia_ukraine_gas
54 Eckel, op. cit.
55 Torbakov, op. cit.
56 'Turkmen–Ukraine Gas Trade', *Global Witness*, April 2006; Washington, D.C.
57 http://www.eurasianet.org/departments/business/articles/ eav090606.shtml
58 It is worth wondering why anyone needs such estimates, since they nearly always turn out to be wrong and our world keeps ticking over, regardless.
59 *Gateway to Russia* (dispatch of 9 February 2005, 12:49 Moscow time): http://www.gateway2russia.com/st/art_267955.php
60 INTERFAX, 10 Jan. 2006, 12:31pm: http://www.interfax.ru/e/ B/finances/26.html?id_issue=11445096
61 *Novosti* website (18 August 2006).
62 Ebel, op. cit., p. 4.
63 US Energy Information Agency: http://www.eia.doe.gov/emeu/cabs/ turkey.pdf. At present rates of increase, Turkey estimates the volume of oil through the straits would reach some 190–200 million tons by 2009.
64 INTERTANKO Tanker Facts 2005: http://www.intertanko.com/ research/fact.pdf
65 US Energy Information Agency website; op. cit.
66 'ENI and Çalik seal contract on construction of new oil pipeline' (15 November 2005): http://www.azertag.com/en/index.shtml? language=english&catid=&news_year=&news_month=&news_day= &newsid=145877&themes_viewing=&themes_page=&themeid= &news_page=
67 http://www.forbes.com/markets/feeds/afx/2006/09/15/ afx3019559.html
68 *Kathimerini* (Athens) (27 September 2006): http://www. ekathimerini.com/4dcgi/news/economy_&xml/&aspKath/economy .asp?fdate=27/09/2006
69 (18 March 2007): http://en.rian.ru/analysis/20070318/ 61932071.html
70 Helmer, J., 'St. Nose is out of joint: Putin to the oil pump', *The Russia Journal*: http://www.russiajournal.com/node/18617

71   http://www.ekathimerini.com/4dcgi/_w_articles_politics_100002_05/09/2006_73836

72   Vladimir Socor (16 March 2007): http://jamestown.org/edm/article.php?article_id=2372014

73   NTVMSNBC (15 March 2007): http://www.ntvmsnbc.com/news/402871.asp

74   'Russia to transport oil through the Balkans' (18 March 2007): http://en.rian.ru/analysis/20070318/61932071.html

75   http://news.xinhuanet.com/english/2007-03/11/content_5827848.htm

76   Barry Wood, 'Putin signs off on $1.2 billion oil pipeline', *Malaysia Sun* (22 March 2007).

77   The industrial and residential sectors account for 20 and 14 per cent, respectively. US Energy Information Agency website: http://www.eia.doe.gov/emeu/cabs/turkey

78   Reed, T. C., *At the Abyss: An Insider's History of the Cold War* (New York: Presidio Press, Random House, 2004). See also Matt Loney (1 March 2004): http://www.zdnet.co.uk/print/?TYPE=story&AT=39147917-39020381t-10000002c [R2-003]

79   Martin, L. L., 'Coercive Cooperation' (Princeton NJ: Princeton University Press, 1992), p. 208.

80   Martin, L. L., ibid., p. 208.

81   Nearly half of the total was spent on the construction of the 396-km marine section and the remarkable high-pressure (250 bar) Beregovaya compressor station on the Russian side: http://www.gazprom.com/eng/articles/article8895.shtml

82   Two parallel 24-in (61-cm) diameter lines were laid down: http://www.offshore-technology.com/projects/blue_stream/

83   In 2010, Turkey is contracted to buy about 15 billion cubic metres of Russian natural gas from Blue-Stream, about 12.5 billion cubic metres Russian natural gas from the 'Progress Line' through Bulgaria, 10 billion cubic metres of natural gas from Iran, and about 6.5 billion cubic metres each from Azerbaijan and the LNG terminal in the Marmara Ereglisi. US Energy Information Agency: http://www.eia.doe.gov/emeu/cabs/ turkey

84   http://www.eia.doe.gov/emeu/cabs/turkey.html

85   $3.20 per million Btu to $2.08 per million Btu.

86   US Energy Information Agency, op. cit.

87   M. Katik (14 July 2003): http://www.eurasianet.org/departments/business/articles/eav071403.shtml

88   Necdet Pamir in the Istanbul daily, *Cumhuriyet* (28 November 2004).

89   US Energy Information Agency, op. cit.

90 Fluctuations in the price of gas during the 18 months it took to draft this book have made it difficult to interpret ongoing developments, of determining who the winners and losers are. It must be more difficult to determine the economics of engineering projects that take several years from inception to operation.

91 http://www.zaman.com/?bl=economy&alt=&hn=29385

92 The 'Nabucco' project for transmitting Iranian gas to East and Central Europe must be in further doubt, now the Iranians have breached some of their agreements with the IAEA about nuclear matters.

93 J. Helmer (26 September 2004) http://archives.econ.utah.edu/archives/marxism/2004w38/msg00343.htm. Also see ref. 70 for same article.

94 Kosyrev, Dmitry; Russian Information Agency *Novosti* (9 December 2004): http://en.rian.ru/rian/index.cfm?prd_id=126&msg_id=5191997&startrow=1&date=2004-12-09&do_alert=0

95 Brezinski, quoted in Jaffe and Manning; op. cit.

96 Jaffe and Manning; op. cit.

Chapter VI

1 Baddeley, J. F., 'The Russian Conquest of the Caucasus' (first published in 1908. Reissued 1969 by Russell & Russell, New York), pp. 20–1.

2 Baddeley, op. cit., p. 18.

3 Cherniaev, V. D., Vdovin, G. A., Yassin, E. M. and Stavrovsky, E. R., 'Oil Transportation', in N. A. Krylov, A. A. Bokserman and E. R. Stavrovsky (eds), *The Oil Industry of the Former Soviet Union* (Amsterdam: Gordon & Breach Science Publishers, 1998), pp. 71 and 187.

4 Cherniaev *et al.*, op. cit., p. 3.

5 The total capacity of the two refineries was some 20 million tons. During the last years of the Union, Western Siberian crude was pumped into these refineries to keep them working. Skagen, O. in H. Amirahmadi (ed.) *The Caspian Region at a Crossroad* (London: Macmillan Press, 2000), p. 58.

6 'Some Common Concerns': http://www.foe.co.uk/resource/reports/common_concerns.pdf; Campagna per la Riforma della Banca Mondiale, CEE Bankwatch Network, The Corner House, Friends of the Earth International, The Kurdish Human Rights Project and PLATFORM. Greg Muttitt and James Marriott of PLATFORM with material from several other collaborators, p. 21.

7 The names of the occupied provinces are Agdam, Fizuli, Jabrayil, Qubadli and Zangilan.

8   Two subsequent presidential elections maintained Aliev in power until his death in 2003. He was replaced by his son, Ilkham Aliev.

9   'Abkhazia', in Britannica 2001 Deluxe Edition, CD-ROM.

10 Fuller, Liz, 'Armenia, Azerbaijan Confront The Return Of The Private Army', Radio Free Europe dispatch (Wednesday, 16 February 2005): http://www.rferl.org/featuresarticle/2005/02/7295292e-ede0-49a9-add0-f09e7f1084ff.html

11 Fuller, op. cit.

12 http://thomas.loc.gov/cgi-bin/query/z?c106:s.con.res.63.is:

13 http://www.state.gov/r/pa/ei/bgn/5275.htm

14 Skagen, O., 'Survey of Caspian's Oil and Gas resources', in H. Amirahmadi (ed.), *The Caspian Region at a Crossroad* (Macmillan Press, London, 2000), p. 58.

15 Amirahmadi, H., 'Challenges of the Caspian Region', in H. Amirahmadi (ed.), *The Caspian Region at a Crossroad* (Basingstoke: MacMillan, 2000), p. 15.

16 'Some Common Concerns' quotes Britain's *Sunday Times*, to suggest that BP and AMOCO were behind the coup that ousted Elchibey, and that, as a result, Azeri's were made to accept a smaller share of the contract. However, the document itself explains that taxes were commensurately adjusted to maintain Azeri income.

17 The remainder of the shares were distributed as follows: Unocal: 10.3 per cent; Lukoil: 10 per cent; Statoil (Norway): 8.6 per cent; ExxonMobil: 8 per cent; Turkish Petroleum (TPAO): 6.8 per cent; Pennzoil: 5.6 per cent; Itochu: 3.9 per cent; Delta Hess: 2.7 per cent.

18 'Some Common Concerns', op. cit., p. 41.

19 Elf and TotalFina from France, Agip from Italy, OIEC from Iran, Winterhall from Germany and the Mobil and Chevron from the USA. Ruseckas, Laurent, 'State of the field report: Energy and politics in Central Asia and the Caucasus' *ACCESS ASIA REVIEW*, 1(2) July 1998.

20 Brezosky, L., *Associated Press*, HoustonChronicle website (27 February 2005, 1:40 a.m.): http://www.chron.com/cs/CDA/ssistory.mpl/metropolitan/3059410

21 Roy, O., 'The Iranian foreign policy toward Central Asia': http://www.eurasianet.org/resource/regional/royoniran.html

22 Dorian, J. P., Rosi, I. S. and Indriyanto, S. H., 'Central Asia's Oil and Gas Pipeline Network: Current and future flows', *Energy & Mineral Series* 9 (November 1994).

23 'Some Common Concerns'. op. cit., p. 29.

24 Manning, R. A., 'The Myth of the Caspian Great Game and the New Persian Gulf', *The Brown Journal of World Affairs*, VII/2 (Summer/Fall 2000), p. 15: http://www.watsoninstitute.org/bjwa/archive/7.2/Oil/Manning.pdf

25 Manning, op. cit., p. 17.
26 Hooman Peimani, 'The Caspian Pipeline Dilemma: Political Games and Economic Losses' (Westport Connecticut and London: Praeger, 2001).
27 Kemp, G., 'ENERGY SUPERBOWL: Strategic Politics and the Persian Gulf and Caspian Basin', The Nixon Center, Washington, DC 1997: http://www.nixoncenter.org/publications/monographs/ENERGY.html
28 BP Statistical Review of World Energy, June 2006.
29 Ruseckas, op. cit., p. 47.
30 http://www.eia.doe.gov/emeu/cabs/azerbjan.html
31 http://www.eia.doe.gov/emeu/cabs/kazak.html
32 BP Statistical Review of World Energy (June 2006).
33 http://www.inform.kz/txt/showarticle.php?lang=eng&id=138949
34 http://www.eia.doe.gov/emeu/cabs/caspian.html
35 For example, see Manning, R. A., op. cit.
36 Helmer, J., 'St. Nose is out of joint: Putin to the oil pump', The Russia Journal: http://www.russiajournal.com/node/18617
37 Novosti, unattributed news dispatch (15 March 2005, 1.22 p.m.): http://en.rian.ru/rian/index.cfm?prd_id=160&msg_id=5461929&st artrow=1&date=2005-03-15&do_alert=0
38 Interfax, unattributed news dispatch (15 March 2005, 8:37 p.m.): http://www.interfax.ru/e/B/0/0.html?id_issue=11255883
39 Abbasov, S., Ismailova, K. 'BTC: Kazakhstan finally commits to the pipeline', EurasiaNet.com: http://www.eurasianet.org/departments/business/articles/eav061906.shtml
40 'Russia to transport oil through the Balkans' (18 March 2007): http://en.rian.ru/analysis/20070318/61932071.html
41 Corso, M. and Devdariani, J., 'Lavrov trip does little to ease Georgian-Russian tension' (18 February 2005): http://www.eurasianet.org/
42 NOVOSTI unattributed dispatch; 'Georgia tries to put pressure upon Russia' (26 February 2005, 5:10 p.m.): http://en.rian.ru/rian/index.cfm?prd_id=160&msg_id=5444019&startrow=1&date=2005-02-26&do_alert=0
43 Civil Georgia; 'Plans to Sell Trunk Gas Pipelines Stir Controversy': http://www.civil.ge/eng/article.php?id=9168
44 Manning, op. cit., p. 10.
45 Irada, A., 'Azerbaijan, Turkey, Georgia to Discuss Major Railway Project', Baku Today (18 August 2005): http://www.bakutoday.net/view.php?d=14479
46 Alkhazashvili, M., 'Armenia against Kars-Akhalkalaki railway' (Monday, 5 September 2005): http://www.messenger.com.ge/issues/0940_september_5_2005/economy_0940_1.htm

47   (25   September   2006):   http://www.zaman.com/?bl=   international&alt=&hn=36774

48   http://www.arminfo.am/news_280806_1.shtml

49   Stepanian, R., 'Armenian officials deny Russian role in 1999 parliamentary carnage' (Wednesday, 4 May 2005): http://www. armenialiberty.org/armeniareport/report/en/2005/05/E9E55A76-7259-4B3E-AA2B-2AFF85232DEE.ASP

50   Jaffe, A., Seminar Report, Main Study, 'The political, economic, social, cultural and religious trends in the Middle East and the Gulf and their impact on energy supply, security and pricing', Rice University, 1997, p. 29: http://www.rice.edu/energy/publications/docs/TrendsinMiddleEast_MainStudy.pdf

51   US Energy Information Agency website for Iran: http://www.eia. doe.gov/emeu/cabs/iran.html

52   Roy, O., 'The Iranian foreign policy toward Central Asia'; http://www.eurasianet.org/resource/regional/royoniran.html

53   Ghorban, N., 'By way of Iran: Caspian's Oil and Gas Outlet', in H. Amirahmadi (ed.), *The Caspian Region at a Crossroad* (London: Macmillan Press, 2000), p. 151.

54   US Energy Information Agency website for Iran: http://www.eia. doe.gov/emeu/cabs/iran.html

55   Hersh, S. M., 'The Price of Oil; What was Mobil up to in Kazakhstan and Russia?', *The New Yorker* (9 July 2001): http://iicas.org/english/Krsten_05_07_01.htm

56   Ibid.

57   *India Daily*; 'India stands firm on the surface on Iran Gas pipeline deal but behind the scene things look different' (18 March 2005): http://www.indiadaily.com/editorial/1949.asp

58   *NewKerala* (16 March 2005): http://www.newkerala.com/news-daily/news/features.php?action=fullnews&id=86701

59   Shipments will rise to 2.3 billion cubic metres per year from 2019 under a 20-year contract. The Moscow Times.com; 3124 (Tuesday, 15 March 2005), p. 10.

60   http://www.bakutoday.net/view.php?d=12865

61   US Energy Information Agency website for Iran: http://www. eia.doe.gov/emeu/cabs/iran.html

62   PanArmenian Network; 'Gazprom fears to lose Armenia' (12 February 2005): http://www.panarmenian.net/details/eng/?id=485&date=2005-02-12

63   Marianna Grigoryan (7 July 2006): http://www.armenianow.com/?action=printable&AID=1615&CID=1731&lng=eng

64   Vladimir Socor; 'IRAN–ARMENIA GAS PIPELINE: FAR MORE THAN MEETS THE EYE' (21 March 2007): http://jamestown.org/edm/article.php?article_id=23720

65 (12 March 2007): http://www.panarmenian.net/news/eng/?nid= 21416;
66 http://www.bakutoday.net/view.php?d=12841
67 Marianna Grigoryan (14 September 2006): http://armenianow.com/ ?action=viewArticle&AID=1692&CID=1815&IID=&lng=eng
68 Khachatrian, R., 'Markarian rules out fresh asset handovers to Russia' (Friday, 13 January 2006): HTTP://WWW. ARMENIAL-IBERTY.ORG/ARMENIAREPORT/REPORT/EN/2006/01/D681F CA3-EAAE-4098-B085-26D8DB505CD8.ASP
69 *Novosti* dispatch; 'Armenia, Russia conclude military exercises' (13 September 2005): http://en.rian.ru/russia/20050913/41384721.html
70 *Novosti* (15 March 2007): http://en.rian.ru/world/20070315/ 62061926.html
71 Interfax-Central Europe (21 March 2007): http://wiadomosci. onet.pl/1506516,10,1,0,120,686,item.html
72 HTTP://WWW.SOFIAECHO.COM/ARTICLE/GAS-PIPELINE-CONSTRUCTION-THROUGH-BULGARIA- HALTED—italian-media/id_21315/catid_69
73 Interfax-Central Europe (21 March 2007): http://wiadomosci. onet.pl/1506516,10,1,0,120,686,item.html
74 Feiveson, H. and Cuk, T., op. cit., p. 22; quoting interview with Ms Epinger at the Caspian Policy Division of the State Department (2 November 1998).
75 Feiveson, H. and Cuk, T., 'Caspian energy and the politics of Caspian states: Kazakhstan and Turkmenistan', Caspian Energy Task Force, 401c (4 January 1998), p. 21: http://www.wws.princeton. edu/~wws401c/1998/tanja.pdf
76 'Pipelines to Progress: FSU Oil Exports Past, Present, Future', Speech by Richard H. Matzke, President of Chevron Overseas Petroleum Inc., to the National Association of Petroleum Investment Analysts (21 May 1997): http://www. chevrontexaco.com/news/archive/chevron_speech/1997/97-5-21-matzke.asp
77 Government of Russia (24 per cent), Government of Kazakhstan (19 per cent) and Government of Oman (7 per cent); ChevronTexaco (15 per cent), ExxonMobil (7.5 per cent) and Oryx (1.75 per cent), Russian-American joint venture LUKArco (12.5 per cent) and the Russian-British Rosneft-Shell Caspian Ventures (7.5 per cent), British Gas (2 per cent), Italian Agip (2 per cent) and Kazakhstan Pipeline (1.75 per cent).
78 http://www.eia.doe.gov/emeu/cabs/kazak.html
79 Novosti Russian Information Agency; unattributed news dispatch, 'CPC Oil pipeline capacity to be more than doubled' (2 March 2005): http://en.rian.ru/rian/index.cfm?prd_id=159&msg_id= 5448520&startrow=1&date=2005-03-02&do_alert=0

80 Feiveson, H. and Cuk, T., op. cit., p. 23.
81 *Novosti* (13 March 2007): http://en.rian.ru/business/20070313/ 61913519.html
82 Manning, op. cit., p. 21. Richardson quoted in Stephen Kinzer, 'On Piping Out Caspian Oil, U.S. Insists, the Cheaper, Shorter Way Isn't Better', *New York Times* (8 November 1998).
83 Feiveson, H. and Cuk, T., op. cit., p. 18.
84 Sergei Blagov (20 March 2007): http://www.eurasianet.org/ departments/insight/articles/eav032007a.shtml
85 Kemp, G., 'ENERGY SUPERBOWL: Strategic Politics and the Persian Gulf and Caspian Basin' (Washington, DC: The Nixon Center, 1997) executive summary quoted in: http://www .nixon-center.org/publications/monographs/ENERGY.html
86 http://www.jamestown.org/edm/article.php?volume_id=407& issue_id=3392&article_id=2369982
87 Olcott, M. B., 'International Gas Trade in Central Asia: Turkmenistan, Iran, Russia and Afghanistan', p. 5: http://iis-db. stanford.edu/pubs/20605/Turkmenistan_final.pdf
88 Proven oil reserves (2003): 0.6 billion barrels in Uzbekistan; 0.5 billion barrels in Turkmenistan. Proven gas reserves (2003): 1.85 billion cubic metres in Uzbekistan; 2.9 billion cubic metres in Turkmenistan. From 'BP Statistical Review of World Energy June 2004': http://www.bp.com/
89 Olcott, M. B., op. cit., p. 24.
90 Ahmedov, F., 'Farhad Ahmedov believes Russia should share part of its European markets with Turkmenistan, Kazakhstan and Uzbekistan'; posted 15 January 2005: http://turkmenistan.ru/index.php?page_id= 8&lang_id=en&elem_id=5980&type=event&sort=date_desc
91 Transcript of THE CNA CORPORATION Energy Conference 'TWILIGHT IN THE DESERT'; Speaker: Matthew Simmons, Chairman, Simmons & Company International (Tuesday, 20 June 2006, 6:00 p.m.), Arlington Virginia. Transcript by: *Federal News Service*, Washington, D.C.
92 Olcott, M. B., op. cit., p. 24.
93 Feiveson, H. and Cuk, T., op. cit., p. 31.
94 For this and the next section, see M. B. Olcott's article, 'International Gas Trade in Central Asia: Turkmenistan, Iran, Russia and Afghanistan': http://iis-db.stanford.edu/pubs/20605/ Turkmenistan_final.pdf
95 Olcott, op. cit., p. 13.
96 Roy, O., op. cit.
97 Olcott, op. cit., p. 12.
98 Rashid, A., *Taliban* (London: I. B. Tauris, republished London: Pan Books, 2001).

99 Olcott, op. cit.

100 Olcott, op. cit., p. 26.

101 Ak&M Analytical Information Agency – Russian Stock Market; 'Gazprom to purchase Uzbek natural gas at $60 per 1,000 cu m' (23 January 2006): http://www.akm.ru/eng/news/2006/january/23/ns1619369.htm

102 Olcott gives two different prices for this same contract: on p. 4, $1.08 per million BTU is quoted, whilst on p. 26, $1.32 per million BTU has been given. The latter price corresponds to $47.50 per 1,000 cubic metres. Blagov gives the slightly lower price quoted elsewhere (21 April 2005):http://www.eurasianet.org/departments/business/articles/eav042105.shtml

103 Blagov, S., 'Russia outmaneuvers Ukraine for Turkmen gas – for now', 4 April 2005: http://www.eurasianet.org/departments/business/articles/eav042105.shtml

104 (21 June 2005): http://news.monstersandcritics.com/mediamonitor/article_1018107.php/Turkmen_leader_accuses_Ukraine_of_not_strictly_following_gas_accord

105 'Turkmen–Ukraine Gas Trade', Global Witness, April 2006; Washington, DC.

106 Kiani, K. (23 September 2005): http://www.dawn.com/2005/09/23/top5.htm

107 'India to join central Asia gas pipeline', Business Standard (India), New Delhi (21 February 2006).

108 Ashgabat, 'China, Turkmenistan Begin Gas Pipeline Talks' (17 January 2006): http://www.newscentralasia.com/modules.php?name=News&file=article&sid=1661

109 Sergei Blagov (6 September 2006): http://www.eurasianet.org/departments/business/articles/eav090606.shtml

110 CASPIAN INFORMATION CENTRE, 'China, Russia want U.S. out of Central Asia' (5 July 2005): http://www.caspianinfo.org/news.php#594

111 Vladimir Socor, Eurasia Daily Monitor (16 March 2007): http://jamestown.org/edm/article.php?article_id=2372014

Chapter VII

1 From 'BP Statistical Review of World Energy June 2006': http://www.bp.com/; and 'BP Statistical Review of World Energy June 2006': http://www.bp.com/; 130 million tons in 2004 according to the IEA Oil Information Book, IEA/OECD Paris, 2005.

2 Much has been made in the literature of the magnitude and speed at which China's imports have grown. In six years (1999–2004), Chinese imports have increased from nearly 40 to nearly 130 million tons. The increase represents less than 2 per cent of global production. Cf. refs, in Kandiyoti, R., 'Development of Oil and Gas Pipelines in North East Asia', in Proceedings of the World Engineers' Convention 2004, Shanghai, China, 2–6 November (2004), pp. 496–502.

3 During the same period (1999–2004), Korean and Japanese imports have remained large but stable, between 110–120 and 210–220 million tons p.a., respectively.

4 Japan's LNG imports during 1999–2003 varied between 72 and 80 billion cubic metres, while those of South Korea rose slowly from 17 to nearly 28 billion cubic metres per year; Kandiyoti, op. cit.

5 Xu, Xiaojie, 'Japanese Energy Security and Changing Global Energy Markets: Sino Russian Gas Connections & Impacts', The Center for International Political Economy & The J. A. Baker III Institute for Public Policy; Rice University, May 2000.

6 21 January 2005.

7 *Strategic Geography* XXI (2003/4).

8 Japan's Marubeni Corp., Japan Petroleum Exploration Co. and Itochu Corp., which together hold a 30 per cent stake, and India's Oil & Natural Gas Corp., 20 per cent.

9 ONGC: India's state owned Oil and Natural Gas Corporation. OVL, the overseas arm of state-run Oil and Natural Gas Corp, purchased a 20 per cent stake in Sakhalin-I project for $1.7 billion in 2001. In November, India had approved $1.1 billion of additional investment in Sakhalin-I. ONGC Videsh plans to ship approximately 700,000 barrels of oil from the Sakhalin-I fields to India every 70 days from April 2006. *Sify Despatch* (Saturday, 1 October 2005, 1:52 p.m.).

10 The developers estimate recoverable reserves of 2.3 billion barrels of oil and 485 billion cubic metres of gas.

11 http://quote.bloomberg.com/apps/news?pid=10000006&sid=aEyVGzRSc_gU&refer=home

12 Shell (55 per cent), Mitsui (25 per cent) and Diamond Gas Sakhalin B.V., a Mitsubishi company (20 per cent).

13 It is estimated that these fields contain recoverable reserves of over 1 billion barrels of crude oil and more than 500 billion cubic metres of natural gas.

14 http://en.rian.ru/business/20051130/42267022.html

15 'Gazprom becomes Sakhalin II majority shareholder' (21 December 2006): http://en.rian.ru/business/20061221/57530281.html

16 http://en.rian.ru/analysis/20050428/39755688.html

17 (19 September 2006): http://news.monstersandcritics.com/ energy-watch/news/article_1203020.php/Energy_Watch_-_Sept_19
18 (25 September 2006): http://usinfo.state.gov/xarchives/ display.html?p=washfile-english&y=2006&m=September&x=200609251528491CJsamohT0.5906488
19 Kandiyoti, R., Herod, A. A. and Bartle, K. D., 'Solid Fuels and Heavy Hydrocarbon Liquids: Thermal Characterization and Analysis' (Oxford, London, New York: Elsevier, 2006) p. 241.
20 Including Azerbaijan, Canada, Kazakhstan, Venezuela, Sudan, Indonesia, Iraq, and Iran: http://www.eia.doe.gov/emeu/cabs/china.html
21 Bajpaee, C., 'China fuels energy cold war' Asia Times online (2 March 2005): http://www.atimes.com/atimes/China/GC02Ad07.html
22 Bajpaee, op. cit.
23 http://www.eia.doe.gov/emeu/cabs/china.html
24 The Japan Times (1 October 2006): http://search.japantimes.co.jp/ mail/nn20061001a1.html
25 Ibid.
26 http://tsedb.theglobeandmail.com/servlet/WireFeedRedirect? cf=GlobeInvestor/tsx/config&date=20050414&archive=ccnm&slug=0414074n
27 Bajpaee, op. cit.
28 http://www.energybulletin.net/4080.html
29 (23 December 2005): http://www.tmcnet.com/usubmit/2005/dec/ 1237451.htm
30 People's Daily (23 December 2005): http://english.people.com.cn/ 200512/23/eng20051223_230202.html
31 http://www.bloomberg.com/apps/news?pid=10000085&sid=aOm4hmgQuuTc&refer=Europe
32 Asia Times (24 August 2005): http://www.atimes.com/atimes/ China/GH24Ad01.html
33 Kennedy, J. L., Oil & Gas Pipeline Fundamentals, second edition (Tulsa, Oklahoma: Pennwell, 1993), p. 2.
34 http://www.amur.org.uk/news_050121.shtml
35 Japan Times (20 May 2005): http://www.japantimes.co.jp/cgi-bin/getarticle.pl5?nn20050520a3.htm
36 Ibid.
37 Novosti dispatch (30 May 2005, 5:26 p.m.): http://en.rian.ru/russia/ 20050530/40441079.html
38 MOSCOW (30 May 2005) (RIA Novosti); also see http://pipeliners. blogspot.com/2005_05_01_pipeliners_archive.html
39 Lavelle, P., 'Outside view: Russian energy and Asia' (UPI, 26 November 2005, 9:44:00 a.m. -0500): http://www.wpherald.com/ storyview.php?StoryID=20051126-113246-4137r

40 Tomberg, I., 'Russia's future: Eastern Siberia and Far East', *Novosti*, Moscow (24 January 2006): http://en.rian.ru/analysis/20060124/43167857.html

41 http://www.prime-tass.com/news/show.asp?topicid=55&id=384969

42 http://news.independent.co.uk/europe/article326603.ece

43 www.amur-leopard.org/assets/pipeline-report-200706.pdf

44 *Vladivostok News* (1 August 2006): http://vn.vladnews.ru/issue529/Business/Transneft_finalizes_oil_terminal

45 (6 September 2005): http://www.prime-tass.com/news/show.asp?topicid=55&id=383329

46 Iwashita, Akihiro, 'An Inquiry for New Thinking on the Border Dispute: Backgrounds of "Historic Success" for the Sino-Russian Negotiations': http://src-home.slav.hokudai.ac.jp/coe21/publish/no6_1_ses/chapter6_iwashita.pdf.

47 http://www.nyconsulate.prchina.org/eng/xw/t191213.htm

48 http://www.interfax.cn/showfeature.asp?aid=3711&slug=CHINA-JAPAN-NATURAL%20GAS-DISPUTE

49 Kandiyoti, R., 'De nouvelles routes pour le pétrole et le gaz', *Le Monde Diplomatique*, May 2005.

50 C. Bajpayee: http://www.isn.ethz.ch/news/sw/details.cfm?ID=10840

51 Bajpayee, op. cit.

52 http://www.interfax.cn/showfeature.asp?aid=3711&slug=CHINA-JAPAN-NATURAL%20GAS-DISPUTE

53 EXPERT Russian Business; http://eng.expert.ru/business/1303neft.htm

54 http://en.rian.ru/rian/index.cfm?prd_id=160&msg_id=5078581&startrow=1&date=2004-11-12&do_alert=0

55 (7 October 2005): http://www.bloomberg.com/apps/news?pid=10000101&sid=aR45Y.Buy2EE&refer=japan

56 (17 September 2005): http://en.rian.ru/russia/20050917/41424965.html

57 Miyamoto, A., in I. Wybrew-Bond and J. Stern (ed.), *Natural Gas in Asia* (Oxford University Press, 2002), pp. 106–87.

58 (17 September 2005): http://en.rian.ru/russia/20050917/41424965.html

59 (14 February 2007): http://www.themoscowtimes.com/stories/2007/02/14/042.html

60 (28 February 2008): http://mosnews.com/money/2007/02/28/japanpipeline.shtml

61 Miyamoto, op. cit.

62 http://www.bloomberg.com/apps/news?pid=10000101&sid=a6K.UlojvPn8&refer=japan#

63 Miyamoto, op. cit.

64 http://en.rian.ru/rian/index.cfm?prd_id=159&msg_id=5083762&startrow=1&find=Sakhalin

65 http://www.eia.doe.gov/emeu/cabs/china.html

66 Gas production has jumped from 3.4 billion cubic metres p.a. to 33.7 billion cubic metres in 2001, and an estimated 48 billion cubic metres p.a. in 2005. IEA Statistics, International Energy Agency, Natural Gas Information 2005, Copyright OECD/IEA 2005, Paris, France; Part I, pp. I.3 and II.5. Estimate for 2005 from: http://www.newsgd.com/news/guangdong1/200512210059.htm.

67 120 billion cubic metres per year by 2010 and 200 billion cubic metres by 2020: http://www.newsgd.com/news/guangdong1/200512210059.htm

68 'PetroChina sources said construction of the new pipeline to Guangzhou will start in 2020 and will have a capacity of 26 billion cubic metres a year, more than double that of the current line to Shanghai': http://www.newsgd.com/news/guangdong1/200512210059.htm

69 Fridley, D., in I. Wybrew-Bond and J. Stern (eds), Natural Gas in Asia (Oxford University Press, 2002), pp. 5–65.

70 The pipeline cost $5.25 billion, with $3.3 billion for upstream investments. The 4,200-km project transmits natural gas from the Tarim basin to the Shanghai region. The western sector of the line has a length of 2,330 km.

71 http://www.eia.doe.gov/emeu/cabs/china.html

72 http://www.bp.com/genericarticle.do?categoryId=2012968&contentId=7014766

73 http://www.bg-group.com/media/archive_2002/260902-sx.htm

74 (8 September 2006): http://www.rferl.org/featuresarticle/2006/09/93A2DB5A-9043-4482-BB4B-681A2BE6F40A.html

75 (18 September 2006): http://www.itar-tass.com/eng/level2.html?NewsID=10801651&PageNum=0

76 (8 September 2006): http://www.rferl.org/featuresarticle/2006/09/93A2DB5A-9043-4482-BB4B-681A2BE6F40A.html

77 (13 July 2006): http://vladivostoktimes.ru/show.php?id=170&p=

78 Yonghun Jung, 'North East Asia Gas Pipeline Development', Asia Pacific Energy Research Centre, April 2000, Institute of Energy Economics, Tokyo, Japan; APEC #00-RE-01.8: http://www.ieej.or.jp/aperc/final/ne.pdf

79 http://www.eurasianet.org/departments/business/articles/eav022502.shtml

80 The 449-km link from Atyrau (former Guriev – on the Caspian), north-east to Kenkiyak (former Shubarshi), has been upgraded from 10 to 14 million tons in 2006. The Kenkiyak–Kumkol link running south-east is under construction by the Kazakh state oil and gas concern, KazMunaiGaz, due for completion during 2006.

81 (4 October 2005): http://eng.gazeta.kz/art.asp?aid=65505

82 *People's Daily* (23 December 2005): http://english.people.com. cn/200512/23/eng20051223_230202.html
83 Yermukanov, M., Friday (18 November 2005): http://www. jamestown.org/edm/article.php?article_id=2370494
84 'China and Kazakhstan discuss gas pipeline' (10 January 2006): http://www.forbes.com/business/feeds/afx/2006/01/10/afx2442265. html

Chapter VIII

1 I owe this classification to Deniz Kandiyoti (personal communication).
2 (21 October 2006): http://www.rferl.org/featuresarticle/2006/10/ 6c7bfd08-ddd8-49dc-af7e-30600c326ec4.html
3 (24 November 2006): http://en.rian.ru/world/20061124/55955862. html
4 Former Russian Foreign Minister and Prime Minister.
5 Emerson, S. A., 'The relevance of Caspian oil for the world market', in *Caspian Energy Resources*, The Emirates Centre for Strategic Studies and Research, 2000, pp. 169–86.
6 Jaffe, A., 'The political, economic, social, cultural and religious trends in the Middle East and the Gulf and their impact on energy supply, security and pricing', Baker Institute for Public Policy, Rice University, 1997: http://www.rice.edu/energy/ publications/docs/TrendsinMiddleEast_MainStudy.pdf
7 Kandiyoti, R., Herod, A. A. and Bartle, K. D., 'Solid Fuels and Heavy Hydrocarbon Liquids: Thermal Characterization and Analysis' (Oxford, London, New York: Elsevier, 2006). See calculation presented in Chapter 9.
8 Calorific values are low; ash properties would cause deterioration of plant performance.
9 I was given this 'best' estimate by my friend Dr J. R. Gibbins, a 'believer', who quoted this price in *defence* of carbon capture and storage.
10 http://www.bloomberg.com/markets/commodities/energyprices. html
11 Personal experience of the levels of training and care required in handling compressed hydrogen.
12 IEA (2005), Energy Statistics of OECD Countries 2002–3, OECD/IEA, Paris.
13 UK Government (2003), Energy White Paper: 'Our Energy Future – creating a low carbon economy', February 2003: www.dti.gov.uk/ energy/whitepaper
14 Gellici, J., *Energeia* 16/4 (2005) 4.

Index

South Ossetia   159–161, 176
Southern Improvement
    Company   10
Spill [oil spillages]   21, 31,
    34–35, 40–41, 119–120,
    141, 157
Stalin, J. V.   47, 157, 222
Standard Oil Company   7, 10
Standard Oil Company of
    California (SOCAL, later
    Chevron)   25, 56, 107,
    150, 165, 180, 186, 197,
    211
Standard Oil Company of New
    Jersey (Exxon)   52,
    165–166, 205
Standard Oil Company of New
    York (SOCONY)   52
Straits of Malacca   1, 82, 203
Sudan People's Liberation Army
    (SPLA)   46
Suez Canal   1, 9, 56, 61, 64,
    66–68, 73, 77, 82, 141, 199
Sukhodolnaya–Rodionovska
    bypass   128
SuMed (Suez–Mediterranean)
    oil pipeline   77, 82
Supsa oil port   165, 169
Swapping oil with Iran
    178–180, 187, 193, 238

Taishet pipeline hub   205,
    212–214, 216, 221–223,
    234
Tanker war   73, 74, 83
Tarbell, Ida   10
Tengiz oil field   9, 129, 143,
    171, 185–188
Texaco   50, 56, 150, 197, 211
Ter-Petrossian, Levon   162
Theft from pipelines
    Nigeria   31
    Ukraine   2, 129, 135
    Russia   119

Thunder Horse   164
Tierra del Fuego   23
TNK-BP company   132, 207
town-gas   19, 224
Trans-Alaska oil pipeline
    (TAPS)   vii, 35, 36, 205
Trans-Alaska gas pipeline   xiii
Trans-Afghan gas pipeline
    109–110, 194, 196–197
Trans-Arabian oil pipeline
    ("Tapline")   vii, 12, 60,
    62–64, 66–70, 81
Trans-Caspian pipelines   108,
    170, 184, 189
Trans-Caucasus   154
Transneft   9, 121, 127–128,
    132, 143–145, 163, 165,
    169, 186, 188, 202, 207,
    217, 222–224, 233
Tuapse   119, 140, 174
Turkish Petroleum Company
    51–53
Turkish straits   1, 129, 140–141,
    143
    Bosporus (Istanbul Boğazı)
        140–142, 147
    Dardannelles (Çanakkale
        Boğazı)   140
Tymoshenko, Yulia   137, 138,
    198

Ulaan Bataar   37, 229–230
Unocal   107–109, 166,
    194–195, 197, 211
Urengoi gas field   147, 191
Uttar Pradesh   88

Vladivostok   213, 217, 234
Vainshtok, S.   132, 217
Ventspils   119, 127
Volga–Ural basin   157

Warsaw Pact   xiv, 11, 94, 116,
    123, 125, 153, 240